D1473133

Foreign policy and human rights

Foreign policy and human rights

Issues and responses

EDITED BY
R. J. VINCENT

Published in association with
The Royal Institute of International Affairs

Cambridge University Press

CAMBRIDGE
LONDON NEW YORK NEW ROCHELLE
MELBOURNE SYDNEY

Published by the Press Syndicate of the University of Cambridge
The Pitt Building, Trumpington Street, Cambridge CB2 1RP
32 East 57th Street, New York, NY 10022, USA
10 Stamford Road, Oakleigh, Melbourne 3166, Australia

First published 1986

Printed in Great Britain at the University Press, Cambridge

British Library cataloguing in publication data

Foreign policy and human rights: issues and responses.
1. Civil rights
I. Vincent, R. J. II. Royal Institute of International Affairs
323.4 JC571

Library of Congress cataloguing in publication data

Foreign policy and human rights.
'Published in association with the Royal Institute of International Affairs.'
Includes index.
1. Civil rights (International law) 2. International relations.
I. Vincent, R. J., 1943–
K3240.4.F67 1986 341.4'81 86-2259

ISBN 0 521 32396 7

CE

Contents

Part Two: Responses

Contributors

J. D. ARMSTRONG is a lecturer at Birmingham University and Director of its Graduate School of International Studies. His publications include *Revolutionary Diplomacy* (University of California Press, 1977) and *The Rise of the International Organisation* (Macmillan, 1981).

CHRISTOPHER BREWIN is lecturer in international relations at Keele University. He has written on the European Community, justice, and human rights, and is currently writing a book on international co-operation.

ROBIN CHATTERJIE joined the Foreign and Commonwealth Office in 1974 and was First Secretary in the United Nations Department with special responsibility for Human Rights and Social Affairs, 1980–83. He is currently on leave working for the European Commission in Brussels.

J. A. FERGUSON is a member of the Australian Department of Foreign Affairs. He has been Ambassador to Peru, and the Australian representative on the Third Committee of the United Nations General Assembly.

RHODA HOWARD is Associate Professor of Sociology at McMaster University in Hamilton, Ontario. She is the author of *Colonialism and Underdevelopment in Ghana* (Croom Helm, 1978) and of several articles on development and human rights. She is currently completing a study on human rights in English-speaking sub-Saharan Africa.

DAN KEOHANE is lecturer in international relations at Keele University. He has published on nuclear arms control and disarmament and nuclear proliferation, and his teaching includes a course on South Africa in International Relations.

JAMES MAYALL is reader in international relations at the London School of Economics. He has written widely on the theory and practice of international relations, and is the author of *Africa: the Cold War and After* (Elek, 1971) and the editor of *The Community of States* (George Allen and Unwin, 1982).

SALLY MORPHET has worked in the Research Department at the Foreign and Commonwealth Office since 1966 specializing first on South and South-East Asia, and, from 1974, on general international and United Nations questions.

FRANCISCO ORREGO VICUÑA is Professor of International Law and Relations at the Institute of International Studies and the Law School of the University of Chile. He is the author of a number of books and articles on international affairs, and specializes on Latin America, the Law of the Sea, and the Antarctic.

ARFON REES is lecturer in politics at Keele University. His doctorate at Birmingham University was on the development of the Soviet system of government in the 1920s. He is currently working on a text-book on Soviet politics.

CHARLES TOWNSHEND is senior lecturer in history at Keele University. He is the author of *The British Campaign in Ireland 1919–1921* (Oxford 1975) and *Political Violence in Ireland: Government and Resistance since 1948* (Oxford, 1983). He is currently completing a general study of counter-insurgency in the British Empire during the twentieth century.

R. J. VINCENT is senior lecturer in international relations at Keele University. He is the author of *Nonintervention and International Order* (Princeton, 1974) and of a forthcoming book on *Human Rights in International Relations*.

CLARE WELLS, a former UNESCO official and lecturer in politics at Lancaster University, is currently on the staff of the parliamentary committee of the European parliament. Her book on UNESCO which is based on her doctoral dissertation at Oxford is forthcoming from Macmillan.

Preface

The question of human rights has come to occupy a more important place in modern international relations than it once did. This is partly due to what critics would dismiss as ephemeral forces, such as the Carter Administration's attachment to human rights as a means of recovering American self-esteem after reverses at home and abroad. Whatever is of interest to a super-power, the same critics would add, naturally becomes of interest to all other powers, including other super-powers. But the assumption of greater importance bears witness to something deeper than this. The year that is often taken to begin the present era, 1945, might come to stand in the tradition of 1776 and 1789: the truths that were self-evident, the men who were born free and equal in rights, then the peoples of the United Nations reaffirming faith in fundamental human rights. Human rights might come to be interpreted as having the same relationship to an international revolution in the twentieth century, as natural rights did to national revolutions in the eighteenth. Whatever shape future interpretations may take, we can observe now a slow change in international society by virtue of which the rights of individuals and of groups other than states are coming to be thought of as having a legitimate place in the world of states rather than being the domestic concerns of states with which outsiders had no business.

Accordingly, it is now harder for the makers of foreign policy to shrug off human rights as things that it would be nice to take seriously but which play no great part in the reality of international politics. So the intrinsic importance of the subject now has some worldly recognition. This is reflected in the attention paid to the subject by political scientists in recent years: human rights are no longer the preserve of lawyers alone, and there is now a considerable literature on human rights in world politics. But one of the features of this literature (apart from its Americanness) has been its division into a concern with issues on the one hand ('dissidents in the Soviet Union', 'multinationals in Latin America', 'civil rights in South Africa'), and with what our response should be on the other ('US foreign policy and human rights'). This book seeks to bring these two concerns together, so that issues and responses are discussed in one place rather than passing like ships in the night.

Most of the chapters of the book were presented first as papers to a conference at the University of Keele. I am grateful to the Nuffield Foundation for making this conference possible. I am grateful also to William Wallace of the Royal Institute of International Affairs whose idea it was that a volume of case studies might well accompany my own book for Chatham House on human rights in international relations and whose encouragement and support has been invaluable. I should also like to thank Betty Appleby, Maureen Simkin, and Kath McKeown for their secretarial help. Pauline Wickham at Chatham House, and Sheila McEnery at Cambridge University Press, worked very hard on a difficult manuscript. I acknowledge with thanks their substantial contribution.

University of Keele R. J. Vincent

I Introduction

R.J. VINCENT

There is no obvious connection between human rights and foreign policy.[1] Human rights, the rights that all people have by virtue of their humanity, tend to be associated with individuals, and if with groups at all then with groups other than states. Foreign policy, which all states have by virtue of their existence in a world of states, tends to be associated only with them. It may be that states which have achieved that status by means of a successful appeal to the principle of self-determination are the beneficiaries of something which has come to be acknowledged as a human right. It may also be that companies like BP, or groups like Amnesty International, have something akin to foreign policies in the sense of organized relations with outsiders. But it would be odd to speak of 'Amnesty's foreign policy' or of the 'human rights of the Soviet Union'. This oddness indicates the lack of obvious connection between foreign policy and human rights.

To students of international relations it is the absence of any connection which is obvious. According to the realist school at any rate, states should pursue interests not rights and attention to the latter would get in the way of the achievement of the former. The United States should ignore the entreaties of dissident individuals within the Soviet Union in order not to confuse the pursuit of security between the two states. Great Britain should trade with the states of Latin America because of the interest of its society in commerce, whatever their domestic human rights records.

Of course, established interests might come to be defended as rights, but these are the rights of states which are likely to pull in a different direction from the rights of individuals: *raison d'état* versus ordinary morality. The principle of non-intervention which stands at the centre of the morality of states, allows the wronged individual no international recourse. Far from Kant's public law of mankind designed to make a violation of right in one place felt in all others, the idea is to desensitize states to each other's internal wrongdoing in the name of order between them. In practice a foreign policy of human rights is rejected as a policy of interference leading to chaos. In principle it is rejected because particular social contracts in separate states come before any obligation to some supposed universal community of right-bearing individuals. The rights of citizens trump the rights of man.

Again from the viewpoint of the student of international relations, these particular social contracts arise from, and then international society allows for, the coexistence of plural conceptions of rights. The difficulty with any one state taking rights, even if it calls them *human* rights, as the touchstone of its foreign policy, is the suspicion that it is seeking thereby to make its particular values general. It is a kind of imperialism. It might be more or less blatant on the part of its propagator. But from the point of view of those on the receiving end, or of observers elsewhere in international society, policies based on or in pursuit of what are called human rights have more to do with local interests than with global values.

These themes recur in the chapters that follow. They condition the discussion of human rights in international relations. But they do not exhaust it. And one of the points of this book is to show through an examination of the issue and responses to it the extent to which the question of human rights has lodged itself in international society in a way that cannot be accounted for simply in the language of imperialism. Human rights have forced themselves into each of what were presented above as the standard perspectives of the student of international relations. The realist dismissal of rights, and especially of individual rights, is confronted, for example, by the observation that denial of such rights might have unfortunate consequences for the states that look the other way: there is a direct connection between the denial of rights in one part of the world and the demand for them in another, as is illustrated by the flood of immigrants and refugees.[2] The noninterventionist insistence on the exclusiveness of the rights and duties of states is confronted by the adoption, by international society itself, of general principles of conduct towards individuals and groups within those states. And the perspective of international society as an arrangement by means of which the several cultures of the world maintain their integrity as independent units is confronted by the emergence of a global cosmopolitan culture which is stretched across all cultures, and of which the international law of human rights is one expression.[3] So these themes too recur below: they involve the study of international relations in the context of world politics as a whole, and they connect up by this means human rights and foreign policy in a way not explicable by reference to the society of states alone.

Definitions and questions

The issue of human rights is often joined precisely on the matter of definition, and of what are the right questions to ask about the subject. Are economic and social rights of the same status as civil and political rights? Do individual rights come before collective rights? Who bears the duties correlative to the lists of rights? Are human rights genuinely universal, or are they the global extension of an internal western discussion? What is peculiar about African, or Islamic or Chinese conceptions of human rights?

These questions are familiar enough, and the contributors to this volume have accepted the task of explaining the particular view of the subject-matter of human rights taken by the societies with which they are concerned. But the book seeks conclusions about human rights in any and all foreign policies, and not in this or that foreign policy, so we need a notion of our subject-matter which can bring together the several discussions rather than allowing each one to speak for itself alone. This might be done as follows. Rights are moral possessions (not necessarily individual possessions). Human rights are the moral possessions to which all human beings are entitled, and each of them equally. (This does not exclude group rights, but to be human rights it would have to be shown that everyone was entitled to them). The possessions consist of important interests like the protection of life against violence, or the provision of subsistence. We may know that a human right exists not by reference to this statute or that contract, but by the appeal its rightness makes to reason. Of any asserted claim to the status of a human right we might ask ought everyone to have it? Are there any reasons for thinking that it should not be distributed equally? And is it of paramount importance?[4] We thus have a set of criteria by which we may judge claims about the existence of human rights, rather than a list of what are said to be human rights.

Rhoda Howard's chapter below (chapter 2) is the one that deals most systematically with questions about the definition of human rights. She assesses the claim that there is a specifically African conception of human rights, scrutinizing its purported communitarianism (compared to Western individualism), its basis in consensus (compared to Western competitiveness), and its redistributive thrust (compared to the Western pursuit of individual profit). Her conclusion about whether there is indeed an African conception of human rights providing a cultural barricade against the rest of the world is sceptical. The importance of her discussion from the point of view of the overall argument of the book is that it raises the question whether, conceptually, it is possible to discuss the matter of human rights in the world as a whole in a single language.

If Rhoda Howard provides us with reasons for using a single language about them, it is then the connection between human rights issues in some parts of the world, and the responses to them in others, that is the central concern of the book. It is a book about the international relations of human rights: the impact of human rights issues on international politics and of international politics on human rights issues. Which human rights issues have gained international prominence? Why? What difference has international attention made? What difference might it make?

The connection between issues and responses is dealt with at two levels. There is, firstly, the main division of the book into a section on issues, and a section on responses, with the authors in the former section dealing with contemporary human rights issues which have gained international prominence, and those in the latter section dealing with responses abroad to them. There is, secondly, the treatment within the issues chapters of the effect of the international response, and within the responses chapters of perceptions of the issues. In this way, there is an attempt to bring together the discussion of issues and responses within each chapter as well as within the covers of a single volume.

The authors of the chapters on issues all deal with the cultural and historical background of their subjects, with the central human rights questions, with why they are a subject of international concern, and with the impact of international attention. The space devoted to each of these questions varies with the subject. Dan Keohane (chapter 3) on South Africa deals with the history of South Africa since the establishment of the Dutch East India Company at the Cape in the seventeenth century, with apartheid and human rights in contemporary South Africa, and with the character and impact of international concern on this isolated country. Arfon Rees (chapter 4) explains the Marxist–Leninist theory which informs the Soviet conception of human rights, takes the dissidents as illustration of the actual impact of the issue in the Soviet Union, and discusses the dilemmas of western policy in response to their claims. In the chapter on Palestine (chapter 5), Sally Morphet handles the issue primarily in the United Nations context, identifying the perplexities of the principle of self-determination, and detailing systematically the response of the international community to the claims of the Palestinians. Francisco Orrego emphasizes the importance of cultural differences in his chapter on Latin America (chapter 6), and argues that the insensitive handling of the human rights issue turns it into a question not of the rights of man but of the interests of imperialists. In his chapter on Northern Ireland (chapter 7), Charles Townshend treats the Irish twist to the doctrine of self-determination, shows how the rights issue has evolved there, and makes clear the limitations of external influence (even from London). In the final chapter of the issues section (chapter 8), Clare Wells discusses the debate on information rights in UNESCO, showing that international organizations are as much to be considered arenas for an argument about human rights as institutions for their implementation.

The chapters in the responses section deal with the attitudes of their societies or organizations to the question of human rights, with their reaction to some or all of the issues raised in the first part of the book, and with an evaluation of the place of human rights in their overall policy: how important it is and why it is there at all. James Mayall leads off this section with his chapter on the United States (chapter 9). In it he deals with the high standards the United States has always set itself in the matter of human rights for foreigners, with what he calls a libertarian and an egalitarian tradition in the American interpretation of human rights, and with the circumstances in which human rights are likely (or not) to become prominent in foreign policy. Christopher Brewin (chapter 10) discusses the reasons for European attitudes on the matter of human rights, and deals with the European response to the issue within its own frontiers, in East–West, and in North–South relations. James Ferguson (chapter 11) assembles a composite Third World response to the human rights issue in the course of which he challenges such conventional distinctions as those between collective rights which the Third World is supposed to believe in and the individual rights supposedly championed by the West. He writes in defence of Third World conceptions but from a first world point of view, and he reinforces Rhoda Howard's challenge to cultural relativism. Robin Chatterjie (chapter 12) treats international organizations as actors (as distinct from Clare Wells' arenas), tracing the evolution of United Nations doctrine on human rights and recording its response to many of the issues in Part One. Finally, in the responses section, J. D. Armstrong writes on the responses of non-governmental organizations to the issue of human rights, dwelling on Amnesty International and the International Committee of the Red Cross, evaluating their impact, and discussing the extent to which they have won a measure of international legitimacy.

Why these particular issues and responses? The issues more or less selected themselves as those that have been prominent in contemporary world politics. But there was also the question of spread. Here, there were two considerations: the first an Amnesty-style concern to include the first, second and third worlds; the second the not unrelated concern to include each of the three groups of rights the discussion of which constitutes the contemporary debate on human rights – civil and political rights (Northern Ireland), economic and social rights (the Soviet Union), and collective rights (black Africa, but also South Africa). (We shall see, however, when these cases are scrutinized that each of them involves all three conceptions of rights.) The responses also sought prominence and spread – but with a bias towards those countries and organizations in whose policies towards outsiders human rights have been a live issue, and not merely a response to developments in the international community. China, it might be said, is a notable absentee from the list of issues. The reason for this we leave to the concluding chapter which seeks to come to a general view about the place of human rights in international relations.

Themes

While one cannot come to conclusions in introductions, it is possible to foreshadow some of the themes of the pages that follow, and on which we shall need to come to a conclusion, and also to set out what were some of the starting places for thought.

The most prominent of these was the political theory lurking behind the questions formulated above in regard to both issues and responses. This is the liberal doctrine that the world consists of a set of self-determining political groupings whose salvation is worked out domestically. If there are questions about human rights within any of these groupings, it is likely that the difficulty is domestically generated and that its solution could not be externally imposed. It is Cobden putting the principle of non-intervention into the mouths of the Hungarian and Italian nationalists. What they wanted was not direct foreign assistance, but the non-interference of outside powers so that they could be left to work out their own destiny.[5]

An extension of this doctrine is the notion of non-intervention as the guardian of a morally plural world against the imposition of the values of a single culture: the anti-imperialist theme that we touched on earlier. This has been and remains a popular defence of the principle of non-intervention. It allows the coexistence of Liberal and Marxist, Northern and Southern, Islamic and Hindu, African and Chinese conceptions of human rights. The *universal* principle is non-intervention, protecting *particular* conceptions of human rights.[6]

This last sentence reveals that while non-intervention may be a productive starting-place for thought about human rights in international relations, it is not an adequate conclusion. For the point about human rights is that they should apply to all human beings and not be prefaced by some adjective – Liberal, African, Islamic – which might serve to restrict human rights rather than enhance them. The idea of African human rights is to make Africans different from the rest of the world. This is the opposite thrust to the notion of human rights which is to make everybody the same, at least in respect of the enjoyment of certain basic rights.[7] We need to think in this regard of human rights setting limits to the domain of non-intervention rather than being ruled out *ab initio* by the 'morality of states' or 'liberal statism'.[8]

A theme for this volume is the exploration of the nature of these limits, not as a legal matter, which is not a subject explored here,[9] but as a matter of international political legitimacy. (The absence of a chapter on international law is deliberate. Human rights has been the province of lawyers. The point here is to subject it to political scrutiny.) To what extent does being a member of international society now involve being more than merely a sovereign state? What evidence is there that 'a particular order of relations between state and individual' is becoming part of the international legitimacy?[10] As a matter of political reality, is there anything in the claim that 'Human Rights is the idea of our time'?[11]

A theme that follows on from this one is whether there is a basis for international action in the new framework of international legitimacy. Or is the framework so rudimentary, and the disagreement about its extension so fundamental that the notion of international public policy, or an international regime in the area of human rights is ludicrously premature. If, as we suggested in the preface, there has been in the twentieth century a revolution in human rights to compare to the eighteenth-century revolutions, then we may extract from it a code for action. What we explore below is, firstly, whether there is any actual community of interpretation of these rules for action, and, secondly, whether rules of action (describing actual behaviour) in any way match the rules for action (what is prescribed). For, as Stanley Hoffmann reminds us, unless a set of rules for action are in part a set of rules of action, they will wither away.[12]

Notes

1 Some of what is written here first appeared in my 'Human Rights and Foreign Policy', *Australian Outlook*, vol. 36, no. 3 (December 1982).
2 See Sandy Vogelgesang, *American Dream, Global Nightmare: the Dilemma of US Human Rights Policy* (New York, Norton, 1980), pp. 18–20.
3 See R.J. Vincent, 'Human Rights and Cultural Relativism', paper presented to 25th ISA Conference, Atlanta, 1984; *Human Rights in International Relations*, ch. 3 (forthcoming).
4 See Maurice Cranston, 'Human Rights, Real and Supposed', in D. D. Raphael (ed.), *Political Theory and the Rights of Man* (London, Macmillan, 1967).
5 Richard Cobden, speech to the House of Commons, June 28, 1850, in John Bright and James E. Thorold Rogers (eds.), *Speeches by Richard Cobden on Questions of Public Policy* (2 vols., London, 1870), vol. 2, p. 226.
6 This was a theme of my *Nonintervention and International Order* (Princeton, Princeton University Press, 1974), stressed in 'Western Conceptions of a Universal Moral Order', *British Journal of International Studies*, vol. 4, no. 1 (April 1978).
7 See Henry Shue, *Basic Rights* (Princeton, Princeton University Press, 1980).
8 See Richard Falk, *Human Rights and State Sovereignty* (New York, Holmes and Meier, 1981), chapter 1.
9 For recent treatments see Ian Brownlie (ed.), *Basic Documents on Human Rights*, 2nd edn (Oxford, Clarendon, 1981); Paul Sieghart, *Human Rights in International Law* (Oxford, Clarendon, 1983).
10 John Gerard Ruggie, 'Human Rights and the Future International Community', *Daedalus*, vol. 112, no. 4 (Fall 1983), p. 96.
11 Louis Henkin, 'Introduction' in L. Henkin (ed.), *The International Bill of Rights* (New York, Columbia University Press, 1981), p. 1.
12 Stanley Hoffmann, 'Reaching for the Most Difficult: Human Rights as a Foreign Policy Goal', *Daedalus*, vol. 112, no. 4 (Fall 1983) p. 26.

Part One: Issues

2 Is there an African concept of human rights?

RHODA HOWARD*

In this chapter I will address the question of whether there is a specifically African concept of human rights, distinct from the Western liberal concept, which by implication would render inappropriate the application of Western concepts of human rights to Africa.[1] I will use examples from English-speaking Africa, specifically from Ghana, Nigeria, Kenya, Malawi, Tanzania, Uganda and Zambia. I will argue that there are some elements of culture and social organization in Africa which are distinct from Western culture and social organization, and which therefore affect ideals about human rights. However, African society also has many aspects which are similar to advanced Western capitalist society, and which create human rights needs and ideals closer to the Western model than to the 'traditional' model of rights and obligations of indigenous Africa.

Two preliminary questions

Before commencing my analysis I wish briefly to dispose of two rather ticklish questions which confront the Western analyst of human rights in the underdeveloped world.

First, is it legitimate for a Westerner to ask, and moreover posit answers to, these questions, given the history of Western imperialism in the underdeveloped world, particularly in Africa? I answer that it is clearly legitimate. Knowledge must be evaluated on its own terms. There can be no boundaries put on its generation such as the ethnicity or the national origin of its practitioner. Moreover, as a sociologist I argue for the validity of the comparative method as practised particularly by Max Weber.[2] That is to say,

* For their comments on an earlier draft of this paper, I am grateful to Jack Donnelly, Graham Knight, Craig Murphy, R.J. Vincent, and Claude E. Welch, Jr. I would also like to thank the Social Sciences and Humanities Research Council of Canada, and the British Council for support for research and travel related to this article.

one can abstract particular features from entire societies and study them in comparison to similar features of other societies; they have a reality apart from their embeddedness in a particular culture. African societies are not merely particular because they are African; they are also universal because they are societies. It follows from this that I reject the extreme view of cultural relativity in which 'Reverence for cultural values, rather than reverence for life, becomes the absolute virtue . . .'.[3]

The second question I wish to dispose of is whether there is any universality to human rights. On a philosophical level, the natural rights perspective is that human rights *must* be universal: they are inherent in one's humanity and are contingent neither upon fulfilment of one's obligations to society, membership of a particular group, nor the decision of the state to 'grant' rights.[4] On an organizational or political level one can argue that universality exists insofar as there are a number of universal United Nations Conventions, representing a broad but not complete consensus among member states, on human rights. However, of the seven countries on which I am basing my analysis, only Kenya and Tanzania have ratified either or both of the International Covenant on Civil and Political Rights, and the International Covenant on Economic, Social and Cultural Rights (as of December 1983). Nevertheless, there is substantial evidence of the universality of human rights on the legal level. Since World War II, the internationalization of human rights has been quite firmly established.

> [T]he plea of domestic jurisdiction cannot any longer be heard to defend inhuman treatment, slavery or forced labour, wrongful arrest and detention, denial of justice in the courts, denial of freedom of religion or of political opinion, the invasion of personal property or family life.[5]

Finally one may also ask whether there is a *sociological* universality of human rights. Can we say that all human beings have the same perceptions of basic rights? The negative case, that there are some situations which all human beings prefer to avoid, is perhaps easier to prove than the positive. Peter Berger suggests that one can condemn certain gross violations with confidence that there is a consensus, emerging 'from all the major world cultures',[6] that these are indeed violations of human rights. Such violations, he argues, include *inter alia* genocide, torture, expulsions, enslavement, and desecrations or destruction of religious or ethnic symbols. In a similar vein, the noted sociologist, Barrington Moore, Jr, provides a list of universal causes of unhappiness:

1 being tortured or slaughtered by a cruel enemy
2 starvation and illness
3 the exactions of ruthless authorities who carry off the fruits of prolonged labour
4 the loss of beloved persons through the actions of others over which one has little or

no control

5 rotting in prison, being burned at the stake, or even simply losing the means of livelihood for the expression of heretical or unpopular beliefs.[7]

Thus there is a reasonable presumption that human rights may indeed be universal. It remains now to be seen whether cultural variations in human rights ideals rule out such possible universality.

What is different about African human rights?

Those who argue that the African concept of human rights differs radically from the Western take as the key to that difference the alleged existence of a *communitarian ideal* in Africa. Within that ideal the group is more important than the individual, decisions are made by consensus rather than by competition, and economic surpluses are generated and disposed of on a redistributive rather than a profit-oriented basis. A quote from the President of Zambia, Kenneth Kaunda, who calls himself an 'African humanist' clearly identifies these three elements:

> the tribal community was a *mutual* society. It was organised to satisfy the *basic human needs* of all its members and, therefore, *individualism was discouraged*... Human need was the supreme criterion of behaviour ... *social harmony* was a vital necessity... [C]hiefs and tribal elders ... adjudicated between conflicting parties, admonished the quarrelsome and anti-social and took whatever action was necessary to strengthen the *fabric of social life*.[8] (Emphasis added).

The President of Tanzania, Julius Nyerere, adopts a similar stance with his contention that 'the idea of "class" or "caste" was non-existent in African society. The foundation, and the objective, of African socialism [communalism] is the extended family.'[9]

Unfortunately such hearkening back to the 'original', pre-colonial model of African communalism obscures the social changes which have taken place in Africa since the European incursion. Ali Mazrui puts it well in his conjectural summary of the 'clash' of European and African cultures. Referring to the ways in which cultures affect individual motivation, he says

> Particularly important as a cultural factor is the balance between the pursuit of individual interests and the pursuit of collective welfare. In traditional African societies the scale was approximately as follows. One was first motivated to acquire enough for his or her basic needs and the needs of the immediate family. The second imperative was the pursuit of conditions to satisfy the basic needs of the wider family and society. The third imperative was the pursuit of personal advancement beyond basic needs. The fourth was the promotion of the welfare of the extended family and wider society beyond their collective needs.
>
> Under the western impact some reshuffling of principles of behavioural motivation took place. The pursuit of basic needs still remains primary in a westernized African.

But next in importance now tends to be the pursuit of self-advancement beyond basic needs. In other words, the basic needs of the wider clan are beginning to be subordinated to the imperative of personal advancement.[10]

Mazrui makes two important points: that in the process of social change Africans, like Westerners, have become more and more motivated by individual, not collective (whether family or societal) advancement, and that the idea of personal advancement was not unknown even in 'traditional' (indigenous, pre-contact) African societies. I will elaborate upon these two points by discussing in detail the three alleged value differences, noted above, between African and Western society.

COMMUNITARIAN VS. INDIVIDUALISTIC ORIENTATION

Kaunda's stress on the mutuality of society, and Nyerere's on society as an extended family, are both understandable if one considers the traditional African concept of 'personhood', ably explained by Menkiti. There is no concept of person in traditional or folk society, Menkiti asserts, independent of that person's fulfilment of the social obligations of his or her role. One *grows* into personhood: 'personhood is the sort of thing which has to be attained, and is attained in direct proportion as one participates in communal life through the discharge of the various obligations defined by one's stations ... It is the community which defines the person ... persons become persons only after a process of incorporation ...'[11] However, as Menkiti himself points out such a concept is not a concept of human rights.[12] There is no humanity in such traditional societies separate from fulfilment of one's obligations and incorporation into the group; those who are not incorporated into the group, such as slaves, strangers, or criminal outcasts, have no rights; indeed, even those who are members of the group, but who fail to fulfil their obligations, such as barren women in societies which highly value children, may be considered less than fully human.

The so-called 'African concept of human rights' is, therefore, actually a concept of human dignity.[13] The individual feels respect and worthiness as a result of his or her fulfilment of the socially approved role. 'Rights' do not inhere in one's humanity, rather they are *contingent* upon one's 'fulfilment of one's obligations to the group'[14] and the subsequent *granting* of rights by the community. Rights are dependent on one's status.

In such a society, the individual lacks many ... of the rights that are so highly valued in the liberal democratic state. However, he has a secure and significant place in his society and has available a wide range of intense personal and social relationships which provide him important material and non-material support. He also has available regularized social protections of many of the values and interests which in the West are protected through individual human and legal rights ... such a society is undeniably morally defensible, is in many ways quite attractive, and can be said to protect basic human dignity.[15]

One can realistically argue that people may well value their dignity, that is their feeling of self-respect and of being respected as a result of their conforming to the roles ascribed to them by their membership in a particular social group, more than their freedom to act as individuals. In relatively homogeneous, static and small-scale societies this tendency is likely to be stronger than the tendency towards individualism. In an insightful essay on African forms of domestic 'slavery', Miers and Kopytoff argue that 'In most African societies, "freedom" lay not in a withdrawal into a meaningless and dangerous autonomy but in attachment to a kin group, to a patron, to power – an attachment that occurred within a well-defined hierarchical framework ... Here, the antithesis of "slavery" is not "freedom" qua autonomy but rather "belonging".'[16] The domestic slave's dignity, if not his freedom, was guaranteed by his incorporation as a junior member of his owner's lineage. On the other hand, slaves were always threatened by the possibility of being victims of mass ritual executions, as when Ashanti (Ghana) kings died; hence their inferior status was openly acknowledged. We have no way of knowing whether group acceptance compensated, for a slave, for the threat, however remote, to that most basic of human rights, the right to life.

In modern terms, a good example of the conflict between individual freedom and group acceptance by conformity to societal custom can be found in an examination of women's rights in English-speaking Africa.[17] Under various United Nations Conventions, a number of common African practices pertaining to marriage, namely bridewealth (by which a suitor must 'pay' for his bride), child betrothal, arranged marriages, and widow inheritance (by which a widow acquires a new male guardian from her deceased husband's lineage), contravene international human rights instruments, ostensibly because all of them interfere with the individual's right of free choice of a marriage partner. Yet all of these are practices which are accepted as legitimate by most Africans. Similarly female genital operations are practised widely in Africa. Yet, according to overwhelming medical opinion, the practice is severely detrimental to the health of both women and their children and is roundly criticized in the West and by many educated Africans. Both the Economic Commission for Africa[18] and the Organization of African Unity[19] have called for its abolition. Yet defenders of the practice argue that it, like the customs regarding marriage, is part of the 'glue' which holds society together, an integral part of what makes an African woman a fully-fledged and respected adult member of her particular ethnic group.[20]

The example of women's rights in English-speaking Africa demonstrates that communitarian, rather than individualistic, modes of thinking are still much stronger in Africa than in the fully capitalistic, ideologically liberal West. The principle of cultural relativity, while it should not be raised to an absolute standard excusing any and all deviations from international human rights standards, is a useful one to keep in mind in this connection. Nevertheless, changes in the direction of increased individual freedom or autonomy are occurring in Africa, partly because of severe structural dislocations and partly because of the introduction of new ideologies. Cultural stasis is unlikely, however 'indigenous' culture may be.

CONSENSUAL VS. COMPETITIVE ORIENTATION TO DECISION-MAKING

The communal model of human rights asserts that the African approach to decision-making is consensual by nature. For example Wai, perhaps the strongest proponent of this approach, states that

> The relationship between the chief and his people is based on a pattern of obligations: from the chief to the people and vice versa ... In the traditional setting Africans had the right to remove chiefs who acted arbitrarily or ruled dictatorially ... Africans participated in the process of decision making through recognized channels and institutions. Discussion was open and those who dissented from the majority opinion were not punished ...[21]

Thus a number of the provisions in the International Covenant of Civil and Political Rights, such as freedom of thought, opinion and assembly, and particularly the right to 'genuine and periodic elections', which are essentially designed to ensure the fairness of a *competitive* political system, are asserted to be irrelevant to African politics.

This view of the consensual nature of African politics is exaggerated. There is a tendency for some writers to over-generalize, as Mojekwu does in extending his analysis of his own (apparently Igbo) sub-unit of Nnewi to all of Africa.[22] It is true that local village decisions in non-state African societies were made by consensus; elected chiefs and elders debated an issue until general agreement was reached, and errant officials who violated the general consensus could be deposed. But not all African societies were of this non-centralized village type, even before contact with the British and formal political colonialism. Some, like the Ashanti in Ghana, were a sort of feudal bureaucracy based on tribute and control of long-distance trade, in which appointed officials from the capital had power over local village chiefs. In Northern Nigeria, there were a number of centralized Muslim states which consolidated their power before British rule and retained it afterwards. According to Beattie, 'the Nupe peasant [in Nigeria] has no say in the appointment of the fief-holding lords to whom he is subject, nor has his Ganda [in Uganda] counterpart any voice in the appointment of the major chiefs'.[23] In his 'Common Man's Charter' President Obote of Uganda specifically rejected preservation of Buganda 'feudalism', because it was detrimental to any true 'move to the left' in Uganda.

> We do not consider that all aspects of the African traditional life are acceptable as socialistic. We do not . . . accept that belonging to a tribe should make a citizen a tool to be exploited by and used for the benefit of tribal leaders . . . [W]e do not accept that feudalism . . . is a way of life which must not be disturbed because it has been in practice for centuries.[24]

In any case, since political independence the local autonomy of villages and even former empires has become confined to matters in which the central and regional governments have no interest.

The myth of the consensually-defined traditional political system is used to buttress claims to a national political system in which no formal opposition is allowed and decisions are supposedly made by consensus within one national party. In Kenya, the government gradually banned all opposition parties during the 1960s. Eventually the only party left was KANU (the Kenya African National Union), and Kenya officially became a one-party state in mid-1982. In practice, there is evidence that within this one-party system some political democracy (in the sense of genuine and periodic elections) does exist. During elections, KANU nominates more than one candidate for each legislative seat. A substantial number of ministers and MPs is overthrown at each election. On the other hand, serious challengers to the power of former President Kenyatta and KANU, such as Oginga Odinga, have been imprisoned. At least one politician who went beyond the accepted bounds of political argument by seriously trying to represent the interests of the poor in Kenya, Josiah Mwangi Kariuki, was murdered. An official commission investigating his murder strongly suggested that it had been arranged by the chief of the Criminal Investigation Department, on orders from above.[25]

In Zambia, similarly, all opposition parties have gradually been eliminated. The ruling and only party, UNIP (the United National Independence Party), nominates all candidates for electoral seats; no independents are permitted to run. Moreover, in some cases elections are by 'acclamation', when UNIP sees fit to nominate only one candidate. Only one presidential candidate, nominated by UNIP, is permitted. No criticism of the president or the government philosophy of humanism is permitted, and the press is controlled.[26]

To conclude, the non-competitive 'palaver' (talking out) state might be one way of running local political affairs, especially in ethnically homogeneous areas with a strong sense of group cohesion, but it is doubtful that it can be implemented in any truly democratic manner on the federal level. Consensual politics (implying local and individual participation in the consensus) are not typical of large-scale indigenous African states; nor can such consensual politics accommodate competing ethnic or class interests except at the long (or even short) run cost of increased state coercion. The one-party 'palaver' state presumes the formation of a ruling elite. Access to the elite may be fairly open and 'democratic' during the early establishment of the political system, but not in the long run.

REDISTRIBUTION OF SURPLUS VS. INDIVIDUAL PROFIT

The 1966 Covenant on Economic, Social and Cultural Rights contains a number of provisions suggesting that basic material security should be considered a fundamental human right. During the 1970s, this early stress on physical security was reinforced by the commitment of the United Nations to the idea of a 'New International Economic Order', in which the material inequalities between rich and poor nations would be alleviated by a restructuring of world trade; and a commitment to the philosophy of 'basic needs'; that is, that minimal physical needs ought to be assured to all human beings. But this philosophy of material security has avoided considering the real inequities of property relationships which are at the basis of the maldistribution of wealth, except for a guarantee in the Covenant on Economic, Social and Cultural Rights of nations' sovereignty over national resources (Article 1, 2).

The charter on human rights of the Organization of African Unity, however, specifies that discrimination based on 'fortune' should be abolished.[27] This suggests that there is at least a philosophical difference between Africa and the Western world with regard to property rights, which are the basis of personal profit; that in principle at least, African governments support the idea of redistribution of wealth. Such a pronouncement at the level of the OAU accords with the communal model of economic justice. The Preamble to the African Charter on Human Rights states, moreover, that 'it is henceforth essential to pay a [sic] particular attention to the right to development'.[28]

Legesse contends that 'Most African cultures, whether they are formally egalitarian or hierarchical, have mechanisms of distributive justice ... Most African kings and chiefs were expected to use their wealth for the welfare of their subjects.'[29] Here the anthropological past is confused with the sociological present. It is accurate to portray the pre-capitalist 'tribal' way of life as one in which neither productive property nor surplus was privately held. In rural agricultural societies in Africa, land was distributed to families for use on the basis of need. A certain proportion of the surplus was given to the chief, but his control over the surplus was as a steward on behalf of the group; he distributed food for ritual occasions or stored it against future poor harvests. Even in societies which were stratified not only by age and sex, but also into castes of nobles, freemen and slaves, each individual was guaranteed adequate land for his or her own sustenance. While one may perhaps attribute this guarantee of livelihood to the African communal culture, economic factors were also influential. Adequate sustenance for all is a relatively costless allocation of resources in a society in which (as in much of Africa until recently) there is a surplus of land and a shortage of labour.

Authors such as Pollis and Schwab, who write that 'in many cultures ... land is owned communally and there is no "right" to individual ownership of holdings'[30] fail to recognize that the past distribution of land had an economic basis which is now breaking down. The initial redistributive economy has now been affected by over five centuries of incorporation into the Western dominated world capitalist economy. Faced with capitalist expansion, many Africans have responded with capitalist 'rationality'. The evidence that social classes based on differential access to private property in tangibles such as land and industry, as well as in intangibles such as knowledge and public office, are emerging in contemporary English-speaking Africa is overwhelming.[31] Except perhaps in the Tanzanian case, there is no evidence that in modernizing Africa, wealth is being redistributed; rather, as the Kenyan situation vividly illustrates, the gaps between rich and poor are rapidly increasing.[32]

In Kenya, the government has used its right of national sovereignty to nationalize property formerly belonging to ethnic non-Africans. Non-citizen ethnic Asians engaged in commercial activities have systematically had their trade and production licences revoked, so that they have been forced to sell their properties to ethnic Africans and many have consequently chosen to emigrate. In the first decade after independence, white settler farmers were bought out, partly with funds provided through British and multilateral foreign aid, and Africans were resettled on the land. However, despite the fact that many of the so-called 'Mau Mau' rebels of the 1950s had been land-poor peasants, the white highlands were 'redistributed' to those Africans who could afford to *buy* the land, and to political leaders and their favoured followers.[33] In the large-scale industrial and commercial sphere, certain sectors have been declared for Kenyans only; in this case again, however, only the wealthy Kenyans can afford to participate.

In contrast to Kenya's explicitly capitalist development policy, with its consequent destressing of basic welfare sharing, is the attempt by Tanzania, under the leadership of Julius Nyerere, to implement a form of 'African socialism' based on cooperative labour on, and ownership of the major means of production, land. The core of Tanzanian policy, known as 'ujamaa', is the voluntary centralization of previously dispersed peasant households into villages where basic government services are located, and out of which large-scale cooperative agriculture backed by state loans can be conducted. The reality of implementation of the policy has deviated from the ideal, however. As a result of the unwillingness of some peasants to move into the villages, a policy of enforced 'villagization' was introduced[34] violating Article 12(1) of the United Nations Covenant on Civil and Political Rights, which guarantees freedom of movement. The policy also resulted in domination of the villages by urban-based bureaucrats[35] thus depriving local groups of their previous autonomy. The bureaucrats tended to give loans and equipment to the richer farmers. Moreover, in some matrilineal areas, women, who had held land in their own right in their original communities, were denied land rights in the new villages;[36] this situation was partially rectified in 1975 when women were granted half the land rights of men.[37] Finally, 'villagization' does not appear to have raised agricultural productivity.[38] This latter may have occurred partly because, despite the ideal of communalism, Africans have not 'traditionally' cultivated land collectively; rather each household has been responsible for its own plot.[39] Thus the Tanzanian experiment in collectivization, or the return to an allegedly indigenous ideal, appears to have exacerbated inequalities between urban bureaucrats and local peasants, between peasants of different levels of wealth, and between men and women, without significantly increasing productivity so as to be better able to fulfil the requirements of the material human rights of its citizenry.

From the example of Tanzania, it is evident that the redistributive model of economic equality will be difficult to implement in sub-Saharan Africa, at least insofar as some civil and political freedom is also allowed. The Kenyan example shows dramatically that redistribution of wealth has taken place at the expense of non-ethnic Africans, but such redistribution has not precluded the rise of new class divisions among Africans. The redistributive ideal, like the ideal of the consensual political system and the community-oriented individual, is based on inadequate understanding of pre-colonial African societies and an ignoring of the profound structural changes which have taken place in African societies as a result of British colonialism and Africa's incorporation into the capitalist world economy.

Discussion

So far, my answer to the question of whether there is a specifically African concept of human rights, has been that there is not. I have maintained that the argument for a specific African concept of human rights is based on a philosophical confusion of human dignity with human rights, and on an inadequate understanding of structural organization and changes in African societies. Underlying this inadequate understanding of structure (by which I mean the basic economic, stratificatory, and political organization of society) are a number of assumptions regarding the meaning of culture which are used to buttress the reliance on the concept of 'cultural relativity', in order to argue that the Western concept of human rights cannot be applied to Africa. In this section, I will discuss the assumptions regarding culture underlying the argument for an African concept of human rights. I will then go on to discuss the question of why, in the face of evidence to the contrary, African intellectuals persist in presenting the communal model as a real model of African social relations. Finally, I will briefly discuss an alternative sociological position.

CULTURAL ASSUMPTIONS UNDERLYING THE COMMUNAL MODEL

The first implicit assumption underlying the communal model of African human rights is that *culture is a static entity*. In sociological terms, this is a functionalist perspective: it assumes that since all aspects of customs, norms and values are functional to the persistence of the social system as a whole, one aspect cannot be changed without the whole edifice's crumbling. I argue rather that even though elements of culture have a strong hold on people's individual psyches, and therefore can persist even when, as in the case of female genital operations they seem eminently 'irrational' to outsiders, nevertheless cultures can and do change. Cultural change can result as an adaptation to structural change. It can also result from individuals' being exposed to and adopting new ideas. Individuals are actors who can influence their own fate, even if their range of choice is circumscribed by the prevalent social structure, culture or ideology. In so doing, both those who choose to adopt 'new' ideals such as the idea of individual choice in marriage, and those who choose to retain the 'old' ideals, may be doing so in their own interests. Culture, like structure, is inherently dynamic; and it is responsive to conflict among individuals or social groups.

A second implicit assumption underlying the communal model of African human rights is that *culture is a unitary whole*; that is, that people are members of one culture or another, hence to attempt to judge African human rights by the so-called 'universal' standards embodied in the main United Nations instruments is to impose one whole culture upon another whole culture.[40] But the evidence suggests that people are quite adept at being 'cultural accommodationists'; they are able implicitly to choose which aspects of a 'new' culture they wish to adopt and which aspects of the 'old' they wish to retain. There is clear evidence of this in the religious syncretism of many African sects, which combine polygyny with Western Christian beliefs. The process of urbanization provides evidence as well; Africans who urbanize do not suddenly adopt 'modern' as opposed to 'traditional' ways; rather they create 'urban villages' in the new cities, retaining ethnic links but adapting ethnic organizations to new social functions.[41]

Thus since culture is neither static nor unitary, one cannot preach a return to the quasi-mythical old ways; *even if* structure were to be successfully transformed, the 'new' ideas would still exist in people's individual choices of how to live. It may well be that both the new ideals of individualism, competition and private profit, and new interpretations of old inequalities such as that between male and female, have been introduced into English-speaking Africa as a result of the ideological imperialism of the Christian missionary and the British educator. Nevertheless, these ideals have been adopted and retained independently by Africans.

A third assumption underlying the cultural model of African human rights is that *culture is unaffected by structure*. It has been an implicit argument throughout this chapter that the opposite is more accurate; that structure does affect culture. Culture is adaptive. One can accept the principle that customs, values and norms do indeed 'glue' society together, and that they will endure, in the typical 'cultural lag' syndrome even when structures have changed, without assuming cultural stasis. To a significant extent cultures and values reflect forms of organization of the productive forces available to a society, and forms of social stratification. This does not mean that beliefs are completely determined by material forces: on the contrary I have argued throughout this essay for the autonomy of the individual impelled by his or her own ideas in determining, within certain boundaries, his or her own fate. It does mean that since the overall economic and social structure of English-speaking Africa no longer adheres, if it ever did, to the small-scale communal model, cultures, values, beliefs, human rights ideals and individual lives will have changed accordingly.

The final assumption, referred to earlier in this chapter, is that *culture is neutral*. Yet very few social practices, whether cultural or otherwise, are entirely neutral in their impact. In considering any cultural practice, it is useful to ask, who benefits from its retention? Do the 'cultural policy makers'[42] have a personal interest in the custom? Those who seek to preserve, as well as those who seek to change, customs may in fact be seeking their individual or group self-interest.[43] Even in ethnic or national groups with coherent, shared customs and values, there can be, and in Africa usually is, social stratification. Those who speak for the group are usually those most capable of articulating the group's values to the outside world; but such spokesmen are likely to stress, in their articulation of 'group' values, those particular values which are most to their own advantage.

REASONS FOR PRESENTING THE COMMUNAL MODEL OF HUMAN RIGHTS

Why, in the face of so much evidence to the contrary, do some African intellectuals persist in presenting the communal model of social organization in Africa as if it were fact, and in maintaining by extrapolation that the group-oriented, consensual, and redistributive value system is the only value system in Africa, hence that it ought to be the basis of a uniquely African model of human rights?

One possible explanation for this phenomenon may be that such African intellectuals are themselves victims of the intellectual imperialism which they so vigorously decry. There is a long-standing Western myth of the 'noble savage', exemplifying the virtues of generosity and self-sacrifice within his own community, virtues which have been lost in the materialistic, profit-seeking Western world. This originally Rousseauian myth has permeated sociological thinking with its fundamental opposition between traditional rural and modern urban society.[44] The noble savage is incapable of a selfish, profit-seeking act; but he is also incapable of the scientific and technological innovation which such selfishness allegedly impels and which is the basis of Western economic, political and cultural dominance in the modern world. The noble African is doomed to stagnation in his closed, isolated, subsistence-level village, while the mundane Westerner pursues individual wealth and collective economic prosperity in the modern city. Such are the two ideal types which permeate Western sociological thinking on how human nature has evolved; by choosing the former instead of the latter, the African intellectual may be as blind to social reality as the 'modernization theorist' who chooses not to consider the real price of a culture of self-interest, both in Africa and in the Western world.

The Ghanaian philosopher J. E. Wiredu suggests that the search for 'authenticity', whether in philosophy or in culture, may be an expression of the continued inferiority complex of Black Africans.[45] Reacting against their former acceptance of all things colonial, African nationalists now 'need' to find their 'authentic' culture. Wiredu is criticizing the contention that there is a unique African philosophy, but his remarks can apply just as easily to the contention that there is a unique African culture.

> African nationalists in search of an African identity, Afro-Americans in search of their African roots and Western foreigners in search of exotic diversion – all demand an African philosophy [culture] that shall be fundamentally different from Western

> philosophy [culture] ... Partly through the influence of Western anthropology and partly through insufficient critical reflection on the contemporary African situation, many very well placed Africans are apt to identify African thought [culture] with *traditional* African thought [culture] ... these Africans have been in the habit of calling loudly, even stridently, for the cultivation of an African authenticity or personality.[46] (Emphasis in original.)

On the other hand, such a call for authenticity, in Wiredu's view, may be 'merely a political slogan'.[47] The advocacy of a theory of African communalism by African intellectuals may very well be in their own self-interest. In general the defence of 'indigenous' customs by African intellectuals may facilitate their 'big-man' domination over local groups who find their cherished values threatened. The defence of customs regarding women may justify the widening inequalities between men and women now that capitalization of land has increasingly deprived women of their economic security, which had been rooted in the indigenous system of land allocation.[48] The myth of the 'palaver state' in which contentious issues are 'talked out' until a consensually agreed decision is reached, may permit the evolution of a one-party dictatorship and eventually of a ruling elite. The Nigerian political scientist, Claude Ake, maintains that African leaders are referring back to the 'traditional' palaver form of government as a means of blocking popular demands for participation in government. The leaders' 'ideology now proclaims the end of internal ideological conflict ... The African tradition of unanimity has to be rehabilitated ... as an argument against dissent, interest articulation, and democratic participation.'[49]

Similarly, the myth of the redistributive economy may permit the 'corrupt' practice of nepotistic allocation of state resources to officials' kinsmen and co-ethnics. Patron–client relationships based on the village model by which the better off assume responsibility for the worse off, may substitute for real structural change in the allocation of resources. All of these ideals allow the new wealthy to justify their retention of power as long as they allocate some of their (or the state's) property to those poorer than themselves; the recipients then become their political supporters in a round of clientilistic or ethnically-based politics which precludes political organization across ethnic lines on a class basis. Keeping in mind, again, that those who seek to retain, as well as those who seek to change, cultures and custom may have a material interest in so doing, it is as well to approach African intellectuals' proponence of the communal model of human rights with a judicious degree of scepticism.

AN ALTERNATIVE APPROACH

In an earlier paper[50] I have argued that one must analyse violations of human rights in Africa, as elsewhere, through a structural approach. While I cannot recapitulate my argument here, I can explain my central methodological principles. Firstly, a comparison with the evolution of human rights in the Western world is essential; such a comparison makes it evident that Western liberal ideals were not implemented overnight; rather they were implemented after individuals had joined together into groups (e.g. as trade unionists, as women, as members of religious minorities) to demand them.[51] Secondly, an understanding of the continuing effects of colonialism and neo-colonialism in Africa is necessary, in order to comprehend the difficulties in obtaining the minimal economic basis for human rights. Finally, one must understand the real social changes in Africa which have resulted in the creation of class-stratified societies ruled by elites who base their power on property, knowledge, and domination of the state.

Thus there is no need to adopt a defensive posture, arguing for the uniqueness of African culture, to explain why Africa *cannot* implement all of the Western and United Nations' ideals of human rights. Human rights cannot be legislated into existence, in Africa or anywhere else, *in vacuo*. They are a function of structural as well as cultural conditions. Indeed, one might well argue that in many African countries, given the underlying structural constraints, a great deal has been done in a very short period of time to grant new human rights to ordinary citizens.[52]

Implication for international human rights action

Given, then, what we know of the real structure underlying the African 'culture' of human rights, what can we expect by way of progress in human rights within English-speaking Africa, and what ought, and will, the Western democracies do to help to implement their human rights?

INTERNAL AFRICAN HUMAN RIGHTS POLICIES

Those individual rights of freedom of choice which do not have a political component, such as freedom within marriage, will probably be the easiest to implement over the short term. Individualism will probably become more pronounced (for good or for ill), and collectivist customs change, through the continued expansion of education and mass communication, and the intensification of the urban experience in Africa. Legislation to abolish customs which are repugnant within the Western individualist tradition is probably unnecessary. Customs ought not to be banned when there is evidence that they do not cause discomfort for the vast majority of people who follow them; legislation should merely assure the individual's right to opt out of a practice or custom when he or she wishes.

With regard to civil and political liberties, the basic freedoms will probably be much more difficult to implement. The optimism which greeted the Nigerian return to constitutional rule in 1979 died with the military coup of December 31, 1983. The pattern in Africa appears to be that either a ruling class (not necessarily capitalist or economically-based) consolidates itself and retains power, frequently by establishing a one-party state: or alternatively, that military dictatorships take over. One possible step towards more political freedom may occur if a ruling class consolidates itself economically, to the extent that it no longer needs direct control over the state; it will then be able to relinquish such control.[53] Indeed, the history of Western democracy seems partly to be that of the opening up of politics to the lower classes once the ruling economic elite had fully consolidated itself.

With regard to economic and social rights, the right to an 'adequate' standard of living will probably be the most difficult for the new African governments to assure. It is unlikely that such a right can be implemented without a vast increase in the gross national product, combined with the granting of political freedoms which will allow the various 'out-groups', such as the landless poor, women, and subordinate ethnic groups, to make demands on the elites for redistribution of wealth.[54] But it will be difficult for Africa to imitate the Western European model in which a vast expansion of wealth was followed by political demands for its redistribution, precisely because, to a considerable exent, Africa's poverty, or underdevelopment, is the obverse side of Europe's wealth, or development.[55] Africa has no colonies, nor does it have captive markets for its manufactured goods or an assured cheap supply of its raw materials, as Western Europe and Britain had during their age of economic expansion. The most optimistic economic projection for Sub-Saharan Africa in the 1980s is zero growth; for the poorest nations of the region, such as Tanzania, a negative growth rate of minus one per cent per year is projected.[56]

INTERNATIONAL ACTION BY THE WESTERN DEMOCRACIES

Generally speaking, it is safe to say that foreign policy will not be dominated in most countries by human rights considerations. A fundamental principle of international diplomacy is the preservation of each country's sovereignty; interference in human rights matters inside other countries can be construed as a violation of sovereignty.[57] International human rights treaties are unenforceable.[58] Human rights considerations will be included in foreign policy only when they are relatively costless, when moral prestige is involved, or when, in a democracy, the government is responding to internal popular pressure.

African states themselves subscribe to the principle of state sovereignty. Given the very fragile borders which are a legacy of the colonial era, the Organization of African Unity opts for the sovereignty of existing independent African states at all costs; only in the struggle against Portuguese colonialism and white settler racist governments has this principle been violated. There was no intervention by the OAU in the Nigerian civil war or in Amin's Uganda. Tanzania's intervention to overthrow Idi Amin in Uganda in 1979 was not sanctioned by the OAU. This OAU policy of backing sovereignty of black-ruled states as a first principle has resulted in accusations in the United Nations that it has a 'double standard'.[59] Mower, however, argues that from the African point of view such differentiation is justified in that South African violation of human rights is a consistently implemented policy, whereas black African violations are more likely to be accidents or acts of omission. African statesmen do take actions through 'quiet diplomacy' against human rights abuses by brother Africans.[60]

Supposing for a moment that human rights were high on the agenda of Western foreign policy, when ought Western governments to intervene in human rights matters in sub-Saharan English-speaking Africa? In the realm of custom, I maintain that Western governments ought to intervene with great hesitancy, if at all, even when, as in the case of female genital operations, there is popular pressure for intervention at home. With regard to political abuse, when internal African practice clearly violates international standards regarding personal safety and insecurity (as in the case of torture or arbitrary arrest), and when moreover one can righly argue that such a violation would be painful to the recipient regardless of the culture to which he or she belonged, then international outrage would be appropriate. As far as the right to a decent standard of living is concerned, the onus in a moral sense is upon Western societies to make the financial sacrifices, as envisaged, for example, through the New International Economic Order, which would permit economic expansion in Third World countries.

Nevertheless, the foregoing is hypothetical only, given that human rights are not an important part of foreign policy consideration in most states. The more important question is, under what conditions are Western democracies *likely* to intervene in human rights matters in Africa?

Western democracies will hesitate to intervene in any human rights matter which violates the principle of sovereignty. During the Nigerian civil war, for example, the Canadian government agreed to allow Biafran separatists currently in Canada to remain in the country, but not as 'refugees'; moreover, the Canadian government did not recognize the existence of an independent Biafra. To have done so would not only have sanctioned violation of Nigeria's sovereignty, but also have helped to buttress the case of Quebec separatists in Canada.[61]

Western governments will take action in human rights issues when there is international outrage and internal popular pressure, but the cost is relatively low. Thus when Idi Amin announced the expulsion of Asians from Uganda in 1972, Canada, traditionally a country of immigration, accepted 7,000 refugees, seventy-five per cent of whom were from the professional, managerial, or entrepreneurial strata of society.[62] By contrast, when in 1968 the Kenyan government announced the gradual removal of Asians with British citizenship from a variety of economic sectors, Britain's response was to pass legislation limiting Asian immigration from East Africa to 1,500 'voucher holders' per year.[63] Britain is not a country of immigration, and it feared racial conflicts. Other African expulsions, such as that of 100,000 non-Ghanaian citizens from Ghana in 1970[64] have gone un-noticed internationally, perhaps because they concerned black Africans rather than Asians or Europeans. Similarly, singularly little has been said in the international arena regarding the persecution of Jehovah's Witnesses in Malawi, a persecution which has included expulsion from jobs and schools, imprisonment, rape and murder,[65] presumably because the Witnesses themselves are not a powerful group and pressure on their behalf by citizens of democratic countries has not been strong enough to create a situation of moral outrage.

As far as the right to a decent standard of living is concerned, neither Western nation-states nor individual citizens are likely willingly to make financial sacrifices for the sake of the poor in Africa. Such sacrifices are unlikely to occur unless there is a clearly perceived threat of war or economic destruction if they are not made; such a threat does not emanate from sub-Saharan Africa. Western liberal citizens who find it personally costless to press for judicial or political human rights in the Third World may well find that to pressure for international redistribution of wealth along the lines of the New International Economic Order will have a real cost for them or for their countries. Western criticisms of internal distribution of income in Third World countries, along the lines of the new stress on 'basic needs', will be answered with charges of imperialistic interference in the internal affairs of new states.[66]

Conclusion

I have argued that although there are real cultural variances between African and Western societies, there is no unique African concept of human rights which precludes comparison of the two forms of societies on human rights issues. On the contrary, there is a real philosophical, organizational and sociological basis for acceptance of the principle of universality of at least some of the more fundamental rights. Violations of human rights in Africa, like violations elsewhere, can be analysed in terms of indigenous custom, but must also be analysed in terms of the existent economic, stratificatory, and political system. Thus, the argument of cultural uniqueness is not sufficient to deny the possible universality of human rights. Such an argument should not therefore deter the critic or human rights activist from his or her activities.

With regard to international foreign policy considerations, whether violations of human rights in Africa can be attributed to a unique African culture or to a structural similarity to Western societies is largely irrelevant. Governments do not look for the causes of such social problems when they make decisions regarding intervention. Rather they intervene when sovereignty is not an issue, when the cost of so doing is relatively low and the prestige to be gained from taking a moral stance relatively high, and when internal popular pressure impels them to act. In the case of the Carter Administration's decision to boycott Ugandan coffee in 1978,[67] for example, the cost was low, as Uganda produced no important goods nor had it any significant strategic value; the moral prestige of condemnation of the regime was high; and there was a great deal of internal popular pressure to take action to end Amin's brutalities. In contrast, the cost of intervention on behalf of Biafrans in the Nigerian civil war was high, given that such intervention would have been a direct attack on Nigeria's sovereignty and given that Nigeria possessed a strategic good, oil. France (along with the Soviet Union) risked supporting Biafra, hoping for an eventual line on the oil the Biafrans temporarily controlled; other Western governments supported the federal Nigerian forces despite considerable pro-Biafra popular pressure, and despite the moral prestige which might have been attached to opposition to the alleged genocide of the Ibo.[68]

These examples demonstrate that in order to ensure that human rights considerations are included in foreign policies, the onus in Western democracies is upon citizens to pressure their governments to set aside considerations of sovereignty or national interest in the name of a higher moral cause. Such pressure can be exerted by individuals, or by human rights non-governmental organizations (NGOs) such as Amnesty International. Indeed, some analysts argue that NGOs are *the* transnational actors in human rights, as they can also make direct criticisms of Third World nations which their own governments might find it politically embarrassing to make. Foreign policy is not, in a democracy, something in which there is no popular input, nor are state apparatuses monolithic.[69] Thus, even given considerations of sovereignty and strategic importance, there is room for citizen advocacy of a human rights stance in foreign policy and for actions to be taken at the level of state-to-state relations.

Notes

1 For arguments that there is a uniquely African concept of human rights, see Asmarom Legesse, 'Human Rights in African Political Culture', in Kenneth W. Thompson, ed., *The Moral Imperatives of Human Rights: A World Survey* (Washington, DC, University Press of America, 1980); Lakshman Marasinghe, 'Traditional Conceptions of Human Rights in Africa: The Nigerian Experience' in Claude E. Welch Jr and Robert I. Meltzer, eds., *Human Rights and Development in Africa* (Albany, NY, SUNY Press, 1984); Chris C. Mojekwu, 'International Human Rights: the African Perspective' in Jack L. Nelson and Vera M. Green, eds., *International Human Rights: Contemporary Issues* (Standfordville, NY, Human Rights Publishing Group, 1980); Adamantia Pollis and Peter Schwab, 'Human Rights: A Western Construct with Limited Applicability', in Pollis and Schwab, eds., *Human Rights: Cultural and Ideological Perspectives* (New York, Praeger, 1979); and Dunstan M. Wai, 'Human Rights in Sub-Saharan Africa', ibid.

2 John Rex, 'Social Structure and Humanistic Sociology: The Legacy of the Classical European Tradition' in Rex, ed., *Approaches to Sociology* (London, Routledge and Kegan Paul, 1974), p. 201.

3 David Bidney, 'Cultural Relativism', *International Encyclopaedia of the Social Sciences*, vol. 3 (Macmillan and the Free Press, 1968), p. 545.

4 Jack Donnelly, 'Human Rights and Human Dignity: an Analytical Critique of Non-Western Conceptions of Human Rights', *American Political Science Review*, vol. 76, no. 2, June 1982, p. 304.

5 J. E. S. Fawcett, 'Human Rights and Domestic Jurisdiction', in Evan Luard, ed., *The International Protection of Human Rights* (London, Thames and Hudson, 1967), p. 301. See also Linda J. Maki, 'General Principles of Human Rights Law Recognized by All Nations: Freedom from Arbitrary Arrest and Detention', *California Western International Law Journal*, vol. 10 (1980).

6 Peter L. Berger, 'Are Human Rights Universal?' *Commentary*, vol. 64 (1977), p. 62.

7 Barrington Moore, Jr, *Reflections on the Causes of Human Misery and Upon Certain Proposals to Eliminate Them* (Boston, Beacon Press, 1970), p. 2.

8 Kenneth D. Kaunda, *A Humanist in Africa* (London, Longmans, 1966), pp. 24–5.

9 Julius K. Nyerere, *Ujamaa: Essays on Socialism* (London, Oxford University Press, 1968), p. 11.

10 Ali A. Mazrui, *The African Condition* (London, Cambridge University Press, 1980), p. 59.

11 Ifeanyi A. Menkiti, 'Person and Community in African Traditional Thought', in Richard A. Wright, ed., *African Philosophy: An Introduction* (2nd ed.) (Washington, DC, University Press of America, 1979), pp. 158, 162.

12 Ibid., p. 167.

13 Donnelly, op. cit.

14 Pollis and Schwab, op. cit., p. 15.

15 Donnelly, op. cit., p. 312.

16 Igor Kopytoff and Suzanne Miers, 'African "Slavery" as an Institution for Marginality' in Miers and Kopytoff, eds., *Slavery in Africa* (Madison, University of Wisconsin Press, 1977), p. 17.

17 Rhoda Howard, 'Human Rights and Personal Law: Women in Sub-Saharan Africa', *Issue*, vol. 12, nos. 1/2 (Spring/Summer 1982).

18 (UN) A/CONF. 94/17, 'World Conference of the United Nations. Decade for Women: Equality, Development and Peace' (Copenhagen 14–30 July 1980), 'Report of the Regional Preparatory Meeting of the United Nations Economic Commission for Africa' (Second Regional Conference for the Integration of Women in Development), pp. 43–4.

19 Organization of African Unity CAGH/ST.4[XVI], 'On the Rights and Welfare of the African Child', in *Africa Contemporary Record*, vol. 12, 1970–80, p. C25.

20 Jomo Kenyatta, *Facing Mount Kenya* (London, Heinemann, 1979, 1st edn, 1938), pp. 131–5.

21 Wai, op. cit., pp. 116–17.

22 Mojekwu, op. cit., p. 94, n. 1.

23 John Beattie, 'Checks on the Abuse of Political Power in some African States: A Preliminary

Framework for Analysis' in Ronald Cohen and John Middleton, eds., *Comparative Political Systems* (Garden City, NY, Natural History Press, 1967), p. 372.

24 Milton Obote, 'The Common Man's Charter' (Entebbe, Uganda Government Printer, 1970), pp. 6–7.

25 'Report of the Select Committee on the Disappearance and Murder of the Late Member for Nyandarua North, the Hon. J. M. Kariuki, M.P.' (June 3, 1975).

26 Wai, op. cit., p. 141.

27 Organization of African Unity, Banjul Charter on Human and People's Rights (Document CAB/LEG/67/3/Rev. 5), Article 2. Printed in *International Legal Materials*, vol. 21, no. 1 (January 1982).

28 Ibid.

29 Legesse, op. cit., pp. 125–6.

30 Pollis and Schwab, op. cit., p. 9.

31 For a good recent summary of such literature, see Richard Sandbrook, *The Politics of Basic Needs: Urban Aspects of Assaulting Poverty in Africa* (Toronto, University of Toronto Press, 1982), especially chapters 4 and 5.

32 Ibid., pp. 93–8.

33 Gary Wasserman, *Politics of Decolonization: Kenya Europeans and the Land Issue 1960–1965* (Cambridge, Cambridge University Press, 1976), pp. 140, 151, 155–6.

34 P. L. Raikes, 'Ujamaa and Rural Socialism', *Review of African Political Economy*, no. 3 (May–October 1975), p. 46.

35 Joel Samoff, 'The Bureaucracy and the Bourgeoisie: Decentralization and Class Structure in Tanzania', *Comparative Studies in Society and History*, vol. 21, no. 1 (January 1979), p. 37.

36 James L. Brain, 'Less than Second-Class: Women in Rural Settlement Schemes in Tanzania' in Nancy J. Hafkin and Edna G. Bay, eds., *Women in Africa* (Stanford, Stanford University Press, 1976).

37 Brain, personal communication.

38 Allan McChesney, 'The Promotion of Economic and Social Rights: Two African Approaches', *Journal of African Law*, vol. 24 (1980), p. 176.

39 Bismarck U. Mwansasu and Cranford Pratt, 'Tanzania's Strategy for the Transition to Socialism', in Mwansasu and Pratt, eds., *Towards Socialism in Tanzania* (Toronto, University of Toronto Press, 1979), p. 13.

40 Legesse, op. cit., p. 123 implies this view.

41 Margaret Peil, *Consensus and Conflict in African Societies* (London, Longman, 1977), p. 268.

42 Milton Singer, 'The Concept of Culture', *International Encyclopaedia of the Social Sciences*, vol. 3 (Macmillan and the Free Press, 1968), p. 536.

43 Barrington Moore, Jr, *Social Origins of Dictatorship and Democracy* (Boston, Beacon Press, 1966), p. 486.

44 For example, see Emile Durkheim, *The Division of Labour in Society* (Toronto, Collier-Macmillan, 1933).

45 Frantz Fanon's *Black Skins, White Masks* (New York, Grove Press, 1967) is a classic statement of how such racial inferiority complexes work.

46 J. E. Wiredu, 'How not to Compare African Thought with Western Thought', in Richard A. Wright, ed., *African Philosophy: An Introduction* (2nd ed.) (Washington, DC, University Press of America, 1979), pp. 140, 135.

47 Ibid., p. 135.

48 See Brain, op. cit., also Jette Bukh, *The Village Woman in Ghana* (Uppsala, Scandinavian Institute of African Studies, 1979) and Achola Pala Okeyo, 'Daughters of the Lakes and Rivers: Colonization and the Land Rights of Luo Women' in Mona Etienne and Eleanor Leacock, eds., *Women and Colonization* (New York, Praeger, 1980).

49 Claude Ake, 'The Congruence of Political Economies and Ideologies in Africa', in Peter C. W. Gutkind and Immanuel Wallerstein, eds., *The Political Economy of Contemporary Africa* (Beverly Hills, Sage, 1976), pp. 205–6.

50 Rhoda Howard, 'The Dilemma of Human Rights in Sub-Saharan Africa', *International Journal*, vol. 35, no. 4 (1980).

51 Robert Justin Goldstein, 'Political Repression and Political Development: The "Human Rights" issue in Nineteenth Century Europe' in Richard F. Tomasson, ed., *Comparative Social Research*, vol. 4 (Greenwich, Conn., Jai Press, 1981).

52 Howard, 'The Dilemma', op. cit., p. 729.

53 For a similar viewpoint see Samoff, op. cit., p. 48.

54 Rhoda Howard, 'The Full-Belly Thesis: Should Economic Rights Take Priority over Civil and Political Rights? Evidence from Sub-Saharan Africa', *Human Rights Quarterly*, vol. 5, no. 4 (November 1983).

55 On the 'underdevelopment' of Africa through colonial and neo-colonial mechanisms, see E. A. Brett, *Colonialism and Underdevelopment in East Africa* (London, Heinemann, 1973), Rhoda Howard, *Colonialism and Underdevelopment in Ghana* (London, Croom Helm, 1978), Colin Leys, *Underdevelopment in Kenya* (London, Heinemann, 1975) and Walter Rodney, *How Europe Underdeveloped Africa* (Washington, DC, Howard University Press, 1974).

56 The World Bank, *Accelerated Development in Sub-Saharan Africa: An Agenda for Action* (Washington, DC The World Bank, 1981), p. 4.

57 For discussions of the question of sovereignty, see Fawcett, op. cit., and R.J. Vincent, 'Western Conceptions of a Universal Moral Order', *British Journal of International Studies*, vol. 4 (April 1978).

58 Richard B. Bilder, 'Rethinking International Human Rights: Some Basic Questions', *Human Rights Journal*, vol. 2, no. 4 (1969), p. 595.

59 Laurie S. Wiseberg, 'Human Rights in Africa: Toward a Definition of the Problem of a Double Standard', *Issue*, vol. 6, no. 4 (Winter 1976).

60 A. Glen Mower, Jr, 'Human Rights in Black Africa: A Double Standard?', *Human Rights Journal* (January–March 1976), p. 53.

61 Rhoda Howard, 'The Canadian Government Response to Africa's Refugee Problem', *Canadian Journal of African Studies*, vol. 15, no. 1 (1981), p. 105.

62 Cecil Pereira, Bert N. Adams and Mike Bristow, 'Canadian Beliefs and Policy Regarding the Admission of Ugandan Asians to Canada', *Ethnic and Racial Studies*, vol. 1, no. 3 (1978), p. 360.

63 *African Contemporary Record*, vol. 1 (1968–9), p. 162.

64 Margaret Peil, 'The Expulsion of West African Aliens', *Journal of Modern African Studies*, vol. 9, no. 2 (1971).

65 Tony Hodges, *Jehovah's Witnesses in Central Africa* (London, Minority Rights Group Report no. 29, June 1976).

66 Johan Galtung, 'The New International Economic Order and the Basic Needs Approach', *Alternatives* IV (1978–9), p. 463.

67 *Christian Science Monitor*, 16 January, 1979, p. 8.

68 Laurie S. Wiseberg, 'Humanitarian Intervention: Lessons from the Nigerian Civil War', *Human Rights Journal*, vol. 7, no. 1 (1974).

69 Laurie S. Wiseberg and Harry M. Scoble, 'Transnational Actors in the Promotion and Protection of Human Rights: An Analysis of the Role and Impact of Non-Governmental Organizations', paper presented at the International Political Science Association, World Congress, 14 August, 1979, Moscow, USSR, pp. 2–4.

3 South Africa

DAN KEOHANE

Introduction

While many states experience severe domestic tension between various segments of their population, no country is more strongly associated with the presence of racial conflict than South Africa. This identification derives largely from the insistence of the government of that state that the ethnic affiliation of individuals and groups is a matter of fundamental importance which determines both the character of and the domain wherein political, economic and social rights may be exercised. Accordingly it seems appropriate to start by outlining the background and characteristics of the main racial groups which comprise the population of South Africa. Secondly the pattern of interaction among these disparate clusters, during the centuries after 1652, especially with regard to the allocation of rights, is examined. Thirdly an analysis is made of the logic of Afrikaner Nationalist rejection of racial equality in a common society and of the assumptions and effects of the policy of apartheid. Thereafter an assessment is offered of the reasons why this policy attracted widespread and persistent international censure and of the impact of the external concern upon South Africa.

South African custom and law recognizes four main racial groups, namely Africans, Whites (Europeans), Coloureds, and Asians (mainly Indians). By 1980 these groups accounted for about 72, 16, 9 and 3 per cent respectively of the population (including 'independent' Bantustans) of some 30 million.[1] Mainly because of recurring epidemics and war in the eighteenth century, the current South African population incorporates few descendants of the original inhabitants, the yellow-skinned Khoikhoi and San hunters and pastoralists. Instead most of the majority African people are related to the four principal Bantu-language groups of the Nguni (including the Zulu, Xhosa and Swazi), Sotho, Tsonga and Venda who migrated to Southern Africa many centuries ago. While the Venda is a relatively homogeneous language group, the Nguni language, which is spoken by about half the entire African population, is divided into some dozen clusters, the Sotho into eleven and the Tsonga into four.[2]

Language group distinctions among Africans have generally corresponded with variations in custom, social structure, food taboos, marriage rules and the means of producing material needs although the law, ritual and language of the major constellations exhibit much similarity.[3] An increasingly high proportion of Africans now earn their livelihood in industry, mining, European-owned farms and the service sector, in contrast with the predominance of hunting, crop cultivation and maintaining animal herds in previous centuries, while the great majority adhere to either independent Black Churches or one of the Christian denominations.

About 80 per cent of the leading White group, the Afrikaners (who constitute about 60 per cent of the European total) originate, in roughly equal proportions, from Holland and Germany, with a sprinkling of French Huguenots, Scottish Presbyterians and others.[4] Since their arrival in South Africa in the 1650s, their social and political attitudes have been keenly influenced by their principal occupation (until this century) as farmers, their relative isolation individually as agriculturalists in a vast country and collectively from their 'home countries' in Europe and by their Calvinist Dutch Reformed Church. During the last half century or so the Afrikaners have developed a common political identity and institutions and have become a predominantly urban people.

English-speaking Europeans, although sharing some political sympathies with Afrikaners, have not in centuries past considered the latter as their equal socially and culturally, while both have regarded Africans as being decidedly inferior. Since they first settled in South Africa in the 1820s, the English have tended to follow urban occupations in commerce and the professions thereby enjoying higher income and status than Afrikaners. They maintained extensive ties with Britain (and other countries) in education, culture, politics, law and religion, links strengthened by regular infusions of immigrants, and they looked to Britain as their protector *vis-à-vis* Afrikaners and Africans.

The Coloured people, who live mainly in the Cape province, are in terms of origin the most heterogeneous group in South Africa. They are descended from diverse unions between Africans, Whites, Khoikhoi, San and slaves imported from East Africa and the East Indies.[5] Except for those possessing links with the Malay Archipelago who sustain their adherence to Islam, most Coloured people are Christians, speak Afrikaans and are employed in agriculture, fishing, manufacturing and the service sector.

Most Asian people in South Africa are related to the indentured labourers brought to Natal's sugar plantations from India after 1860. The great majority reside in the province of Natal, engage in manufacturing, transport, white-collar, technical and professional occupations, subscribe to the Hindu (the largest number) or Muslim religion and many speak Indian languages (e.g. Tamil, Gujarati, or Hindi).

Overall, every major group in South Africa's population enjoys significant connections with peoples in various parts of the world which thus tends to intensify foreign interest in developments within the Republic. Geographically the country is part of the African continent and its majority population is one of the largest African groups south of the Sahara. Yet its politically dominant group, which is the biggest White population on the continent does not fully identify with Africa and is out of sympathy with post-colonial Europe which is increasingly multi-racial in composition and committed to universal norms on rights.

Government and race relations in South Africa 1652–1947

NETHERLANDS EAST INDIA COMPANY AT THE CAPE

Under its Charter the Netherlands East India Company had a monopoly of Dutch navigation and trade between the Straits of Magellan and the Cape of Good Hope and the right to wage war, make treaties and administer stations.[6] The company's expedition led by Jan Van Riebeeck landed at the Cape on 7 April 1652 and it established a refreshment station to supply fresh water, vegetables and meat to Dutch ships. Despite company efforts to maintain orderly group relations, armed conflict developed between the European newcomers and the indigenous Khoikhoi over ownership of cattle and rights to land for cultivation or grazing. The Khoikhoi felt keen grievance over their loss of land and stock to the colonists who in turn considered these late Stone Age pastoralists with their 'strange' social, cultural and religious notions and customs to be very primitive.[7]

The importation of slaves after the early years of White settlement encouraged Europeans to view manual labour as suitable only for slaves. It also promoted an 'almost unbridgeable legal and social divide',[8] between those enjoying civil rights (e.g. to own property, marry) and the slaves who possessed only natural rights (e.g. right not to be deprived of life without good cause).[9]

European settlers, although drawn from a number of countries, converged around the Dutch language, the Dutch Reformed Church and opposition to the arbitrary rule and trading monopoly of the Netherlands East India Company. They were also united in their concern for the security of themselves, their land and their stock against their African (mainly Xhosa) neighbours. This conflict in the latter part of the eighteenth century between two land-hungry groups of pastoralists resulted in loss of life and considerable mutual hostility.

BRITISH RULE IN SOUTH AFRICA

In the first half century after Britain assumed government at the Cape in its own right in 1806 (rather than in the name of the exiled Prince of Orange 1795–1803) the status of and relations between the main population clusters underwent major change. The introduction of the English language and of English legal doctrines and principles together with the arrival of 4,000–5,000 British immigrants greatly diminished the Dutch-Afrikaner ethos of life at the Cape. Protestant missionaries were instrumental in obtaining full legal equality for the Coloured people (1828)[10] and they were prominent (along with others influenced by Enlightenment ideas) in securing the end of slavery throughout the British Empire (1834).

In the Constitution of 1853, which was an important milestone in the Cape's movement towards representative self-government, race was disregarded in deciding the franchise qualification.[11] But following the annexation of territories with predominantly African populations, White opinion ensured the erection of more stringent financial, property and educational tests for the vote in the latter decades of the nineteenth century. Thus the non-White proportion of the electorate was reduced and restricted so that by 1909 it accounted for 77 per cent of the population but held only 15 per cent of the votes.[12] In the province of Natal the operation of formidable franchise tests meant that in 1907 the Whites who were a minority of the population had 99 per cent of the votes.[13]

Impelled by severe land shortage and by resentment of both the measures and humanitarian ideas of British officials, about 12,000 Boer colonists began the Great Trek into the interior of South Africa in the mid-1830s. Mainly because they possessed superior weapons and greater awareness of the operation of the market, the Boers overcame African claims to fertile land in their trek. Boer history, custom and Calvinist religion sanctioned the view that Africans (and Coloured people) were a different sub-species, and the two groups held disparate notions on communal and individual ownership, monogamy and polygamy.[14] In the Boer Republics of the Transvaal and Orange Free State with their small European population and limited economic resources, non-Whites 'were not permitted to own land, firearms, or horses, to participate in the political process, or to be at large without passes signed by their white employers'.[15]

In the latter part of the nineteenth century British administrations sought to end the political fragmentation of South Africa, and their interest in bringing the Afrikaner Republics, the African chiefdoms and the two British colonies under one government (leaving the conduct of external affairs with the Imperial authority)[16] was increased by the discovery of diamonds (1867–71) and gold (1886). The imposition of White control upon the African people[17] involved the use of military force and political pressures and was facilitated by the work of missionaries (undermining traditional customs and institutions), traders and labour recruiters for the mines, while Britain's willingness to wage a costly and bitter war against the Afrikaner states (who remained anxious to maintain their independence) in 1899–1902 produced relatively favourable conditions for the unification of the four provinces in 1909–10.[18]

The National Convention (1908–9) appointed to settle a draft constitution for a united South Africa, included no African, Asian or Coloured person but embraced 'the full spectrum of white South African leaders'.[19] In effect the convention postponed a clear decision on entitlement to the franchise and accepted a compromise position which permitted the Transvaal and Orange Free State to maintain their exclusively White (male) electorates while the Cape province retained its substantial proportion of African and Coloured voters. Only a two-thirds majority of the two Houses of Parliament sitting together could alter the non-White franchise of the Cape, and membership of parliament was limited to males of European descent.[20] The 'most Liberal Parliament which ever sat at Westminster'[21] recognized that the goal of unification, which had primacy, could not be secured peacefully on a non-racial basis. It expressed clear misgivings about the exclusion of non-Whites from the South African parliament and from much of the electorate and passed the South Africa Act, making the country a self-governing dominion on 31 May 1910.[22]

GOVERNMENT AND RIGHTS UNDER WHITE RULE, 1910–47

From 1910 the dominant interest in the exclusively White legislature, the Afrikaner farmers, pursued their advantage in a determined manner assisted by the constitution (i.e., the South Africa Act 1909) which made parliament the supreme law-making institution on domestic affairs.[23] The White 21–22 per cent of the population recognized that the Black people were increasingly seeking the same objectives as themselves, namely land, economic opportunities and political power. Accordingly Europeans employed their near-monopoly of the franchise to separate and restrict African political rights in the Cape and to segment land and labour markets according to race.

The proportion of Black voters in the Cape electorate was diminished by almost 50 per cent when the universal adult franchise was conferred on European women (1930) and men (1931) only. Half a decade later the removal of Africans from the Cape common voters roll meant that henceforth they were represented 'not as citizens but as Africans'[24] and they lost the means of influencing a number of constituency electoral contests.

Probably no legislation of the Union of South Africa had a greater impact upon both Africans and Whites than the Land Acts of 1913 and 1936.[25] These restricted the two-thirds of the population who were African to owning or occupying land in the Native Reserves which equalled about 13 per cent of the country. In this way, competition by Africans with Whites for land in 87 per cent of the total territory of South Africa was eliminated and land-starved Africans were impelled to seek employment on White farms and in the mines.

The 'civilised labour' policy instituted by the Nationalist–Labour Pact Government (elected by the votes of White farmers and urban workers in 1924) and which set the pattern for succeeding decades likewise aimed to prevent direct competition between Black and White in the labour market. This policy provided for job reservations, statutory minimum wages and new industrial councils designed to protect the job security and income of White employees,[26] while Africans were for the most part excluded from membership of registered trade unions and thus from influencing their wages and conditions. Moreover, strikes by African workers were defined as criminal acts, discriminatory laws severely restricted the choice of job for Africans and rendered them extremely vulnerable to arrest and detention, while most Africans in the Reserves were subject to the extensive powers vested in the Governor-General.[27]

Apartheid and human rights

AFRIKANER NATIONALIST REJECTION OF RACIAL EQUALITY AND INTEGRATION

Since the beginning of European settlement in South Africa, most Whites have considered the pigmentation, level of technology, beliefs, customs and way of life of the indigenous people to be quite inferior to their own. Largely because the Europeans were more advanced technologically they were able to maintain and reinforce this idea of primacy by distributing rights and opportunities unequally between themselves and non-Whites.

At no time since 1652 have the majority of Akrikaners supported in an unqualified manner concepts of political liberalism like 'equal rights for all civilised men' and non-racial suffrage. On the contrary they repudiated such ideas when they undertook the Great Trek, in the allocation of rights in the Boer Republics and when they succeeded in terminating Africans' non-racial franchise in the Cape (1936). In Afrikaner history these liberal notions are associated with 'ignorant' interference by locally-based Christian missionaries and humanitarians from a European urban background (in the nineteenth century) and with fears of British Imperialism using non-White voters against themselves. More recently Afrikaner Nationalists have connected support for racial equality, which they consider fosters negative attitudes among Africans toward apartheid, with 'reprehensible' external entities like 'the United Nations, Communist Russia, "semi-Communist India" and the British Labour Party', and domestically with African Nationalists, liberals and communists.[28]

Of supreme importance in explaining Afrikaner Nationalist rejection of proposals for a universal franchise in a unitary political system, and in the Nationalist view central to African support thereof, was and remains the facts of demography.[29] If an ethnically and racially heterogeneous society, and one where differences in income, status and authority correlate closely with membership of racial categories, proceeded towards an egalitarian polity, a White minority of one-sixth or one-seventh of the electorate might reasonably expect to find itself in 'permanent subjugation'. Thus it would become an impotent group, shorn of its political and social privileges, if not of its customs and culture. It might, if experience in other divided societies is a guide, be vulnerable along with Asian, Coloured and some African groups, to systematic exploitation and have no recourse to effective protection.[30] Perhaps a constellation which has managed political power so unreservedly for its own advantage, finds it specially difficult to envisage a relationship of racial equality rather than of domination and subordination. The comparative success of the Afrikaner National Party since 1948 (increasing its percentage of the votes among the White electorate from about forty to around sixty (1970s)) together with the lack of sizeable electoral support for a policy of universal franchise, suggests the party probably broadly reflects White preferences on this issue.

During the decades of the 1930s and 1940s processes of major change affecting the economic opportunities, aspirations and attitudes of millions of Afrikaners, Africans and others, imparted great urgency and significance to determining whether the country should follow a course of racial equality and political, economic, social and cultural integration. For many Afrikaners these years were a time of great insecurity and social change, deriving from their leaving a familiar rural community for an English-speaking urban environment where they were viewed as culturally inferior and unsophisticated, and lacking relevant occupational skills. In their new circumstances they were thought by leading Afrikaner Nationalist intellectuals and politicians to be vulnerable to competition from equally skilled Africans demanding lower wages, to the appeal of class-conscious socialist trade unions and to the pressures of anglicization.[31]

The movement of numerous Africans from the Reserves and White farms to jobs in the expanding urban-based manufacturing sector during World War II was facilitated by the suspension of Pass Laws regulating entry to the major towns between 1942 and 1946 (partly to assuage Africans' sense of grievance at a time when a Japanese invasion of South Africa was feared).[32] Prime Minister Smuts and the Native Laws (Fagan) Commission (1946–8) accepted that African urbanization could not be halted or reversed and that many Africans formed part of the settled urban population. The war and urbanization fostered a reduction of racial antagonism, the growth of African trade unions and bargaining power, and the development of common attitudes and the acquisition of Western aspirations by Africans from disparate backgrounds. From the mid 1940s a new generation of African leaders based in the urban areas (the Youth League of the African National Congress) emerged, who felt frustrated by and sceptical of institutions like the Native Representative Council and who advocated forceful ways of attaining political rights such as boycotts, strikes and civil disobedience.

The Purified Nationalist Party (of D.F. Malan) which evolved in the mid-1930s perceived its major tasks to be the protection of the 'identity' of the Afrikaner people against racial, ideological or cultural dilution and to unite them, with the aim of securing the government of the country, thereby attaining the means of shaping the entire society. Specifically the party repudiated any notion that a government composed of its members should respond passively to those processes producing greater economic interdependence between the races, or positively to African Nationalist demands for equal political and other rights. In close and extensive cooperation with Afrikaner religious, economic, cultural and educational organizations, the National Party sought, with considerable success, to unite Afrikaners with various interests around promises of economic benefit and appeals to attain their God-given destiny and special role in leading South Africa.[33]

APARTHEID: IDEOLOGY AND GOVERNMENT RACIAL POLICY SINCE 1948

The consistency, coherence and consequences of the policy of apartheid may be comprehended more fully if first its ideology is outlined. Secondly, official policy is sketched and thereafter an assessment is made of the relationship between the two and of the assumptions underlying the ideology. A political ideology, that is a set of ideas and beliefs, interprets reality by selecting specific aspects of a situation, identifies the goals to be followed by its adherents and furnishes justification for the pursuit of these aims. In May 1959 Dr DeWet Nel (a government minister, speaking in parliament) enunciated divine sanction for apartheid. According to him, all Peoples have been given a calling by God which should not be denied, all Peoples have the inherent right to develop, and the 'personal and national ideals of every individual and every ethnic group can best be developed within its own national community. Only then will the other groups feel that they are not being endangered.'[34]

The ideology of apartheid as it evolved in the decade or so after 1948 can be analysed in terms of its component elements of separation, separate development and homeland development.[35] Afrikaner Nationalists, whose basic unit of analysis is the group (i.e., nation) rather than the individual, have since their rapid urbanization in the 1930s assigned enormous importance to protecting their 'identity' and 'survival'. It is essential, they argue, to establish and maintain separate institutions and structures (e.g., for education, housing, employment, sport, public amenities, and to prevent miscegenation) so as to protect the distinctive values and culture of Whites. Further it is suggested that separation prevents and diminishes friction, competition, intense conflict, chaos, and bloodshed between different races who are likely to be highly antagonistic and prejudiced towards, and ignorant about, each other.

The rationale for separate development, articulated by Prime Minister Verwoerd and others from the end of the 1950s, postulated that different nations, taking nations to mean culturally homogeneous entities possessing a collective identity (indicated in their needs, values and way of life), have dissimilar aspirations. Therefore the separate nations such as the Zulu, Venda, Xhosa or Indian people need their own domain to pursue their ambitions. While the Coloured and Indian peoples' lack of their own geographical area could affect its manner and timing, it would not prevent the implementation of what was called parallel development. The commitment to separate development apparently provided, for the first time, the opportunity for non-Whites to determine their own government. Thus it had the positive aspect of seeming to replace a 'horizontally stratified racial pattern with the Whites forming the privileged stratum, trying to entrench their dominant status through discriminatory practices' with a 'vertically stratified racial division with each race constituting an independent socio-cultural unit'.[36]

Homeland development is a logical extension of separate development in that the various African 'nations' are supposed to follow their political, cultural and economic aspirations in the territory with which they are historically associated and as delineated in the Land Acts of 1913 and 1936.

Since 1948, three relatively distinct phases in the official policy of apartheid may be identified, each partly reflecting the specific circumstances of the time. During the first decade or so, sometimes denominated as the era of negative apartheid, measures were taken to enforce racial segregation in almost all areas of human contact. African representation in parliament and Indian rights thereto, were terminated, Coloured representation was altered from an individual to a communal basis while government assumed wide-ranging emergency powers to suppress intense opposition of African Nationalists and their allies.

During phase two of the policy starting about 1958, which coincided with and was to a degree influenced by rapid decolonisation in Africa and international condemnation of racial policies, Africans were offered the 'freedom' to develop and attain self government in their own Homeland while those living in 'White' South Africa lost whatever limited political rights they held. Concurrently African political movements (e.g. African National Congress: the Pan Africanist Congress) and multi-racial political and social organizations and activities were suppressed and Coloured parliamentary representation was ended.

The third stage of government racial policy dating from the mid-1970s, reflecting pressures and demands arising from economic imperatives, the changing social composition of the Afrikaner National Party (after thirty years in power) and dissatisfaction with the results of some apartheid policies, exhibits a more complicated pattern than earlier phases. On the one side four African Homelands have been granted 'independence' since 1976, and the White government appears anxious to consult with them and the 'non-independent' Bantustans on various issues. On the other side the White regime indicates a determination to continue the suppression of any manifestation of African Nationalism.

Alongside this continuity of policy, leading members of the National Party and government and prominent reformist Afrikaner intellectuals have advocated change of apartheid ideology and policy, thereby deepening divisions within Afrikaner institutions and producing the formation of the sizeable right wing Conservative Party in 1982. Many of the measures of separation of earlier decades (e.g. public amenities, sport, entertainment, job reservations) have been discreetly reversed in part or totally, some Africans in urban areas have secured improved rights of residence, while trade union rights, of a regulated and restricted character are now available to a number of African workers. In November 1983, South Africa's White electorate approved the new constitution which centralises power in the presidency and provides for a tri-cameral parliament with separate chambers for Whites, Coloureds and Asians. The change of constitutions, which is 'a corollary of the "total national strategy"'[37] is supposed to give Coloureds and Asians a voice in the government of their own and common affairs. This development constitutes a direct reversal and repudiation of the rationale offered and action taken by the Nationalists in the 1950s and 1960s although being substantially consistent with the advocacy of an earlier (1910–40) Afrikaner leader, General Hertzog, who favoured Coloured participation in the White legislature.

In a number of respects the assumptions of the ideology of apartheid and the fidelity of official policy thereto are not beyond criticism. Firstly in accordance with the canons of separate development, the various African 'nations', defined by their common descent and pursuit of shared cultural values (e.g. language, traditions, kinship) are (often involuntarily) assigned to eight to ten domains. Yet Afrikaners who may be thought to have many cultural affinities with Coloured people are not combined with them but with English speakers with whom they share colour. This categorisation of Whites into one unit, together with the argument that separation protects White 'identity' and 'survival', underlines the primary importance of race rather than ethnic affiliation in apartheid policy.

Secondly the manner of implementing homeland development suggests it is a questionable model of self-determination. The strong demands of African nationalism, whose focus was all of South Africa, were violently rejected and instead an outside agency, the government, selected the unit of self-rule almost solely on the criterion of ethnic affiliation. Such a foundation for these entities may be considered tenuous if it is thought probable that the processes of urbanization, industrialization and social change affecting Africans, produce other sources of identification. Because most of the Bantustans are incapable of supporting more than half their 'citizens', mainly because of their restricted land area and South Africa's reluctance to provide investment, these 'nations' cannot attain the objective postulated for them by the ideology of apartheid. Neither can their numerous 'citizens' living in White South Africa, who outnumber the Europeans, attain their cultural and ethnic goals.

Thirdly, although racial separation may reduce or prevent occasions of severe friction and even loss of life, it also seems likely to promote the opposite effect. An ideology which stresses the importance of racial and ethnic distinctions, and a policy requiring the involuntary removal of thousands from their homes and the forced cessation of much multi-racial activity, and which through prohibiting inter-racial marriage offers insult to Coloured people, provides a fertile base for the generation of racial antagonism and feelings of grievance. At the same time the maintenance by Whites of racial contacts (on an unequal basis) which serve their economic and domestic needs (e.g. African servants) is incongruent with a serious commitment to separation.

To date, the promise of advocates of separate development to replace hierarchical racial stratification with a parallel order for each ethnic group seems far from realization. Rather the continuing strong correspondence between status, income and racial affiliation, along with the formidable barriers to movement between the ethnic groups, bestows a caste-like character upon South African society.[38] The fact that South Africa's racial policies deliberately confer extremely unequal benefits upon the different ethnic groups suggests that the ideology of apartheid acts both as a motivating belief in, and a rationalization of, White domination.

APARTHEID: THE VIOLATION OF HUMAN RIGHTS

Here human rights refers principally to the civil and political (e.g. rights to life, liberty and property, the right to take part in the government of one's country, equality of rights regardless to race, colour, sex, language, religion or origin) and economic and social (e.g. free choice of employment, right to adequate living standards, right to form and join trade unions, right to education) entitlements of the United Nations Universal Declaration of Human Rights. The Declaration, which was issued (with South Africa among eight abstaining states) in the year when apartheid was inaugurated (1948) offers an authoritative guide to interpreting the human rights provisions of the United Nations Charter and is considered by some observers, but not by South Africa, to represent customary international law binding on all states.[39]

According to Mr R. F. Botha, South Africa's current Minister of Foreign Affairs and Information, his country's conflict with the United Nations on human rights is principally about methods, that is separate development versus integration, because its aims 'are the same as those set out in the Charter' (1967). These objectives in his view are to secure 'justice for all on the basis of equal concern for each and every population group', acknowledging 'the just claims and moral rights of each group to advance towards self-determination'.[40] The international community regards apartheid and in particular the creation of 'independent' Bantustans as a deliberate strategy to dispossess the overwhelming majority of the people of South Africa of their rights in their own country. Thus separate development, which denies Black Africans the possibility of exercising their rights, except in a very diluted manner, in an impoverished, truncated and small area of South Africa, is viewed as a fundamental denial of rights and not as a slightly flawed way of protecting them.

South Africa's allocation of rights to individuals only in the context of their membership of a community, while not homologous with international human rights instruments, which tend (not exclusively) to focus on the individual, does not on its own offer an inescapable indication of their infringement.[41] Rather the violation is recognizable by the selection of a group for unfavourable treatment on grounds which are irrelevant (i.e., race). The republic's general approach to human rights is especially vulnerable to serious criticism regarding the primary issue of its racially discriminatory laws and policies. On three separate but interdependent counts they fail to meet the criterion of reasonableness. Neither is it immune from censure on the consequent matter of political repression which has become increasingly prominent in recent years.

Firstly, on the assumption that human beings are equal in their dignity as persons and equal before the law, the fact that the people of a country belong to various races, whereby their physical attributes (i.e., facial features, hair texture, skin colour, skeletal structure, blood) differ, does not by itself provide a proper basis for assigning them disparate rights and status.[42] Unless and until the government of South Africa ends the racial classification of the entire population together with the major discriminatory measures following therefrom, its assurance that 'it does not condone discrimination purely on the grounds of race or colour'[43] is not credible.

Secondly, because criteria are not available to distinguish racial or ethnic groups (i.e., those with common descent and culture) in a clear-cut manner, the distribution of different entitlements by race typically produces arbitrary and humiliating results. Thus South Africa's racial laws lack a uniform definition of race and involve enquiries into a person's 'family history, social habits and physical appearance'.[44] Each year the racial classification of a number of persons (e.g., 192 in 1978) is altered with immense implications for their whole existence.[45]

Thirdly, the unreasonableness of using race as a basis for allotting status and rights and the capricious effects of operating with this criterion, would be greatly mitigated if it affected only minor aspects of individuals lives. No alleviation of this kind applies in South Africa where a person's racial categorization is 'of cardinal importance to him since it affects his status in practically all fields of life, social, economic and political'.[46] Neither does this different treatment bear any justifiable relation to a person's race nor their ethnic group.

With respect to the racial dimension of South Africa's infringement of human rights (the other aspect concerns political repression) the majority population, the Africans, experience cumulative political, legal, economic, social and cultural deprivation, although retaining equality under the common law. They are denied a voice in parliament and government and in political decisions regarding the allocation of society's resources. With the advent of 'independent' Homelands, millions have been deprived of their South African citizenship although still domiciled in the republic. The Lands

Act of 1913 and 1936 preclude them from owning land in most of the country, while their numbers have increased three-fold in the last half-century. Within the labour market, the bar on African admission to apprenticeship, adequate training, certain jobs, recognized trade unions (until the late 1970s) along with the restrictions on their choice of employment and freedom of movement, have contributed very substantially to their low average incomes of 15–35 per cent that of Whites.[47] This income disparity influences and is paralleled by African reliance upon highly inadequate and limited accommodation and unequal provision in health, welfare and education services.[48]

Because the courts were insisting upon the provision of equal facilities for different races, the Reservation of Separate Amenities Act (1953) was introduced explicitly permitting the assignment of separate but unequal amenities according to race in public transport, cinemas and on beaches. However, the cause of probably the most extensive feeling of bitterness among Africans are the Pass (i.e., reference book with details of identity, employment etc) Laws which severely limit their freedom of movement and result in hundreds of thousands of prosecutions annually. Even greater deprivation may be inflicted upon the security of millions of African families by the migrant labour system which derives from the ban on employees having their relatives living with them in urban areas.

In response to strong African and other opposition to the policy of apartheid, the South African government (assisted by the principle of the supremacy of parliament), enormously enhanced the legal powers of the executive and police, sharply diminished the role of the courts in reviewing cases of detention and administrative action, and severely reduced the freedom from arbitrary arrest of persons of all races.[49] Under laws initially introduced as emergency powers required to deal with 'threats to internal security', which are now part of 'normal' law (e.g., the Terrorism Act 1967, the Sabotage Act 1962, Suppression of Communism Act now the Internal Security Act), the Communist Party was banned in 1950 as were the two African political movements in 1960 and many Black Consciousness organizations in 1977. Thus planned opposition to apartheid was stifled, thousands of persons were detained, many of these indefinitely in conditions of solitary confinement, significant numbers were tortured in detention resulting in some unexplained deaths, and many political activists lost their freedom of movement, speech and assembly through 'banning'.[50]

In general, the restriction of rights has a clear logic of maintaining White domination and privilege although at a 'price' of diminishing their own freedom (e.g., choosing a marriage partner regardless of race). While some racially discriminatory laws have been modified or applied in a more relaxed fashion in recent years, 'security' laws continue to be enforced rigorously.

Therefore the verdict that apartheid 'is an almost clause-by-clause denial' of the civil, political, economic and social rights of the United Nations Universal Declaration of Human Rights remains true.[51]

International concern about apartheid

WHY APARTHEID EXCITED INTERNATIONAL CONCERN

Fifty years ago, South Africa's law and custom on human rights and race relations were not discordant in a fundamental way with colonial-ruled Africa and other parts of the world. After World War II, fought against a state (Nazi Germany) characterised by its gross abuse of human rights and adherence to racist notions, the international community made a strong commitment to promoting human rights and ending racial discrimination as is indicated in the United Nations Charter and the Universal Declaration of Human Rights. In the three decades after 1945 the anti-colonialist movements dissolved the European empires in Africa and Asia, transformed the composition and the priorities of many international organizations, and helped to establish the norm of racial equality. Within South Africa similar demands for majority participation in political affairs and colour-blind laws, were forcefully muzzled by a White minority regime whose ideology bore a resemblance to that of the Nazis.[52] Thus South Africa became increasingly isolated from the rest of the world and aroused a strong expression of concern therefrom.

Because of its basic assumptions and affinities, and the methods employed to enforce the policy and its consequences, South Africa's racial programme alienated it from the international community. It instituted the policy, making race the basic organizing principle of society, at a time (1948) when disclosures about the results of Nazi rule impelled other states to unambiguously dissociate themselves from plans based upon ideas of racial inequality. Moreover post-war studies of race had depreciated its usefulness as a means of classifying human beings and undermined suppositions that certain races possessed particular cultural characteristics.[53]

If the policy of apartheid had been implemented after the majority had been consulted and given their assent, it would be much more difficult for external bodies to declare it illegitimate. In fact, government 'beheaded' organized dissent, diminished the freedoms of the entire population, strengthened the powers and resources of the police, the security services and the armed forces, and made the country akin to a 'police' state. Outside observers found evidence of the malign effects of apartheid not only in the extensive violation of rights coupled with the large racial disparities in resource allocation but especially in the manner in which the authorities responded to occasional 'explosions' of Black resentment as at Sharpeville (1960) and Soweto (1976).[54]

The motivation, intensity and term of external concern about apartheid is not evenly distributed among the actors in international politics. Incidents like the Sharpeville shooting led to the United States and Britain declaring disquiet about South Africa's racial policy from 1960. Other factors conducive to these expressions were Western competition with the East for the sympathy of the newly independent states of Asia and Africa, the direct demands of these countries made at the United Nations, at Commonwealth meetings and at the Organization of African Unity, the increasing domestic sensitivity of race relations, and their adherence to the view that 'individual merit, and individual merit alone, is the criterion for man's advancement whether political or economic'.[55]

In the case of the Soviet Union, itself a large multi-racial state, its unambiguous condemnation of apartheid from the earliest years placed it alongside the new states. This however was a bonus resulting from its posture, not the inspiration thereof. The latter can be found in Soviet ideology, longstanding Soviet ties with the Communist Party of South Africa and latterly with the African National Congress, and in South Africa's obsessive hostility to communism.

For the developing ex-colonial states of Africa, Asia, the Caribbean and Pacific, who seek a more equal relationship with the rich and mainly white West, South Africa 'is the epitome of their universal struggle and a symbol of all that runs counter to their aspirations'.[56] In the perception of most of these countries apartheid is a major bone of contention. Thus India, the leading member of the non-aligned movement in the 1950s, strongly criticized the treatment of South African Indians (which at the turn of the twentieth century included Mahatma Gandhi) at the United Nations from 1946 because it regarded the denial of racial equality as an insult to the honour of India and Indians.[57]

To the fifty African states which have displaced European rule since 1950, and the few African countries independent before that, apartheid constitutes on balance a unifying factor but offers as well an especially acute challenge to their self respect. This is not only because racial conflict within the republic imposes grave and increasing costs (e.g., refugees, armed attack, additional military spending) upon its neighbours. It is also due to Africans' awareness that 'the most blatantly racialist regime in the world',[58] is both a lively reminder of past humiliation and a present insult to their racial dignity, which can be obliterated only when White minority rule in South Africa is terminated.

Unlike the circumstances of some other instances of human rights violations, those experiencing severe oppression in South Africa enjoy strong and direct affinities with countries composing one-third of the total membership of the United Nations and significant ties of sympathy with many others. This factor more than any other explains why international opposition to apartheid reached a high level about 1960, and with intermittent upward variation, continued thereafter. The nature of this international opposition was strongly influenced by the fact that the states which best appreciated the oppressive character of apartheid lacked the means to make their concern effective.

THE CHARACTER AND OBJECTIVES OF INTERNATIONAL CENSURE OF APARTHEID: RADICALS AND MELIORISTS

For some two decades the international community has maintained accord in recognizing that apartheid is not essentially within the domestic jurisdiction of South Africa, declaring its illegitimacy as a theory and policy, and in responding to conspicuous demonstrations of its inhumanity by taking limited action against the republic. Likewise no state (except South Africa) has recognized the four 'independent' Bantustans, which are perceived to be a central element in apartheid policy and a grave violation of the territorial integrity of the country. There is also wide agreement that domestic forces have the principal part in determining the future of South African society, although external agencies and pressures can exert a significant but secondary effect. In other important respects apartheid does not evoke a united international reaction. Instead, it is possible to identify two rather loose coalitions of governmental and non-state actors each offering a distinctive view on matters like the international significance of apartheid and the desirability, nature and probable efficacy of external action against South Africa.[59]

The radical coalition

The radical grouping includes African and most non-White Third World states, the exiled South African nationalists, the Organization of African Unity (especially the Liberation Committee), the United Nations (particularly the Special Committee on Apartheid), the British-based Anti-Apartheid Movement and other organizations. It enjoys consistent multidimensional support from communist countries and significant sustenance or sympathy from additional states. In the dominant radical perspective, South Africa is not only a grotesque realm where the peaceful route to racial equality and majority rule was and remains violently shut by the White regime but is also an issue of central political and moral importance in international politics and within many states. Under the conditions of heavily suppressed racial conflict present in South Africa, it is thought illusory to expect the Europeans to be the agency of fundamental change and misleading to advocate exclusively peaceful change.[60]

Instead the radicals concentrate on identifying how best to assist the majority attain what is considered their eventual assured goal of full participation in government. To this end multiple support (e.g., refuge, bases, affirming that their struggle is legitimate) is supplied to exiled opponents of apartheid, while efforts are made to weaken and isolate the South African polity, recognizing however that because of their economic integration with and heavy dependence upon the republic, her Black neighbours can take only limited action.[61] After years of intense military and economic pressure by South Africa, the leading radical states of Mozambique and Angola submitted to its demands in February and March 1984.[62] Thus Mozambique signed a non-aggression pact whereby it accepted a commitment to prevent ANC guerrillas from operating out of its territory against South Africa and Angola adhered to a disengagement agreement which requires it to deny SWAPO the use of bases and facilities in the area contiguous with Namibia. These two accords not only expose a division of interest and tactics between the liberation movements and the Black governments of Southern Africa. They also seem to challenge radical assertions that foreign investment in the White-dominated republic is a partisan intervention in an existing conflict which makes the Blacks' 'struggle much more difficult and certainly more violent than it needs to be otherwise'.[63]

Using its majority position in the United Nations, the Commonwealth, the Organization of African Unity and other international organizations, the radical coalition has maintained a momentum of pressure, whereby South Africa has become isolated and ostracized since the mid 1960s. In contrast with countries where thousands of people have perished through acts of genocide by government, a 'publicity war' of debates, surveillance, conferences and reports was conducted against the Republic.[64] It has been suspended from the United Nations (since 1974), excluded from the Commonwealth, and many United Nations agencies (e.g. FAO and UNESCO) and has been unable to establish diplomatic relations with most of its African neighbours and the majority of states. Its racial policy has attracted the condemnation of such varied non-governmental bodies as the World Council of Churches, the World Alliance of Reformed Churches, the Olympics Committee (from whose activities it has been excluded), the International Confederation of Free Trade Unions and Amnesty International. South Africa is probably the only instance of a state being the specific target of an international convention, that on the Suppression and Punishment of the Crime of Apartheid, (1973), though the convention is defined in general terms.

The meliorist coalition

What may be designated the meliorist coalition is composed of predominantly White developed countries of the North Atlantic area like Britain, France, West Germany, and the United States along with Japan and those multinational corporations maintaining important economic relations with South Africa. The states comprising this group are South Africa's pre-eminent economic partners and, excepting Japan, have extensive contacts and ties of history, kin and culture with its European people, but few affinities with the majority population. While viewing South Africa as an abnormal society manifesting grave if understandable racial injustice, meliorists do not regard it as the worst instance of inhumanity extant, nor generally as the most pressing issue on their international agenda.

Given that substantial benefits and costs (e.g., in their relations with Afro-Asian states) accrue to meliorist countries because of their links with South Africa, they naturally favour developments within the republic (and external pressures which they consider will promote these changes) which would reduce or eliminate the costs while retaining the advantages of the relationship. Among the benefits none are more important than their economic interests in South Africa which are to maintain stable and profitable investment opportunities, assured supplies of its critical minerals (e.g., gold, manganese, chromium) and access to its substantial export markets.

Although keenly impressed by the economic and military strength and determination of the White government and aware of divisions among the Black population on how to attain major change, the meliorist coalition fears that racial discrimination and oppression will eventually produce violent revolutionary change. This might well result in the replacement of the existing anti-communist regime in Pretoria with a pro-communist government and it could gravely damage Western economic and strategic interests in South Africa. Moreover the occurrence of prolonged and violent racial conflict in the republic might inspire serious tension within multi-racial countries like Britain and the United States.

Accordingly meliorists give general support to a strategy of 'managed or controlled change'. Thus they favour plans for economic and social reform to improve conditions for non-Whites (e.g., employment, housing, training) and for negotiations on power-sharing in the political realm. Typically they consider it ill-advised for outsiders to offer South Africans of whatever race or ideology blueprints about their ultimate political arrangement (although the USA and UK indicated support for the new constitution in 1983) but hope for the evolution of the regime whose pigmentation and policies foster economic, political and racial stability.

The radical–meliorist debate on action against apartheid

While willing to register its reprobation of apartheid in international organizations, the meliorist group, particularly its permanent members of the United Nations Security Council, refused to act against South Africa under chapter 7 of the charter (i.e., action with respect to threats to peace, breaches of the peace and acts of aggression) until November 1977. At the time a combination of 'auspicious' circumstances (strongly influenced in some instances by world economic conditions) at the domestic, regional, continental and global levels, produced the 'elevation' of the existing (since 1963), often disregarded embargo on the supply of arms to the republic, into a mandatory ban.

Domestically these conditions included the Soweto uprising and killings of 1976 together with the death in detention of Steve Biko (the Black Consciousness leader) and the banning of Black organizations and publications in 1977. South Africa's armed attacks, using weapons of Western origin, against contiguous states, its intransigence regarding Namibian independence and alleged attempt to test a nuclear device, comprised the regional aspect while the continental dimension refers to the greater impact of African demands in the light of Nigeria's possession of scarce oil. The global level alludes to the advent of a United States administration sensitive to the claims of the Third World, concerned about human rights internationally and anxious to minimize anti-Western influence in Southern Africa. Impetus was given to this anxiety through Soviet and Cuban involvement in that previously exclusively Western sphere of interest following the end of Portuguese rule.[65]

In the radical view, Western acceptance of a mandatory ban, though indicating vulnerability to the charge that it 'armed apartheid', represented a second-best answer to their repeated calls for mandatory economic sanctions. For some years consumers in Western countries had boycotted South African goods[66] (with little effect) as did a number of radical states, and from 1973 Arab members of OPEC banned the supply of oil to South Africa. While the meliorist coalition would with some misgivings consider the application of economic pressures against the external behaviour of other states, members like Britain and the multinational companies would be extremely reluctant for reasons of ideology and interest, to seek to alter the domestic arrangements of a friendly country like South Africa in this way.

The costs, economic and political, of cutting all major economic ties with the republic would be significant for most meliorist governments (in terms of industrial disruption, employment losses, higher import costs, unpopularity with groups affected economically and those with relatives in South Africa and increased leverage for the Soviet Union in the sale of critical minerals) and probably forbidding in a few cases. Moreover if it were to be effectively implemented, which might present extreme difficulty, it could well require a naval and air blockade and the application of armed force against the target. Even then, according to the meliorist analysis, there would be no assurance of achieving majority rule but the certainty that all the people of Southern Africa, and especially the Blacks would bear heavy costs.

Compared to such a prospect, the promulgation in 1977 of a voluntary Code of Conduct for EEC (member states) employers operating in South Africa, and the restriction by some Western governments of state support (e.g., export and tax credits) for investment therein, seemed highly attractive. The EEC and other Codes (e.g., Sullivan code – USA) identified standards for African employees' bargaining rights, wages, training and social provision and are an exemplar of meliorist methods of advancing reforms in South Africa. They might also be expected to deflate radical (both domestic and Third World) allegations that foreign investors profited from apartheid's non-unionised and highly regulated labour.[67]

THE IMPACT OF EXTERNAL DEMANDS UPON SOUTH AFRICA

The effects of outside pressure upon South Africa may be assessed on the basis that the international community sought to punish, compel and reform the 'offender' namely the White regime and to encourage the 'victim', the Black population, while noting that radicals tended to stress retribution, compulsion and assistance, and meliorists accentuated reform.[68] Since 1960 the rest of the world has imposed significant political, economic and military costs upon the republic. The country's severe loss of status and of legitimacy in the world, together with its exclusion from many international bodies directly restricts the effective pursuit of important state objectives, as well as preventing its people participating in many cultural and sporting activities.

South Africa's large-scale information–propaganda programme in Western countries, coupled with the sponsored visits for overseas figures, indicates an anxiety to communicate with an important 'public' and to prevent its isolation becoming more complete. On the African continent, South Africa's outward looking foreign policy which aimed to reverse the tide of isolation and ostracism, and gain access to essential trading and investment opportunities, had few achievements. Nevertheless Pretoria's relentless pursuit of a strategy of destabilizing its neighbours since the late 1970s did produce accords with Angola and Mozambique and thereby helped to diminish South Africa's isolation. In terms of international acceptance the granting of 'independence' to four Homelands had failed.

Because of external hostility substantial additional resources were required to meet the threat to the state's security. The difference observable between South Africa's current position as the strongest military power south of the Sahara, and the level the armed forces might be expected to reach if it enjoyed relatively harmonious relations with African states, is related to two factors. These are the dissociation of Western countries from direct involvement in South Africa's military defence combined with the perceived requirement to possess adequate means to deter attack by various antagonistic states.

Similarly the possibility of the refusal of all major oil exporters to supply South Africa, has led to an expensive programme to stockpile sufficient oil, firstly to discourage the cut-off of supplies and secondly to withstand such measures if they were taken. This threat also stimulated research into alternative energy sources thereby perhaps producing some distortion in overall resource allocation therefor. Evidently the boycott by Arab members of OPEC (1973) and Iran (1979) of oil supplies to South Africa, forced the country to pay especially high prices for its requirements in the period 1979/80, and to become heavily dependent upon, and thus vulnerable to, the few exporters willing to supply it.[69]

Arising out of the United Nations ban on arms for South Africa, that country developed its arms industry to a point close to self-sufficiency considerably more quickly than it might otherwise have done. Therefore, as in other instances, it was probably a less efficient programme that it would be under 'normal' conditions. In combination, the attention devoted by Western journalists and analysts to the racial instability manifest during the Soweto riots and killings of 1976, the United Nations condemnation thereof and the consequent erosion of confidence among foreign investors, produced a highly damaging net outflow of capital in 1977–8.[70]

The coincidence in time between strong international demands for conformity to the norm of racial equality and some limited moves in this direction within South Africa since the mid 1970s, insinuates that the latter is at least partly attributable to the former. Yet in most instances reliable evidence of a direct relationship between the two is not available. In the late 1950s and early 1960s, Prime Minister Verwoerd acknowledged that the evolution of 'negative' apartheid into the more positive model of Homeland Development leading eventually to independence, was significantly influenced by the desire to make apartheid more acceptable to international opinion.[71]

The commitment of the Pretoria government to move away from 'unnecessary' discrimination based on race or colour in October 1974, was mainly due to the collapse of the 'physical and psychological buffer'[72] of Portuguese rule in Southern Africa. Thus it recognized that without this 'support', the pressures of continuing international criticism, the demand for improved relations with neighbouring states and domestic needs, could not be resisted.[73]

International boycotts appear to have induced the South African authorities to permit the introduction of multi-racial teams in a few sports and to allow non-racial facilities for spectators. With respect to the introduction of bargaining rights and other opportunities for African employees in the late 1970s, the pressures of some multinational companies and the example offered by the application of the EEC Code of Conduct, appear to have made a marginal if positive contribution.[74]

In the period between 1945 and the early 1960s, South Africa's Black leaders received considerable support and inspiration from the United Nations, India, and Nkrumah's Ghana.[75] More recently the success of African nationalists in displacing White-minority rule in Mozambique, Zimbabwe and Angola and the seeming 'defeat' of South African forces in the latter country in 1976, stimulated further internal opposition to apartheid. Although the White government's extensive censorship, prohibition of travel abroad by Black opponents of its racial policy, and refusal to admit opponents of the regime, prevents the dissemination of full information about international condemnation of apartheid and support for majority rule, a limited awareness of this sympathy is probably present among some Blacks. Certainly the morale of government supporters is not raised by the knowledge that various state and other actors provide political, humanitarian, financial, and military aid to refugees from, and nationalist opponents of apartheid, thus permitting the latter to make (occasional) armed attacks within the republic.

South Africa's rulers have refused to meet the cardinal demands of the outside world mainly because of the intensity, nature and source of those claims. Firstly 'the strength of White South Africa'[76] is based upon the weakness of the African states who are the core group seeking change in the republic. Secondly, the target was requested to concede the fundamental values of the governing elite and not some peripheral interest. Thirdly it would be quite illogical for the Whites to make strenuous efforts to suppress African nationalism within their own boundaries only to concede to that force without. Moreover many of those who demanded these changes were silent about grave breaches of human rights in other African states.[77] Although the international pressures have failed to attain their declared objectives that is quite different from asserting that they had no impact. It may be the case that the most positive achievement of international concern and surveillance has been to prevent the taking of additional lives in situations of conflict, through knowledge of the hostile reaction this would induce.[78]

Notes

1 Sources on population totals and percentages are, *South Africa 1982: Official Yearbook of the Republic of South Africa* (Johannesburg, Chris Van Rensburg Publications, 1982) and *Survey of Race Relations in South Africa, 1982* (Johannesburg, South African Institute of Race Relations, 1983).

2 *South Africa 1982* above.

3 M. Wilson and L. Thompson (eds.), *The Oxford History of South Africa*, Volume 1, *South Africa to 1870* (Oxford, The Clarendon Press, 1969) p. 182.

4 *The Cambridge History of the British Empire*, Volume 7, *South Africa, Rhodesia and the High Commission Territories* (Cambridge, Cambridge University Press, 2nd edn, 1963) p. 874.

5 See T. H. R. Davenport, *South Africa: A Modern History* (London, Macmillan, 1977) and United Nations: Unit on Apartheid: Department of Political and Security Council Affairs, Notes and Documents, Number 18/72, *Apartheid and the Coloured People of South Africa*, by A. La Guma (September 1972).

6 M. Wilson and L. Thompson (eds.), note 3 above, p. 185.

7 Consult *The Cambridge History of the British Empire*, note 4 above, p. 280.

8 T. H. R. Davenport, note 5 above, p. 21.

9 To some extent 'widespread miscegenation between Whites, slaves, Khoikoi and San', mitigated the cleavage between the slaves and those with rights. See M. Wilson and L. Thompson, (eds.), note 3 above, p. 184.

10 The missionaries observed that Coloured people 'were esteemed more lightly even than slaves'. See *The Cambridge History of the British Empire*, note 4 above, p. 291.

11 Moreover the relatively low income or property qualification permitted about 80 per cent of adult males to acquire the vote – *The Cambridge History of the British Empire*, note 4 above, p. 384.

12 M. Wilson and L. Thompson (eds.), *The Oxford History of South Africa*, Volume 2, *South Africa 1870–1966* (Oxford, Clarendon Press, 1971), p. 338.

13 H. R. Hahlo and E. Kahn, *The Union of South Africa: The Development of its Laws and Constitution* (London, Stevens and Sons, 1960), p. 71, note 44.

14 See M. Wilson and L. Thompson (eds.) note 3 above, pp. 268–9 and T. Dunbar Moodie, *The Rise of Afrikanerdom: Power, Apartheid and the Afrikaner Civil Religion* (London, University of California Press, 1975), pp. 5–7.

15 M. Wilson and L. Thompson (eds.), note 3 above, p. 367.

16 M. Wilson and L. Thompson (eds.), note 12 above, pp. 248 and 290: T. H. R. Davenport, note 5 above, pp. 127–146.

17 Bechuanaland and Basutoland Protectorates retained much of their traditional powers while most chiefdoms 'survived as territorial based corporate entities under white over-rule'. See M. Wilson and L. Thompson (eds.), note 12 above, pp. 339–43.

18 For an analysis of the conditions favourable to conciliation between Britain and the Boers in the period 1907–9, see M. Wilson and L. Thompson, (eds.) note 12 above, pp. 339–43 and L. Thompson, *The Unification of South Africa 1902–1910* (Oxford, Clarendon Press, 1960).

19 See M. Wilson and L. Thompson, (eds.), note 12 above, p. 348. By 1908 no non-White person had been elected to the Cape Parliament.

20 The Governor-General's eight nominated members of the Senate were supposed to include four with special knowledge of the 'reasonable wants and wishes of the Coloured races'.

21 J. A. Hobson, *The Crisis of Liberalism: New Issues of Democracy: Introduction and notes*, by P. F. Clarke (Sussex, The Harvester Press, 1974), p. 243.

22 The decision of the British parliament in 1909, was the logical culmination of Britain's acceptance of the exclusion of non-Whites from the franchise in the Afrikaner provinces (so as to foster conciliation between Britain and the Afrikaners) in the Treaty of Vereeniging (1902) following the Boer War and also in the consequent grant of responsible self-government to them in 1906 and 1907. High Commissioner Lord Selbourne had signalled to the National Convention that Britain would probably accept their 'compromise' on the franchise – see M. Wilson and L. Thompson (eds.), note 12 above, p. 355. Britain had indicated to the South African leaders that the more rigid were the exclusions based on race, the less probable

it was that the three High Commission Territories would be transferred to the Union of South Africa, and was aware of the deep resentment felt by Afrikaners over 'interference' by British officials, and missionaries on behalf of Africans and Coloured people.

23 The similarity between South Africa's Constitution and that of Britain is discussed in H. R. Hahlo and E. Kahn, note 13 above, chapter 4.

24 E. H. Brookes and J. B. Macaulay, *Civil Liberty in South Africa* (Cape Town, Oxford University Press, 1958) p. 142.

25 The Acts 'largely ratified the conquests of the nineteenth century'. See M. Wilson and L. Thompson (eds.), note 12 above, p. 438.

26 Ibid., pp. 137, 145, 206 and R. Horwitz, *The Political Economy of South Africa* (London, Weidenfeld and Nicolson, 1967).

27 E. H. Brookes and J. B. Macaulay, note 24 above, p. 158.

28 This characterization is attributed to Prime Minister Malan – J. Robertson, *Liberalism in South Africa 1948–1963* (Oxford, Clarendon Press, 1971), p. 130.

29 For a discussion of White rejection of majority rule, see J. Robertson, *Liberalism in South Africa*, note 28, p. 31 and N. J. Rhoodie, *Apartheid and Racial Partnership in Southern Africa* (Cape Town, Academica, 1969), pp. 8, 28–30.

30 Some official South African publications devote considerable attention to examples of intense conflict in other heterogeneous societies, note the breakup of states like the West Indies, Malaysia and British India (1947) argue that parliamentary government has failed in African countries and suggest or imply that these external phenomena indicate the wisdom of separate development. See *Multi-National Development in South Africa: The Reality* (Pretoria, Compiled and Published by the State Department of Information, 1974).

31 These issues are analysed in H. Adam and H. Giliomee, *Ethnic Power Mobilized: Can South Africa Change* (New Haven, Yale University Press, 1979), chapters 4 and 6, and T. Dunbar Moodie, *The Rise of Afrikanerdom: Power, Apartheid and the Afrikaner Civil Religion*, note 14 above.

32 M. Benson, *The African Patriots* (London, Faber and Faber 1973), pp. 98–100.

33 See H. Adam and H. Giliomee, *Ethnic Power Mobilized* and T. Dunbar Moodie, *The Rise of Afrikanerdom*, both note 31 above.

34 Ibid., p. 265.

35 This division is employed by F. Van Zyl Slabbert, 'Cultural and Ethnic Politics', in P. Randall (ed.) *Towards Social Change* (Johannesburg, SPROCAS, 1971), chapter 2.

36 N. J. Rhoodie, *Apartheid and Racial Partnership in Southern Africa*, note 29 above, p. 397, note 41.

37 Quote from K. W. Grundy, 'South Africa's Domestic Strategy' in *Current History*, volume 82, no. 482 (March 1983). See also J. E. Spence, 'Reform in South Africa – A Tangled Web' in *Contemporary Review* (January 1984).

38 South Africa's caste-like characteristics are discussed by P. Randall (ed.), *Towards Social Change*, note 35 above, chapter 2, and in L. Thompson and A. Prior, *South African Politics* (London, Yale 1982), pp. 107–90.

39 See R. Higgins, *Human Rights – Prospects and Problems* (Leeds, Leeds University Press, 1979), p. 7. This analysis is apparently supported by J. D. Van der Vyver, *Seven Lectures on Human Rights* (Cape Town, JUTA, 1976), p. 128 but opposed by L. Henkin, *How Nations Behave: Law and Foreign Policy* (New York, Columbia University Press, 2nd Edn 1979) pp. 231–4.

40 J. Carey (ed.), *International Protection of Human Rights* (Dobbs Ferry, NY, Oceana Publications, 1969), p. 50–1.

41 Note the International Convention on the Elimination of All Forms of Racial Discrimination, 1966, provides for group rights (Article 1, Clause 4, Article 2, Clause 2) while countries like Fiji, Cyprus and Belgium assign rights by group, without attracting general external censure.

42 See the discussion of equality in the dissenting opinion of Judge Tanaka, *South West Africa Cases* (Second Phase, 1966) in Reports of Judgements, Advisory Opinions and Orders, of the International Court of Justice (1966), pp. 284–316 also quoted in I. Brownlie (ed.), *Basic Documents on Human Rights* (Oxford, Clarendon Press, 1971).

43 Statement by South Africa's Ambassador to the United Nations, Mr R. F. Botha in 1974. See *UN Monthly Chronicle*, no. 10 (1974).

44 J. Dugard, *Human Rights and the South African Legal Order* (Princeton, New Jersey, Princeton University Press 1978) pp. 59–63 on race classification.

45 See *Survey of Race Relations in South Africa* 1979 (Johannesburg, South African Institute of Race Relations 1980), p. 72 on changes of race classification in 1977.

46 Dugard, note 44 above, p. 62.
47 For figures on income consult *Survey of Race Relations in South Africa, 1982* and other years (note 45 above) and S. T. Van Der Horst and J. Reid, *Race Discrimination in South Africa: A Review* (Cape Town, David Philip, 1981). The ratio between White incomes and that of Coloured and Asian employees is substantially smaller than that for Africans.
48 Statistics on provision in health and welfare facilities are available in the *Survey of Race Relations*. According to the 1978 *Survey* (p. 399) per capita expenditure was 654 Rand for specified White pupils and 49 Rand for Africans.
49 For an analysis of South Africa's suppression of political rights consult Dugard, note 44 above, J. D. Van der Vyver, note 39 above, and 'Infringements of the Universal Declaration of Human Rights in South Africa' by the International Commission of Jurists, in *Objective: Justice*, vol. 5, no. 4 (October, November, December 1973).
50 See *Political Imprisonment in South Africa* (London, Amnesty International, 1978).
51 L. Kuper, *Genocide* (Harmondsworth, Penguin, 1981), p. 197.
52 Ibid., p. 198.
53 Regarding studies of race, see J. Rex, *Race Relations in Sociological Theory* (London, Weidenfeld and Nicolson, 1970), pp. 3–4.
54 For details of disparities in allocation of resources by race, consult recent issues of the *Survey of Race Relations in South Africa.*
55 Extract from Prime Minister Macmillan's 'Wind of Change' speech to the South African parliament in 1960, wherein he noted the competition between East and West and the strength of African nationalism. Britain's response to apartheid at this time is examined by G. Berridge, *Economic Power in Anglo-South African Diplomacy: Simonstown, Sharpeville and After* (London, Macmillan Press, 1981).
56 F. McA. Clifford-Vaughan, *International Pressures and Political Change in South Africa* (Cape Town, Oxford University Press, 1978), p. 5.
57 See J. Barber, *South Africa's Foreign Policy 1945–1970* (London, Oxford University Press, 1973), pp. 30–3.
58 A. Mazrui, *Africa's International Relations: The Diplomacy of Dependence and Change* (Edinburgh, Heinemann Educational Books, 1977), p. 216.
59 This categorization is influenced by, but different from that examined in T. Shaw, 'International Organizations and the Politics of Southern Africa: Towards Regional Integration of Liberation?', *Journal of Southern African Studies*, volume 3, no. 1 (October 1976), pp. 1–19.
60 The *Lusaka Manifesto* of Central and East African states of 1969 (later endorsed by the OAU and the UN) stated a clear preference for ending apartheid by peaceful means, but seemed to imply that an exclusively peaceful option was no longer available. The current United States Assistant Secretary of State for African Affairs, Mr Crocker, unlike some US officials in the 1970s, notes 'it is misleading to speak in terms of a simple choice between peaceful and violent change'! – C. A. Crocker, 'South Africa: Strategy for Change', *Foreign Affairs*, volume 59, no. 2 (Winter, 1980), p. 344. For a criticism of advocacy of peaceful change in the South African context, see A. S. Minty, The 'Case for Disengagement' in *Investment in South Africa: The Options* (London, Christian Concern for Southern Africa, 1976).
61 Radicals oppose avoidable ties with South Africa like Western investment or trade by most African countries, but recognize that Lesotho could not survive without extensive relations with South Africa.
62 For an analysis of South Africa's military and economic pressures against neighbouring states consult C. Coker, 'South Africa: A New Military Role in Southern Africa 1968–82' in *Survival*, volume 25, no. 2 (March/April 1983), Simon Jenkins, 'Destabilisation in Southern Africa', *The Economist* (July 16, 1983) and B. Munslow and P. O'Keefe, 'Energy and the Southern African Regional Confrontation', *Third World Quarterly*, volume 6, no. 1 (January 1984).
63 Source, Minty, note 60 above, p. 22. Besides the states of Southern Africa, South Africa conducts some 'backdoor' trade with other African countries, who publicly deplore such relations. South African leaders held talks with a number of African governments in the years 1974–6 mainly on the Rhodesian question. See R. W. Johnson, *How Long Will South Africa Survive?* (London, Macmillan, 1977), chapter 7.
64 On the comparative lack of publicity for instances of genocide, and the reasons, therefore, consult L. Kuper, *International Action against Genocide* (London, Minority Rights Group Report, Number 53, 1982). The pressures used against South Africa are analysed in R.

Bissell, *Apartheid and International Organizations* (Boulder, Colorado, 1977) and M. Doxey, 'Strategies in Multi-lateral Diplomacy', *International Journal*, volume 25, no. 2 (Spring, 1980).

65 For a detailed review of the circumstances leading up to the mandatory arms ban, see A. S. Minty 'The Anti-Apartheid Movement and Racism in Southern Africa' in P. Willetts (ed.), *Pressure Groups in the Global System* (London, F. Pinter, 1982), pp. 28–45. For many years Mr Minty has been a leading representative of the Anti-Apartheid Movement.

66 This consumer boycott and later demands for the economic isolation of South Africa, were inspired by the experience of Black boycotts within South Africa in the 1950s – see M. Benson, note 32, pp. 256–63 and J. V. Gbeho, *Africa's Call for Sanctions against South Africa* (London, The Africa Centre, 1982).

67 A full review of the Codes of Conduct is available in A. Akeroyd *et al.*, *European Business and South Africa: An Appraisal of the EEC Code of Conduct* (Mainz, Grünewald, Müchen, Kaiser, 1981).

68 For a brief discussion of the aims of the African states on South Africa see A. A. Mazrui, note 58, pp. 203–6.

69 For a discussion of South Africa's oil supplies see M. Bailey, 'Sanctions busting again', *New Statesman* (18 June, 1982). The costs for South Africa of avoiding the oil embargo are analysed in B. Munslow and P. O'Keefe, 'Energy and the Southern African Regional Confrontation', note 62 above.

70 L. Katzen, 'South Africa's Vulnerability to Economic Sanctions', *Review of International Studies*, volume 8, no. 2 (April 1982), pp. 96–7.

71 See J. Barratt, 'South Africa in a Changing World' in E. Hellmann and H. Lever (eds.), *Race Relations in South Africa 1929–1979* (London, Macmillan, 1980), pp. 213–48.

72 Ibid., p. 240.

73 In the view of one South African scholar, the change owed much to international criticism at the UN. See J. D. Van Der Vyver, note 39, p. 146.

74 On the EEC Code's contribution, consult Akeroyd, note 67. The role of multinational employers is noted in R. M. Price and C. G. Rosberg (eds.), *The Apartheid Regime: Political Power and Racial Domination* (Berkeley, University of California, 1980), pp. 190–1.

75 See Wilson and Thompson, vol. 2, note 12 above, pp. 509–11, J. Robertson, note 28 and G. M. Gerhart, *Black Power in South Africa: The Evolution of an Ideology* (London, University of California Press, 1979), pp. 212, 270, 306.

76 H. Adam, *Modernising Racial Domination* (London, University of California Press, 1971), p. 136.

77 For an explanation of African states' approach to human rights see A. G. Mower Jr, 'Human Rights in Black Africa: A Double Standard?, *Human Rights Journal*, vol. IX: 1 (January/March 1976).

78 See L. Kuper, note 51 above, p. 209.

4 The Soviet Union

ARFON REES

Human rights became a central issue in international relations in the seventies, introducing a new element into inter-state relations and bringing together external and internal influences on the political process in individual countries into a new conjuncture. This development was exemplified in the USSR's relations with the West. This chapter explores the interaction of external and internal pressures in influencing human rights observance in the USSR. It examines the Soviet conception of human rights, the way in which rights have been interpreted in accordance with Marxist–Leninist ideology, and their practical application. The human rights problem in the USSR has been inextricably bound to the question of dissent and here the Jewish emigration campaign is used to illustrate the general problem of strengthening human rights in a state socialist system.

Human rights doctrine and practice in the Soviet Union

MARXISM–LENINISM AND HUMAN RIGHTS

Human rights in the USSR are founded on a philosophical basis quite different from that of Western liberalism. They draw on the early humanistic writings of Marx which were developed as a critique of the claims of the American and French revolutions to have established the universal, rational, equal, inalienable rights of man.[1] Marxism–Leninism in the USSR is a state ideology interpreted by the Communist Party which claims to provide a scientific world view guiding the party's work in all areas of policy as part of a total conception of communist construction.

For the liberal, human rights are premised upon a belief in moral absolutes, such as the inviolacy of the individual, which transcend all national, cultural and class characteristics. The individual human being possesses certain inalienable rights which may not be abrogated, and which the state is duty bound to respect and safeguard. The extension of human rights observance is dependant also on the development of 'civil society' itself, the growth in the power of subordinate social groups and the cultivation of new values and expectations. The state can influence these changes in part, but excessive interference by the state can itself undermine civil rights which are the basis of a free and open society.

In class society, Marxists argue, the prevailing morality usually expresses the interests of the ruling class, and the state itself is an instrument of class domination.[2] Human rights cannot be discussed in abstraction from the realities of class rule. As long as class society exists all moral slogans employed by the ruling class will be deceptions designed to secure its interests, to legitimize its power and maintain its ideological hegemony over society. Under capitalism the proclamation of juridical equality stands in contrast to the realities of class inequalities which are founded on the rights of private property. These realities are concealed behind the facade of 'bourgeois democracy'.

Since true freedom and equality can only be established with the abolition of class exploitation, it is argued, the development of rights can be understood only in relation to the historical process by which class society is transcended. The transition from capitalism to socialism requires that the rights of the exploiters be restricted and those of the exploited enhanced. The state in this period, representing the 'dictatorship of the proletariat', has the task of suppressing the old exploiting classes. With the transition to the classless, self-administering communist society the state itself 'withers away'. The building of socialism involves the eradication of 'bourgeois' consciousness, the re-education of society, the re-moulding of the psychology of the individual, and the creation of the 'new socialist man'.

For the Marxist–Leninist human rights do not inhere in individuals by virtue of their common humanity. They are instead concomitants of a concept of 'social being' which can emerge only after capitalist relations of production have been replaced by socialist relations of production. Human rights are thus also contingent upon the development of a 'socialist personality' acquired in the process of education in a socialist community. Individuals who fail to develop this complex of socially useful properties simply fail to qualify for the citizenship status whose rights the socialist states guarantees and develops.

Marxism–Leninism thus accords priority to the maintenance and development of the socialist order as a condition for the extension of human rights. Emphasis is placed on economic, social and cultural rights which are the prerequisite to the flowering of this socialist consciousness. Priority is accorded also to the collective rights of the proletariat as a class and, later, the socialist community itself above the rights of the individual. Human rights can only be universalized by the action of the proletariat as the 'universal class' fulfilling its historic mission.

The Russian revolution installed the communist party in power which, guided by Marxism–Leninism, established the 'dictatorship of the proletariat', nationalized the means of production, eliminated the property-owning classes and began constructing the economic foundations of socialism. In the process the state engulfed 'civil society'. Socialism was officially established in the USSR by 1936. The Stalin era saw an unprecedented extension of state power, and in the use of coercion to effect this transformation. In the post-Stalin era state repression was slackened. Ideologically this was associated with the transition from the 'dictatorship of the proletariat' to 'the state of the whole people', and the passage to the stage of 'developed socialism'.[3]

THE SOVIET LAW AND HUMAN RIGHTS

The USSR's commitment to human rights is enshrined in various state enactments such as the Declaration of the Rights of the Peoples of Russia (1917) and the Declaration of Rights of the Toiling and Exploited Peoples (1918), as well as in successive constitutions. The rights, freedoms and duties of citizens have been extensively discussed by Soviet legal theorists.[4] The USSR declined to vote for the UN Declaration of Human Rights (1948) because of the importance the declaration assigned to property rights, but it has signed and ratified other international agreements. The USSR has ratified the UN Covenant on Civil and Political Rights (1966) and the UN Covenant on Economic, Social and Cultural Rights (1966), both of which are legally binding but leave considerable discretion to the signatory states on their interpretation. In 1975 the USSR signed the Final Act of the Conference on Security and Cooperation in Europe, at Helsinki, with its basket three provisions on human rights.

The Soviet Constitution of 1977 placed new emphasis on human rights, incorporating in part the provisions of the UN Covenants cited above.[5] The rights to food, clothing, shelter, work, rest and education constitute basic rights which socialism must advance and protect. Only after these rights, which are integral to the full development of the worker, have been guaranteed does the constitution move on to ensure the civil rights which are most prominently enshrined in 'bourgeois' constitutions.[6]

The classic political and civil rights, it is argued, are placed on a materialist foundation in the USSR. The state superstructure itself mirrors the socialist relations of the system's economic and social foundations. Rights are dispensed by the state, which reflects the interests of the whole, in accordance with the scientific evaluation of the system's progress from socialism to communism. In the West, it is argued, rights are determined by the continuous struggle between antagonistic social classes and interests. Rights and freedoms won by subordinate classes may, in periods of intensified class conflict, be suspended or abrogated.

The Soviet constitution emphasizes the contingency of rights. Civil and political rights must be exercised 'in accordance with the interests of the people – to strengthen and develop the socialist system'. Moreover, the exercise of the citizens' rights 'must not harm the interests of society or of the State' and is 'inseparable from the performance of their duties and obligations'.[7] The individual's duties include the obligation to work, to preserve socialist property, to defend the motherland, to protect the constitution, and to uphold the honour and duty of Soviet citizenship.

The Soviet constitution is in part programmatic and not only outlines the workings of the system but also presents the regime's aspirations. The status of the constitution limits the guarantees outlined in its clauses.[8] It enshrines the party's leading and directing role in Soviet society. The task of interpreting and enforcing the constitution is assigned to the courts but the judiciary's power is constrained by the system of political controls.

The political rights of citizens are limited by the political offences listed in the Criminal Code. The main offences are covered by the catch-all articles 70 and 72, which deal with 'anti-Soviet agitation and propaganda', and 'anti-Soviet organization' which weaken or seek to overthrow the political system. Less serious offences can be dealt with under articles 190 and 191 on 'deliberate fabrications which discredit the Soviet political and social system'. Laws against social 'parasitism', and regulations on residence permits have also been used for social control.

THE SOVIET RECORD ON HUMAN RIGHTS

The Soviet response to human rights must be seen in historical perspective. Marxism–Leninism from the first combined a commitment to socialist humanism and a class approach to politics which did not abjure the use of force for securing political ends. The Stalin era was marked by mass repression, terror on an unprecedented scale and a system of political control and coercion unchecked by law. Under Khrushchev the terror machine was substantially dismantled, 'socialist legality' strengthened and political controls relaxed.[9]

The political system, dominated by a highly centralized pervasive party-state apparatus, is imprinted with the tradition of tsarist authoritarianism and Stalinist totalitarianism. This stands in marked contrast to western, pluralistic conceptions of government with their constitutional guarantees and institutional checks. State censorship, control of the mass media and of education, provide powerful channels of indoctrination and social control. The sphere of state activity is greatly enlarged with the subjugation of autonomous social organizations and the careful channelling of political participation.

The political system retains a strong element of arbitrariness. The state has recourse to a panoply of laws to defend its interests. Through the KGB and the courts tight internal control is maintained. In safeguarding itself against any challenge the state also has recourse to non-legal means – the use of administrative measures, intimidation, threats and violence. Labour camps, strict regime prisons, and psychiatric hospitals are used in controlling its opponents.[10]

The October revolution, the first Marxian inspired socialist revolution, brought to the fore a new conception of human rights. The elimination of private ownership of the means of production, it is argued, eliminated the basis of class exploitation. Similarly, the regime has worked to reduce social, racial, national and sexual inequalities by the exercise of positive discrimination. Socialist construction included a policy of 'cultural revolution' to raise the people's educational and cultural standards to overcome prejudices, superstition, religious belief, to develop a rational, scientific world view and to raise socialist consciousness.

The USSR's achievements in different fields of human rights vary greatly. In the economic and social fields impressive achievements have been registered in securing rights to employment, education, housing, social welfare, and leisure, albeit within the restricted resources of the Soviet economy. However, since these services are administered by party controlled agencies they can be subject to political pressures. Rights can thus be deprived by administrative fiat to enforce political conformity and are thus dependent on political acquiescence.

It is in the area of political and civil rights that the main criticisms arise. Through its political monopoly the party can define what rights are granted and how they should be interpreted. The party's control over state and public organizations, control over the media, and the system of internal controls, greatly limits if not negates the rights of those with opinions at variance with those officially prescribed. Rights are thus subject to shifting political and administrative interpretation by unrepresentative and unaccountable officials and their agencies.

Soviet 'socialist legality' was strengthened in the post-Stalin era but is still constrained by the power of the state. The weakness of Soviet 'civil society' as a check on the state is reflected in the lack of autonomous institutions, and the absence of democracy. Within this framework the role of the judiciary as an independent force, as interpreter of law and guardian of rights and liberties, is severely circumscribed.[11] The struggle for human rights in the USSR is inseparably linked with the struggle to strengthen the rule of law. The protests of dissidents against the authorities are often couched in the form of demands to enforce existing laws and constitutional provisions.

The Soviet system displays a fastidious, bureaucratic concern for legality. On the other hand the concept of 'socialist legality' stresses the importance of political and class considerations in determining cases. Chalidze, a leading dissident jurist, stresses the lack of development of 'legal consciousness' amongst the Soviet public and their political leaders, and the weakness of Soviet 'civil society' as a check on the state.[12]

In the high noon of post-Stalin liberalism – the late fifties until the mid-sixties – legal procedural norms were strengthened. Individuals were in some cases able to appeal successfully against violations of legality and to seek redress against the authorities by mobilizing influential opinion amongst leading representatives of the Soviet intelligentsia.[13] Although legal norms exist to prevent abuses, the problem arises in gaining information about these procedures and ensuring their enforcement.

The dissidents in contemporary world politics

THE EMERGENCE OF THE DISSIDENT MOVEMENT

The post-Stalin period saw the emergence in the USSR of a dissident movement as part of the repoliticization of Soviet society.[14] The movement developed its own loose organization, a clandestine press (samizdat), and used appeals and petitions to highlight grievances and secure redress. After 1966 the movement grew substantially with the trial of the two writers Sinyavsky and Daniel threatening a more repressive policy by the government.

The movement, initially united by the common objectives of strengthening socialist legality, increasing political and social freedoms, in the sixties split along ideological lines. On the right, individuals like Solzhenitsyn sought answers to the shortcomings in the Soviet system in a religious and moral renewal. Liberals like Sakharov drew inspiration from the Western liberal tradition with the checks built in against authoritarian government. Marxist reformers such as Medvedev argued for the democratization of the system and reform inside the Leninist tradition.

The movement became increasingly diverse, broadened its focus, and sought more vigorously to propagate its views and win adherents. A wide variety of currents emerged promoting the rights of different nationalities, religious denominations and professional groups. Demands were raised for greater freedom from the artistic and scientific communities. Samizdat proliferated with the emergence of sophisticated underground journals such as the Chronicle of Current Events. Small minority groups, which were quickly suppressed, took up the rights of industrial workers and women.[15]

The dissident movement highlighted widespread human rights violations in the USSR. The significance of that movement, in spite of its limited size, lay in the breadth of the issues raised and the challenge which it posed to the existing order. That challenge focussed particularly on the weakness of organizational safeguards of rights already provided for. The publicity given to this movement in the West introduced a new dimension into the situation.

The most powerful and effective force within the dissident movement was the Jewish campaign for the right to emigrate. Although to some extent at odds with other groups concerned with internal reform, this movement well illustrates the problems of safeguarding human rights in the USSR.

HUMAN RIGHTS AND THE JEWISH EMIGRATION ISSUE

The position of the Jews as a distinct nationality in the USSR is beset by anomalies. The question of Jewish emigration which emerged in the seventies has to be seen against the background of the position of Jews in the USSR.[16]

Under the tsar the Jews in the Russian empire were concentrated in the Jewish Pale in the western provinces, the Baltic regions and Poland. By the beginning of the 1880s latent anti-semitism had turned into systematic persecution, utilized by the regime as a scapegoat mechanism. The May Laws of 1888 and the subsequent pogroms confined the Jews to the Pale. The Jews were subject to severe legal restrictions. In 1903 occurred the government inspired pogroms at Kishinev and Gomel. Russia produced in this period a torrent of anti-semitic literature and anti-semitic movements, such as the Black Hundreds, with state backing.

The turn of the century saw a mass emigration of Jews from the Russian empire to Western Europe and the United States. Many Russian Jews became early adherents of Zionism, whilst others embraced Marxian socialism. The Jews provided a disproportionate number of political leaders and theorists within the revolutionary movement. The new Soviet communist regime after 1917 counted many Jewish activists and intellectuals amongst its leaders.

The Soviet regime set the elimination of discrimination against national minorities, and the eradication of anti-semitism, as an essential objective, following in the tradition of Marx's celebrated article 'On the Jewish Question'.[17] The two decades following the revolution saw great social and educational advances by the Jews in the USSR and a major cultural revival. In the 1930s an autonomous Jewish republic, Birobidzhan, was established in the Soviet Far East, conferring upon them the status of a fully fledged national group. Birobidzhan, however, never became a centre of large Jewish settlement. At this time the Jews were willingly being integrated and assimilated into Soviet society.

The problem of anti-semitism persisted in spite of party sponsored education campaigns to stamp it out. The collaboration of some Soviet nationals with the occupying Nazi forces in 1941–5 in the massacre of Soviet Jews underlines this continuing tradition. The experience of the 'holocaust' and the founding of the state of Israel in 1949, supported by the USSR, rekindled Jewish national consciousness. This in part nurtured a new official anti-semitism within the Soviet political establishment, witnessed by the 'anti cosmopolitan' campaigns of the 1940s and the notorious 'doctors plot' of 1952/3 which were directed against Jewish intellectuals and officials.

The Jewish population in the USSR until the 1960s appeared to be well integrated. In the 1979 census only 1.81 million or 0.68 per cent of the population were registered as Jews although Israeli and Jewish sources estimated the real Jewish population at between 3.0 million and 3.5 million.[18] Unlike most other Soviet minority nationalities the Jews are geographically dispersed with a heterogeneity of language and culture. In the Russian Soviet Federative Socialist Republic (RSFSR) Jews are highly urbanized, well-educated, occupy important positions in the professions and have the highest level of party saturation of any nationality group. Amongst this section of the community there is a high level of acculturisation and inter-marriage with Russians. In the Caucasus, the western Ukraine, Belorussia, and the Baltic republics, Jews are in a much less privileged position, are less assimilated and cling more tenaciously to their culture.[19]

Jewish nationality is recognised in the USSR and is used in registering births and in passport entries. Official Soviet spokesmen stress that Jews are treated on a par with other nationalities, that equality of rights has been achieved and anti-semitism extirpated. However, Jews received few of the advantages enjoyed by other national minorities as a result of government policy. From the late forties onwards Jewish cultural institutions received only scant support, and many institutions were closed down. At the same time the Jews suffered certain restrictions on access to education and the professions, which were keenly felt by a socially ambitious group.[20]

The emergence of the issue

The growth of a mass campaign for emigration surprised and alarmed the authorities demonstrating the USSR's vulnerability to external influences. The movement was triggered by the Arab–Israeli Six Day War of 1967 in which the USSR supported diplomatically and militarily the vanquished Arabs.[21] The stridency of Soviet propaganda against Israel and Zionism, with its anti-semitic overtones, sparked a revival of Jewish national consciousness. This movement gathered force particularly amongst the least assimilated Jews in the western parts of the USSR (the *zapadniki*) and the Caucasus.

Even amongst the more assimilated Jews the sense of estrangement from Soviet society was deepened. Amongst the many Jews active in the dissident movement, this coincided with disillusionment with the prospects of internal reform following the invasion of Czechoslovakia in 1968 and the general clampdown on dissent. Emigration was taken up by other Jews for family, economic, political, cultural and personal reasons.[22]

The continuing tension in the Middle East through the seventies, and especially the Yom Kippur War of 1973, kept Israel as the national and spiritual home of the Jews at the centre of attention. Soviet backing for the Arab cause alienated many Soviet Jews from their own government. The anti-Zionist campaign was continued and intensified in part to discourage Jews from demanding the right to emigrate and to maintain pressure for assimilation.[23]

The campaign challenged the regime's claim to have solved the nationalities problem and to have eradicated anti-semitism. The official view that the transition to communism involves the drawing together (*sblizhenie*) of nationalities was thrown into question.[24] In a multi-national state dominated by its Russian majority such a process must threaten the identity of the national minorities and may deepen resentment against a cultural policy which smacks of Russification. The campaign directly challenged the regime's right and ability to remould society in accordance with its ideological precepts.

The resurgence of Jewish national consciousness was linked to a revival of Zionism, increased identification with the state of Israel, and a renewed interest in Judaism and Jewish history, culture and language. This directly challenged the atheistic premises of official ideology and the long established antipathy of Marxism–Leninism towards Zionism as a species of bourgeois nationalism which allegedly manifests national chauvinism, racism, anti-Soviet and anti-communist attitudes.[25]

The Israeli state has been condemned by the Soviet government as racist, expansionist and an outpost of US imperialism in the Middle East. Official publications attacking the state of Israel have, on occasions, resorted to crude anti-semitic propaganda. Jewish activists identifying with Israel were ideological outcasts, openly disloyal, and thus offensive to nationalistic and patriotic sentiments.

The internal and external campaign

The Jewish emigration campaign was well organized, articulate, and fuelled by nationalistic and religious zeal. Socially it was broadly based but regionally strongest in the western regions and the Caucasus. It developed its own samizdat literature as a medium of information which broke the state's monopoly on communication. Its methods of operation included appeals and petitions to Soviet authorities. Increasingly more militant actions were deployed – demonstrations, occupations, sit-ins, hunger strikes and an attempted airline hijack.[26]

From the outset the campaigners recognized the importance of outside help. Appeals for support were addressed to the Israeli government, Western governments and the United Nations. The Soviet Jews enjoyed an advantage shared by virtually no other group in the USSR, the Germans excepted, in the shape of a politically powerful lobby in the West. In the 1970s the Soviet dissident movement, and especially the Jewish emigration campaigners, became a central preoccupation of the Western media in its coverage of the USSR when Western public opinion sympathized strongly with the Israeli government and the Jewish cause.

The sympathy expressed by many Western radicals for the Jewish cause was also important because it was these forces the Soviet Union wished to court. The attitude of US politicians – especially Democrats sensitive to liberal Jewish votes – was an important consideration. Amongst those communist parties where the Euro-communist tide was rising, an increasingly critical stance was taken towards Soviet policy in the Middle East and the tone of Soviet anti-Israeli, anti-Zionist statements. The Soviet Union's domestic record was also seen as an electoral liability for these parties.[27]

The external pressures on the Soviet government were by no means one way. The alarm of the Arab states at Israeli expansionism was important in sustaining the Soviet hard line on Jewish emigration. The 1975 UN resolution equating Zionism with racism revealed strong Third World hostility towards Israeli policy which could be mobilized.[28] Within the USSR itself the large Muslim population in Central Asia provided a strong body of pro-Arab sympathy.

The leadership's objectives

In March 1971 the Soviet government suddenly eased its controls on Jewish emigration. The decision was taken immediately prior to the twenty-fourth party congress in Moscow, which could have provided an opportunity for Jewish activists to further embarrass the authorities. At this congress

Brezhnev launched his Peace Programme initiating the strategy of détente with the United States.

The resolution of the emigration issue was complicated by political differences within the Soviet leadership concerning détente. Opponents of détente feared their excessive dependence on the West and their ideological neutralization. The hesitancy, inconsistency and reversals in Soviet policy on emigration may also have been influenced by institutional rivalries, between those concerned with the need to continue the policy of détente for military and economic reasons and those alarmed by its internal security implications and the associated loss of skilled manpower.[29]

The emigration campaign spurred an upsurge of anti-semitism in sections of the Soviet media. Attempts were made to exploit anti-semitism to discredit the whole dissident movement. The image of the Jews as a 'fifth column' in league with Western powers fused together anti-semitism and anti-western prejudices in a potent mixture. This current was fostered by right-wing Russian nationalist elements in the political establishment and mirrored a similar trend in Poland in the seventies. This tendency in the USSR was checked after 1974 but remains a shadowy force in Soviet politics.[30]

The authorities sought to isolate the dissidents from the rest of the Jewish community. They wished also to limit the campaign's effect on other groups to discourage attempts at emulation. In an extremely complex, heterogeneous, multi-national state with a profusion of cultural differences such nervousness is not surprising. The regime's concern throughout has been to retain for itself the power to order relations between the different social, national and cultural groups which comprise the USSR.

Emigration, Soviet law and human rights

The Soviet constitution recognizes no right to emigrate. The demands of Jews to be allowed to emigrate was, however, based on an appeal to international agreements signed by the USSR. The International Covenant on Civil and Political Rights, which the Soviet Union has ratified, includes the right of an individual to choose freely his citizenship and the country in which he wishes to reside. Soviet jurists and official spokesmen have acknowledged this right, with some qualifications.

The Helsinki Final Act, signed by the USSR in August 1975, included various provisions on the issue of emigration, including pledges to 'facilitate freer movement in general, and a reaffirmation of other international instruments – the 1948 Universal Declaration of Human Rights and the 1965 International Convention on the Elimination of All Forms of Racial Discrimination – which proclaim the general freedom to leave one's country'.[31]

Many administrative hurdles were placed before the would-be emigrant. Procedures are deliberately complex, lengthy and uncertain. Jewish emigration has been allowed in the past on an individual basis only. Officially it has been judged on the principle of family unification. This requires that a formal invitation be received by a would-be emigrant from relatives abroad. It is then necessary to obtain an exit visa which has to be accompanied by a character reference. Soviet citizenship is automatically withdrawn once permission to emigrate has been granted.[32]

Intense pressures were placed on individuals and families to discourage applications, including dismissals, demotions, harassment and threats. In 1973 the authorities attempted to introduce an education tax to increase the cost of emigration for educated Jews. Following the Helsinki agreement the rules regulating this procedure were modified. These administrative procedures make emigration a privilege to be granted by the state. Only the Soviet Jews and Germans have been granted this right in any number. After 1979 the rules concerning emigration were severely tightened up.

The politics of détente

Brezhnev's policy of détente (*razryadka* – lessening of tension) from 1971 onwards was motivated by various considerations. It was intended to curb the arms race, to reduce international tension and was aimed particularly to neutralize improvement in Sino-American relations. The Soviet government also sought access to Western supplies of grain, advanced technology, and credit facilities. This strategy made the Soviet government susceptible to Western pressures.

In the period 1972 to 1974 détente between the United States and USSR reached its height with the signing by Nixon and Brezhnev of a series of agreements on nuclear arms control as part of the SALT 1 process. These were coupled with measures to improve Soviet–US trade. These important agreements were concluded in spite of strong reservations on détente within the political establishments on both sides.

United States congressmen sympathetic to Jewish emigration seized the opportunity to pressurize the Soviet government. In October 1972, Henry Jackson introduced in the Senate his Amendment to the US Trade Reform Act and in February 1974, Charles Vanik presented the same measure to the House of Representatives. This specified that no 'non-market economy country' shall be eligible for 'most favoured treatment' or to participate in credit programmes or investment guarantees as long as it 'denies its citizens the right or opportunity to emigrate'. The amendment won strong congressional support with the result that the Trade Bill was held up for two years.

The Jackson–Vanik amendment was strenuously opposed by Nixon and Kissinger who feared it would damage détente of which trade was an essential component. The administration stressed the virtues of quiet diplomacy. Nixon and Kissinger held that their 'structure of peace' was more important than individual rights, and that linkages could only be used selectively. Fulbright, chairman of the Senate Foreign Relations Committee, condemned the amendment as an attempt to interfere in Soviet internal affairs.[33]

Amongst Soviet dissidents the amendment provoked conflicting reactions. The liberal Sakharov welcomed the move urging more energetic use of external pressure to open up the USSR, stressing the moral issues involved and the possibility that progress on the emigration front could ease progress in other areas of human rights, strengthening the influence of the dissidents.[34] The reformist Marxist Medvedev condemned the move as inept and counterproductive, an empty political gesture aimed at humiliating the Soviet leadership. The move, he argued, would strengthen the hand of conservative forces in the Soviet leadership.[35]

After Nixon's resignation, which the Soviet leadership lamented, repeated efforts were made to rescue détente. An informal assurance was given by Brezhnev, Gromyko and Ambassador Dobrynin to the Ford–Kissinger administration concerning the criteria to be applied in handling future emigration applications. This was intended to ease the passage of the Trade Bill. In October 1974 in an exchange of letters between Kissinger and Jackson the tacit agreement was made public. It provoked an outspoken attack from Gromyko and from TASS denouncing US distortions of the USSR's true position.

The agreement on Jewish emigration enabled the Ford–Kissinger administration to get its Trade Bill through Congress. In December 1974, however, the Senate set new low ceilings on credits to the USSR which effectively undid the measure's intended goal. Predictably the USSR in January 1975 revoked the October 1972 trade agreement which it had striven so hard to secure.[36] This development led to a general cooling in Soviet–American relations. Jewish emigration from the USSR declined as a consequence.

Whereas the Nixon–Kissinger administration had pursued détente with the USSR with little regard to the regime's internal policies, the Carter administration from 1976 onwards sought to combine détente with support for Soviet human rights campaigners. This became part of the general foreign policy strategy of the new Democratic administration. The reassertion of moral issues in the conduct of foreign policy stood in sharp contrast to the hard-nosed pragmatism of the Nixon era.

The attempt to limit the nuclear arms race resulted in negotiations, SALT 2, in 1978/9. The USSR was anxious for agreement to ease the strain placed on its economy and to maintain the existing global balance of forces. The SALT 2 agreement was aborted by congressional opposition. NATO's decision to deploy a new generation of missiles in the autumn of 1979 finalized the break. The Soviet intervention in Afghanistan put the matter beyond doubt. Soviet controls over Jewish emigration, which had been relaxed to assist the Carter administration's détente policy, were tightened.

The impact of the campaign

The Jewish emigration campaign has been the most successful dissident campaign to date. It secured, temporarily at any rate, its objective of freer emigration. From 1968 to 1970 only 4,300 Jews emigrated from the USSR. In the decade 1971 to 1981, 246,000 Jews left the USSR, most for Israel although after 1976 a great many went to the United States. The peak years of emigration, 1972–4 and 1978–80, coincided with the two high points of détente.[37] Increased emigration was used by the Soviet authorities both as a bargaining counter and as a token of good faith, to ease the détente process.

The campaign's effect on the position of Soviet Jews was contradictory. Officially it is claimed that the majority of Jews applying for emigration visas were allowed to leave the USSR.[38] Jewish organizations, however, repudiate this claim and argue that administrative restrictions were used to staunch the flow, and that emigration policy was dictated mainly by foreign policy considerations. Some concessions were won in the cultural field. At the same time the position of the Soviet Jews was weakened – the strength of Jewish dissent sapped. Educational and occupational opportunities for Jews were further restricted. Also significant was the growth of popular anti-semitism.

These developments created a vicious circle and may fuel a continuing demand from Soviet Jews for the right to emigrate.[39] A new phase in East–West détente in the future may again see a relaxation of Soviet emigration controls.

Soviet responses to the human rights issue

THE REJECTION OF WESTERN CRITICISM

In the Helsinki Final Act of 1975, human rights issues were for the first time recognized as factors affecting interstate relations between the USSR and Western governments. Under Ford and especially during the Carter administration, from 1976 to 1980, human rights issues were thrust into the forefront of United States–Soviet relations. The Soviet response to the Carter administration's strictures on its human rights record was fierce and pointed, reflecting both the ideological gulf that separated the two superpowers and the profound differences in their political systems and attitudes.

Western criticisms of the Soviet record on human rights are depicted by the Soviet press as part of an ideological campaign to discredit the USSR internationally. By concentrating attention on an unrepresentative dissident movement, it is argued, the human rights situation in the USSR had been misrepresented and counterposed to a narrow Western capitalist conception of rights. More seriously the campaign attempted to exploit internal difficulties in the USSR, and to challenge Soviet sovereignty. The campaign, it is further argued, tried to distract attention from shortcomings in the West – unemployment, racial tension, poverty and human rights violations. It sought to burnish the United States' tarnished image internally and externally in the wake of Vietnam, Watergate and the Lockheed scandal. The campaign served to mobilize Western public opinion through anti-Soviet propaganda. It could thus be dismissed as a cynical manoeuver, an arrogant affront to national pride by a US government that has traditionally taken a sanctimonious attitude to the USSR.[40] Radical Western scholars of foreign affairs share a similar cynical evaluation of Western governments' motives behind the human rights campaign. The Carter administration's human rights campaign underlined for the USSR the pitfalls of détente and the dangers of being drawn into an excessively dependent relationship with the West.

Soviet press articles and scholarly works, vigorously rebut Western criticism and restate the Soviet view on human rights. Brezhnev and other leaders have noted the significance of human rights issues in the ideological struggle between socialism and capitalism.[41] In the international arena the Soviet government claims much of the credit for extending the concept of rights in the economic, social and cultural field.[42] In this way Soviet spokesmen seek to defend the USSR record on human rights and to guard ideological orthodoxy domestically and in the international communist movement.

RIGHTS AND CHANGE IN THE SOVIET UNION

The Soviet case raises fundamental questions concerning the problem of political development and the conditions under which institutional guarantees of human rights can be established. In all systems human rights are subject to some degree of political determination and may be withdrawn, suspended or redefined. The problem in the USSR is how powerful centrifugal forces can be handled in a heterogeneous society with innumerable lines of latent cleavage, which has no real experience of open, representative government. Human rights provides a banner around which a fragmented dissident movement might rally and which could in the long term jeopardize the regime's stability.[43]

The Soviet case highlights a central ideological dilemma in the field of human rights – the tension between political and civil rights on the one hand and economic and social rights on the other. In the USSR economic and social rights have been given precedence. The CPSU's political dominance allows it to impose its priorities on the society. The democratization of the system might strengthen political and civil rights but in the process erode those economic and social rights which have been secured already, which legitimize the regime and serve to maintain popular support.

The adaptation of the existing highly centralized party–state apparatus to a more open representative system poses formidable problems. Soviet reformers argue that democratization would reinvigorate the system. The risks involved, however, are considerable. Dissent is treated by the authorities as a solvent which erodes the cement which holds this cumbersome edifice together. Within the political establishment powerful interests can be expected to resist change.[44] The main stimulus for political reform is likely to come as a result of pressure for reforming the Soviet economic system.

The regime's authoritarian character is sustained by a political culture that emphasizes moral certainties, conformism, unity and discipline, which stresses respect for authority and upholds the rights of the collective against individual and sectional interests.[45] The state's authority in the past has been buttressed by a dread of internal disorder and the fear that the regime might regress into the repression of the past. The apparent immovability of the ubiquitous and unified party–state apparatus itself reinforces conformist attitudes in a system where individuals have little confidence in their ability to bring about change.

The dissident movement never numbered more than a very small minority within the intelligentsia which is by no means all liberal in outlook.[46] Amongst the reformers, what is seen as the political immaturity of the people, inhibits demands for change. Soviet public opinion, in so far as it was aware of the movement, appears to have reacted to it with indifference, suspicion and even hostility. The regime rests on a broad base of popular support and acceptance. Against such dissident groups anti-Western, anti-liberal, anti-intellectual, nationalistic sentiments can be mobilized.

THE WEST AND DOMESTIC CHANGE IN THE SOVIET UNION

The Conference on Security and Cooperation in Europe (CSCE) with its regular follow up conferences provide a means whereby compliance with the Helsinki Final Act can be monitored. The Helsinki Final Act resulted in an important innovation – the establishment of monitoring groups in the signatory countries to check on its observance. In the USSR there was established the Helsinki Watch Group with affiliated groups throughout the country.[47] The Helsinki Watch Group petitioned the authorities against violations of the Final Act and appealed to other signatory governments to bring sanctions to bear against their own government for breaches of its provisions.

External pressure on the Soviet authorities in this period was directed principally by Western governments. Western broadcasting agencies provide an alternative source of information and ideas to official Soviet programmes and play an important part in keeping people informed of events and play a part in monitoring developments within the USSR and without. Non-governmental organizations have also played a key role in monitoring human rights violations. However, no other groups in the West have been able to organize the sustained pressure of the Jewish lobby.[48]

The sensitivity of these issues explains the prickliness of the Soviet response to Western protests against human rights violations in the USSR.[49] The Carter administration's human rights crusade drove the Soviet government into a defensive stance. The vulnerability of the regime on such issues produced a strategy which combined détente with a clamp-down on internal dissent. This may have been part of a political bargain to reassure internal opponents of détente who feared its impact on domestic policy.[50]

The campaign's impact was weakened by divisions between the Western governments especially the divisions between the United States and Europe.[51] Most of the pressure on the Soviet government came from the United States. This reflects not only US influence and power, but also the openness of the US political system to interest group pressure and the more strident anti-communist tradition of that country.[52]

Western pressure on the Soviet authorities undoubtedly tempered their actions. Critical publicity damaged the country's reputation abroad. It adversely affected those in the legal and medical professions involved in implementing official policy. External pressure gave heart to internal campaigners, and encouraged them to speak out. Outside agencies, by providing information and ideas, helped overcome the isolation of campaigners struggling against official repression. For those dissidents who were unknown in the West outside pressure probably had no beneficial effect. Western pressure proved incapable of preventing the dissident movement being suppressed.

Whilst the authorities' methods in handling dissidents were tempered, their effectiveness was not diminished. From 1966 onwards official repression was intensified. Under KGB direction, a ruthless but sophisticated campaign was waged to eliminate organized dissent. Dissidents were encouraged to emigrate or pressurised to conform. Growing use was made of psychiatric hospitals to deal with those considered politically deviant. By the late seventies the dissident movement had been effectively destroyed. In 1982 the Helsinki Watch Group finally abandoned its work which had been made impossible by the authorities.

External pressures secured some minor modifications in Soviet policy and practice but no dramatic breakthroughs. Neither the pragmatism of the Nixon administration nor the moral crusade of the Carter administration had any significant effect on Soviet domestic policies. On domestic issues internal political considerations override all others. The Jackson–Vanik amendment affair demonstrated the Soviet government's willingness to bargain minor domestic policy concessions for economic and other political objectives so long as the costs incurred were not excessive.[53]

This episode illustrated also the limits of external pressure where essential Soviet interests are seen to be at stake. For ideological and more practical reasons, the Soviet leadership cannot allow major concessions. The vast resources of the USSR limit its dependence on the West and restrict the scope for economic sanctions. Political ostracisation is also ineffective given the regime's policy of self-isolation. The USSR's position in the communist bloc and the Third World makes it also partly impervious to Western pressures.

Soviet dissidents are divided on the question of the efficacy of external pressures in strengthening human rights observance in the USSR.[54] Socialists close to the Marxist–Leninist tradition like Medvedev stress the need for incremental change as part of a renewal of that tradition. In this respect Soviet achievements on the human rights front have to be assessed alongside the failures. The advancement of human rights is inextricably bound to the democratization of the system. External pressure is most effective when applied by governments and movements sympathetic to socialism. The interest of right-wing forces in the West in human rights in the USSR is seen as one sided, politically motivated, and likely to damage the prospects for reform.[55]

Non-socialists, like Sakharov, closer to the Western liberal democratic tradition, elevate the question of human rights to a fundamental principle of universal significance. This tradition is pessimistic about the possibility of internal reform, and sees the existing political structures as inimical to any serious advance. Sakharov stresses the need for voluble and energetic pressure from the West from all political quarters. He urges the West to use its economic and military leverage to open up Soviet society and allow internal movements to press for the strengthening of human rights.[56]

Whereas Medvedev sees improved relations between the West and the USSR as a necessary precondition for internal reform, Sakharov sees internal change in the USSR as an essential precondition for improved Soviet-Western relations and for world peace. Medvedev sees the problem of world peace in terms of competition between the USSR and an embattled West whose imperial order is slowly disintegrating. Sakharov, together with many Western commentators, sees the threat to peace being posed by an expansionist Soviet totalitarian state.

Western pressure on the human rights front in the USSR has been focussed principally on the demands of dissident groups as the most effective means of pressurising the authorities. Internal reform, however, is unlikely to come from the activities of small dissident groups which can be easily contained. Such changes will come most probably from reformers within the political establishment. Radical changes as envisaged by either Sakharov or Solzhenitsyn are unlikely barring some cataclysmic shock to the system. Reform as envisaged by Medvedev offers the best, ideologically least offensive, prospect although even here the room for manoeuvre is limited. Such a strategy probably requires détente as an essential precondition.

Conclusion

The study of human rights observance in the USSR highlights a major philosophical and ideological problem regarding the way in which rights are defined and the priority which they are accorded. It illustrates also the problem of how rights are enforced and the circumstances under which they are established, extended or withheld. These are ideological and practical problems which allow no simple solutions. Notwithstanding these problems Soviet dissidents exposed widespread abuses of human rights in the USSR. Without democratizing the structure of government and without strengthening the rule of law rights which are acknowledged by the authorities themselves will remain as concessions to be dispensed at their convenience.

Western pressures on the Soviet authorities on human rights issues yielded only limited concessions. Given the traditions of the country, the nature of the regime and the kind of internal problems it faces it is difficult to see how else the Soviet government could have reacted. The heated exchanges between Western governments and the Soviet government over human rights illustrate the ideological chasm which divides them and which inhibits constructive dialogue. In the case of the Jewish emigration campaign, concessions were made without significantly changing the regime's human rights policy. The Carter administration's failure to influence Soviet policy and the demise of the dissident movement led to the waning of Western interest and concern with human rights problems in the USSR in the early eighties.

The problem as to how the West might assist the process of change in the

USSR remains unresolved. Given the antagonism between these two systems, Western initiatives in this field will invariably be regarded with the greatest suspicion. Western policy is caught between two options – the exploitation of human rights to weaken the system internally, or the development of conditions under which the internal reformers can gain greater influence. The former strategy serves to discredit the internal reformers, whilst the latter course is more difficult to chart, carries no clear prospect of success, and offers little immediate political recompense.

Notes

1 L.J. Macfarlane, 'Marxist Theory and Human Rights', *Government and Opposition*, vol. 17, no. 4 (Autumn 1982), pp. 414–28. See also, Alice Erh-Soon Tay, 'Marxism, Socialism and Human Rights', in Eugene Kamenka and Alice Erh-Soon Tay, *Human Rights* (Edward Arnold, London, 1978), pp. 104–12.

2 The following section draws heavily on the article by Mary Hawkesworth, 'Ideological Immunity: The Soviet Response to Human Rights Criticisms', *Universal Human Rights*, vol. 2, no. 1 (January–March 1980), pp. 69–74.

3 A.B. Evans, 'Developed Socialism in Socialist Ideology', *Soviet Studies* (July 1977).

4 A.Y. Vyshinsky (ed.), *The Law of the Soviet State* (New York, 1961), ch. 9; L. Grigoryan and Y. Dolgopolov, *Fundamentals of Soviet State Law* (Moscow, 1971), ch. 4.

5 Aryeh L. Unger, *Constitutional Developments in the USSR* (Methuen, London 1981).

6 *Constitution (Fundamental Law) of the Union of Soviet Socialist Republics* (Novosti Press Agency Publishing House, Moscow, 1977), see chapter 6, 'Citizenship of the USSR. Equality of Citizens' Rights', and chapter 7, 'The Basic Rights, Freedoms and Duties of Citizens of the USSR.

7 Ibid., p. 50.

8 Robert Sharlet, 'De-Stalinization and Soviet Constitutionalism' in S.F. Cohen, A. Rabinowitch R. Sharlet (eds.), *The Soviet Union Since Stalin* (Macmillan, London, 1980), pp. 93–112. Robert Sharlet, 'Constitutional Implementation and the Juridicization of the Soviet System' in D.R. Kelley (ed.), *Soviet Politics in the Brezhnev Era* (Praeger, New York, 1980), pp. 200–34.

9 Frederick C. Barghoorn, 'The Post-Krushchev Campaign to Suppress Dissent', in R.L. Tokes, *Dissent in the USSR* (Johns Hopkins University Press, Baltimore, 1976), p. 59.

10 Amnesty International, *Prisoners of Conscience in the USSR* (London, 1980). The number of labour camp inmates in the USSR is estimated at between 1 and 2 million, of whom perhaps 10–20,000 might properly be classified as political prisoners.

11 S. White *et al.* (eds.), *Communist Political Systems* (Macmillan, London, 1981), chapter 6.

12 Valery Chalidze, *To Defend These Rights* (Collins and Harvill Press, London, 1975).

13 Zhores A. Medvedev and Roy A. Medvedev, *A Question of Madness* (Macmillan, London, 1971).

14 On the difference between 'dissent' and 'opposition' see: P. Reddaway, 'The Development of Dissent and Opposition', in A. Brown and M. Kaser (eds.), *The Soviet Union Since the Fall of Khrushchev* (Macmillan, London, 1978), pp. 122–3.

15 On the dissident movement in general see, Rudolf L. Tokes (ed.), *Dissent in the USSR* (Johns Hopkins University Press, Baltimore, 1975); Abraham Brumberg, *In Quest of Justice* (Pall Mall Press, London, 1970); Michael Meerson-Aksenov, Boris Shragin (ed.), *The Political, Social and Religious Thought of Russian 'Samizdat' – An Anthology* (Nordland Publishing Company, Belmont, Mass., 1977); P. Reddaway (ed.), *Uncensored Russia: The Human Rights Movement in the Soviet Union* (Jonathan Cape, London, 1972). For particular studies of aspects of the dissident movement see Ihor Kamenetsky, *Nationalism and Human Rights* (Libraries Unlimited, Littleton, Colo.), Viktor Haynes and Olga Semyonova, *Workers Against The Gulag* (Pluto Press, London, 1979). On the Soviet human rights movement see Joshua Rubenstein, *Soviet Dissidents: Their Struggle for Human Rights* (Beacon Press, Boston, 1980).

16 Zev Katz, 'The Jews in the Soviet Union', in Zev Katz (ed.), *Handbook of Major Soviet Nationalities* (Free Press, New York, 1975), pp. 355–90.

17 Karl Marx, Frederick Engels, *Collected Works* (Lawrence and Wishart, London, 1975), vol. 3, pp. 146–74.

18 Zev Katz, op. cit., p. 365.
19 Alec Nove and J.A. Newth, 'The Jewish Population: Demographic Trends and Occupational Patterns', in L. Kochan (ed.), *The Jews in Soviet Russia Since 1917* (Oxford University Press, Oxford, 1978), pp. 132–67.
20 B.D. Weinryb, 'Antisemitism in Soviet Russia', in L. Kochan, *The Jews in Soviet Russia Since 1917*, pp. 300–32. On the attitude of Jewish emigres on antisemitism in the USSR see Zvi Gitelman, 'Soviet Political Culture: Insights from Jewish Emigres', *Soviet Studies*, vol. 39, no. 4 (October 1977), p. 551.
21 Zev Katz, 'After the Six-Day War', in L. Kochan, *The Jews in Soviet Russia Since 1917*, pp. 333–48.
22 Zvi Gitelman, 'Moscow and the Soviet Jews: A Parting of the Ways', *Problems of Communism* (January–February 1980), p. 25.
23 Mikhail Zand, 'The Jewish Question in the USSR: Theses', Stephen F. Cohen (ed.), *An End to Silence* (W.W. Norton, New York, 1982), pp. 245–9.
24 Zvi Gitelman, 'Human Rights and Jewish Nationalism in the USSR', in Ihor Kamenetsky (ed.), *Nationalism and Human Rights in the USSR* (Libraries Unlimited, Littleton, Colo., 1977), pp. 217–27.
25 Zev Katz, 'After the Six-Day War', in L. Kochan, *The Jews in Soviet Russia Since 1917*, pp. 347–8, 335.
26 Lukasz Hirszowicz, 'The Soviet-Jewish Problem', in L. Kochan, ibid., pp. 395–400.
27 Philippa Lewis, 'The Jewish Question in the Open: 1968–71', in L. Kochan, *The Jews in Soviet Russia Since 1917*, pp. 356–362.
28 Lukasz Hirszowicz, 'The Soviet-Jewish Problem', in L. Kochan, *The Jews in Soviet Russia Since 1917*, pp. 368, 399.
29 W. Korey, 'Soviet Decision-Making and the Problem of Jewish Emigration Policy', *Survey*, vol. 22, no. 1 (Winter 1976), pp. 112–31. See also, L. Schroeter, *The Last Exodus* (New York, 1974).
30 A. Yanov, *The Russian New Right* (Institute of International Studies, University of California, Berkeley, 1978). See also, P. Reddaway, 'The Development of Dissent and Opposition', in A. Brown and M. Kaser (eds.), *The Soviet Union Since the Fall of Krushchev*, pp. 143–6. Wlodzimierz Rozenbaum, 'The Jewish Question in Poland Since 1964', in George W. Simmonds (ed.), *Nationalism in the USSR and Eastern Europe in the Era of Brezhnev and Kosygin* (The University of Detroit Press, Detroit, 1977), pp. 335–41. Zev Katz, 'After the Six Day War' in L. Kochan, *The Jews in Soviet Russia Since 1917*, pp. 336, 338, 339, 341. Maurice Friedberg, 'AntiSemitism as a Policy Tool in the Soviet Bloc', in J. Jacobson (ed.), *Soviet Communism and the Socialist Vision* (Transaction Books, New Brunswick, 1972).
31 Lukasz Hirszowicz, 'The Soviet-Jewish Problem', in L. Kochan, *The Jews in Soviet Russia Since 1917*, pp. 377–8.
32 Philippa Lewis, 'The Jewish Question in the Open: 1968–1971', in L. Kochan, *The Jews in Soviet Russia Since 1917*, p. 360.
33 Lukasz Hirszowicz, 'The Soviet-Jewish Problem', in L. Kochan, *The Jews in Soviet Russia Since 1917*, pp. 375–6.
34 Andrei D. Sakharov, *Alarm and Hope* (Collins and Harvill Press, London, 1979), pp. 26, 109, 165, 178.
35 Roy Medvedev, *Political Essays* (Spokesman Books, Nottingham, 1976), p. 68. Ken Coates (ed.), *Détente and Socialist Democracy* (Spokesman Books, Nottingham, 1975), pp. 148–9.
36 Lukasz Hirszowicz, 'The Soviet-Jewish Problem', in L. Kochan, *The Jews in Soviet Russia Since 1917*, pp. 376–7.
37 The figures available for the number of Jews emigrating from the USSR are given as follows:

1948–68	7,641	1976	14,261
1969	2,979	1977	16,736
1970	1,027	1978	22,000
1971	13,900	1979	51,000
1972	31,651	1980	21,470
1973	35,000	1981	9,460
1974	20,628	1982	2,700
1975	13,221	1983	1,300

Sources: Figures for 1948–79 in J. Lowenhardt, *Decision Making in Soviet Politics* (London, 1981), p. 79, and L. Kochan (ed.), *The Jews in Soviet Russia Since 1917*, pp. 366–7. Figures from 1980–1 from *The Times*, 17 November 1982. Figures for 1982 from *The Daily Telegraph*, 29 January 1983. Figure for 1983 from *The Guardian*, 28 December 1983.

Between 1971 and 1981, 246,000 Jews left the USSR, of whom only 154,160 went to Israel. The majority of the others went to the United States, *The Times*, 17 November 1982.

38 Lukasz Hirszowicz, 'The Soviet Jewish Problem', in L. Kochan (ed.), *The Jews in Soviet Russia Since 1917*, p. 369.

39 Zvi Gitelman, 'Moscow and the Soviet Jews: A Parting of the Ways', *Problems of Communism* (January–February 1980), pp. 18–34.

40 Mary Hawkesworth, 'Ideological Immunity: The Soviet Response to Human Rights Criticisms', *Universal Human Rights*, vol. 2, no. 1 (January–March 1980), pp. 74–83. See the article by Alexandrov, 'Concerning Freedoms, Real and Imaginary', *Pravda*, 20 February 1976, reprinted in English translation in *The Current Digest of the Soviet Press*, vol. 28, no. 7, pp. 1–6.

41 L.I. Brezhnev, *Socialism, Democracy and Human Rights* (Pergamon Press, Oxford, 1980), pp. v–viii; L.I. Brezhnev, *Peace, Détente and Soviet American Relations* (Harcourt Brace, Janovich, New York, 1979), pp. 61–3.

42 N.K. Mikhailovskii, A.M. Ossyuk, Yu. I. Nikoporko, A.D. Buteiko, *Pravoi cheloveka i sovremennyi mir* (Naukova Dunka, Kiev, 1980), pp. 20–66. G.S. Ostapenko, *Bor'ba SSSR v OON za sotsial'no-ekonomocheskie prava cheloveka 1945–1977gg* (Nauka, Moscow, 1981).

43 David Kowalewski, 'Trends in the Human Rights Movement', in D.R. Kelly, *Soviet Politics in the Brezhnev Era* (Praeger, New York, 1980), pp. 168–74.

44 On the problem of internal reform in the USSR see Stephen F. Cohen 'The Friends and Foes of Change: Reformism and Conservativism in the Soviet Union', and R. Medvedev, 'The Stalin Question' in S. F. Cohen, A. Rabinovich and R. Sharlet (eds.), *The Soviet Union Since Stalin* (Macmillan, London, 1980).

45 Stephen White, *Political Culture and Soviet Politics* (Macmillan, London, 1979).

46 Frederick C. Barghoorn, *Détente and the Democratic Movement in the USSR* (The Free Press, New York, 1976), pp. 165–9.

47 Joshua Rubenstein, *Soviet Dissidents: Their Struggle for Human Rights* (Beacon Press, Boston, 1980), pp. 213–50.

48 Teresa Rakowska-Harmstone, 'The Struggle for National Self-Assertion and Liberalisation in the Soviet Union', in R.D. Gastil (ed.), *Freedom in the World* (Freedom House, New York, 1979), pp. 100–10.

49 Karl E. Birnbaum, 'Human Rights and East–West Relations', *Foreign Affairs* (July 1977), pp. 794–5.

50 Roy Medvedev, *Political Essays* (Spokesman Books, Nottingham, 1976), pp. 17–20.

51 See Sakharov's strictures on the 'weakness' of the European governments over the provision of credits to the USSR after the US Senate in 1974 had limited credit provisions as a result of the row over Jewish emigration – A.D. Sakharov, *My Country and the World* (Collins and Harvill Press, London, 1975), pp. 51–61, 'The Freedom to Choose One's Country of Residence'.

52 Roy A. Medvedev and Zhores A. Medvedev, 'The USSR and the Arms Race', *New Left Review*, no. 130 (November–December 1981), p. 10 – 'The absence of American socialism and the long isolation of American politics from the affairs of the European state system have contributed to the underdevelopment of a rational understanding of the international politics in the United States.' The American perception of Soviet intentions and objectives had been shaped also by other factors – the USA's role in the post-war period as the West's international policeman, and the influence of East European emigres within the American academic and political community.

53 Jeremy Azrael, 'The Nationality Problem in the USSR', in Seweryn Bialer (ed.), *The Domestic Context of Soviet Foreign Policy*, (Westview Press, Boulder, Colorado, 1981), pp. 148–9. The risks run by the Soviet government in bargaining with the US government over Jewish emigration are recounted by Azrael as follows:

First, the very fact of bargaining over what are widely regarded as basic rights exposes the Soviet regime to a certain amount of international opprobrium. Moreover, the regime's willingness to bargain is tantamount to a public admission of its serious need for outside economic assistance, if not to a public affirmation of the legitimacy of foreign intervention in

Soviet internal affairs. Third, every bargain it strikes weakens the argument that intervention cannot yield positive results and thereby strengthens the hands of would-be interventionists, including those who, like the Arab states in the case of Jewish emigration to Israel, may feel that a bargain has been made at their expense. Finally any sign of vulnerability or susceptibility to foreign pressure is likely further to destabilize the 'nationality front' by convincing Soviet citizens that more impressive feats of national self-assertiveness could result in stronger foreign intervention on their behalf. [Azrael adds] The history of the Jackson–Vanik Amendment suggests that the regime is so sensitive to these risks that it will repudiate bargains that involve public commitments and formalised agreements.

54 R.N. Dean, 'Contacts with the West: The Dissidents' View of Western Support for the Human Rights Movement in the Soviet Union', *Universal Human Rights*, vol. 2, no. 1 (January–March 1981).

55 Medvedev, *Political Essays*, p. 25. Ken Coates (ed.), *Detente and Socialist Democracy* (Spokesman Books, Nottingham, 1975).

56 Andrei Sakharov, *Alarm and Hope* (Collins and Harvill Press, London, 1979), p. 109. A similar strategy is advocated by western liberal democrats – Raymond D. Gastil, *Freedom in the World* (Freedom House, New York, 1979), pp. 85–100.

5 The Palestinians and their right to self-determination

SALLY MORPHET*

The issue

The issue of the Palestinians and their rights, in particular their right to self-determination (and what that entails), is now a staple of international politics. The following is designed to show what the issue is, and how it has been handled since 1947, when the General Assembly of the United Nations passed a resolution dividing Palestine into eight parts: three going to form a Jewish state, three an Arab state, a seventh (Jaffa) an Arab enclave in Jewish territory and the eighth (Jerusalem) a *corpus separatum* under a special international regime. This resolution, like the bulk of General Assembly and Security Council resolutions, constituted a recommendation. It asked Britain as the mandatory power together with the other UN members to adopt the partition plan.[1]

In 1948, the year Israel declared its independence 'by virtue of our natural and historic right and on the strength of the resolution of the United Nations General Assembly', the Arab population of Palestine was 1,432,545 (65.2 per cent) and the Jewish population 759,100 (34.8 per cent). Palestine had been taken from the Turks, who had governed it as part of the Ottoman Empire, by the British in 1917/18 and the Palestine Mandate was given to Britain by the League of Nations in 1920. The purpose of the A Mandates under which Palestine was classified was for the territory under Mandate to be given 'administrative advice and assistance by a Mandatory until such time as they are able to stand alone'. They were regarded as having 'reached a stage of development where their existence as independent nations can be provisionally recognised'. However this particular mandate was complicated by the fact that the British Foreign Secretary, A.J. Balfour, had declared in 1917, that Britain would support a Jewish national home in Palestine providing 'nothing

* The views expressed in this chapter are the author's and do not necessarily represent those of the Foreign and Commonwealth Office.

shall be done which may prejudice the civil and religious rights of existing non-Jewish communities in Palestine'. Fifty-six thousand (8 per cent) Jews out of a total population of 680,000 were then living in Palestine. Religious Jews had always been concerned with returning to Zion but the idea took on political nationalist overtones with the foundation of the World Zionist Organization by T. Herzl in 1897 which aimed at the establishment of a Jewish state.

Palestinian Arab opposition to Zionism was first expressed through violence in 1920. Jewish opposition to the British government's efforts to control immigration was mainly political and directed against the British government in the United Kingdom. The actions of the Nazi government in Germany in the 1930s made many in the West more sympathetic to Jewish aspirations. The first partition plan for Palestine was suggested by the British Peel Commission in 1937: it was accepted as a basis for negotiation by the Jews but rejected by the Arab Higher Committee. Both sides took to guerrilla warfare which was suspended by the Jews at the beginning of World War II. Jewish terrorist groups nevertheless became active in the middle of the war against the British government and the Arab community. In April 1947 the British government requested a special session of the General Assembly to consider the appointment of a special committee to make recommendations concerning the future government of Palestine. This special committee was set up and suggested either partition with economic union or a federal state. In November, the General Assembly accepted the partition plan (GA 181 II) by thirty-three for (Australia, Belgium, Bolivia, Brazil, Byelorussian SSR, Canada, Costa Rica, Czechoslovakia, Denmark, Dominican Republic, Ecuador, France, Guatemala, Haiti, Iceland, Liberia, Luxembourg, Netherlands, New Zealand, Nicaragua, Norway, Panama, Paraguay, Peru, Philippines, Poland, South Africa, Soviet Union, Sweden, Ukrainian SSR, United States, Uruguay, Venezuela) – thirteen against (Afghanistan, Cuba, Egypt, Greece, India, Iran, Iraq, Lebanon, Pakistan, Saudi Arabia, Syria, Turkey and the Yemen) – and ten abstaining (Argentina, Chile, China, Colombia, El Salvador, Ethiopia, Honduras, Mexico, United Kingdom, Yugoslavia).

The Assembly had previously rejected three resolutions. The first had raised the question of the competence of the United Nations to recommend any solution contrary to the UN Charter and against the wishes of the majority of the people of Palestine and suggested that an advisory opinion be sought from the International Court of Justice on a number of questions, including 'whether the indigenous population of Palestine has not an inherent *right* to Palestine and to determine its future constitution and government'.[2] The second had called for international cooperation over the resettlement of

Jewish refugees in their countries of origin and in the territories of member states, and the third had called for the establishment of an independent, unified Palestine.

One Jewish commentator[3] writing at the end of 1947 described the partition resolution as 'the recognition of Jewish nationhood by the supreme forum of world opinion', despite the fact that he recognized that out of the total population represented in the General Assembly only 33.6 per cent voted for partition and the proportion would have probably become even smaller if it was taken into account that more than 400 million people were not represented in the Assembly. He noted that Nehru had stated in 1947 that Palestine was, in the opinion of India, an Arab country.

> There is no doubt that these words expressed the feeling of most African and Asiatic peoples, and although we never intended to treat the Arabs as a colonial people, in their eyes we are linked up with the imperialist Powers on whom we have so largely relied. The votes on the Palestine question in the General Assembly were an exact reflection of this fact, and all peoples whoever in the past, directly or indirectly, were the objects of colonial policy were in opposition to the establishment of a Jewish state.

He also pointed out that the neighbours of the new Jewish state were united in their opposition to its creation; that many of those opposed to partition were sincerely convinced that legal and moral right was on their side and that the establishment of a Jewish state under existing conditions was a breach of the law and a violation of the established principles of national freedom and personality.

The partition plan assigned, with the exception of Jerusalem, about 60 per cent of the land to the Jewish state and 40 per cent to the Arab state. By 1949 Israel was accepted as a member of the United Nations through Security Council and General Assembly resolutions (in March and May). In the armed violence that followed the partition resolution, it had taken 77 per cent of the land of the mandate. The preamble to the General Assembly resolution accepting Israel's membership had however recalled both the partition resolution and a further resolution, GA resolution 194 III of December 1948, which had *inter alia* resolved that refugees wishing to return to their homes and live at peace with their neighbours should do so and that compensation should be paid for the property of those choosing not to return, and for the loss of or damage to property. This, as regards boundaries, appeared to mean that the United Nations recognized as Israel's boundaries those laid down in the partition resolution and not the *de facto* boundaries established by the Armistice Agreements made in 1949 with Egypt, Lebanon, Jordan and Syria.

In September 1948 the Provisional Government of Israel had passed an ordinance extending its laws for the state of Israel (i.e. the area it should have occupied under the 1947 partition plan) to any part of Palestine which the

Minister of Defence had defined by proclamation as being held by the Defence Army of Israel. In December 1949 the General Assembly passed a resolution placing Jerusalem under the UN Trusteeship Council. Israel defied this (and others) by moving its capital to West Jerusalem in 1950 when it also passed its Law of Return. In April 1950 the remaining area of the former Palestine Mandate (except the Gaza strip) was formally brought under Jordanian control by legislation confirming 'the reservation of all Arab rights in Palestine'. The Egyptians maintained control of the Gaza strip. By the end of 1949 about 75 per cent of the Arab population had left the area which had come under Israeli control. The situation in terms of numbers of refugees[4] was as follows:

area of Palestine Mandate:

- a 31,000 Palestinians in Israel as constituted by the partition plan and in the Israeli occupied territories
- b 200,000 Palestinians on the Gaza strip (the original population numbered 70,000)
- c 280,000 Palestinians on the West Bank (the original population numbered 460,000)

- d 97,000 Palestinians in Lebanon
- e 75,000 Palestinians in Syria
- f 70,000 Palestinians in Jordan
- g 4,000 Palestinians in Iraq
- h 7,000 Palestinians in Egypt.

Palestinians today live outside the Middle East in West Germany, the United States and Latin America. There are 400,000 living within Israel's pre-1967 *de facto* boundaries plus 1 million under Israeli occupation (since 1967) on the West Bank and Gaza strip, 1 million in Jordan, 358,000 (Lebanon), 299,000 (Kuwait), 222,000 (Syria), 136,000 (Saudi Arabia), 100,000 (other Gulf States), 45,000 (Egypt), 23,000 (Libya) and 20,000 (Iraq).

The response

A number of questions about rights are relevant to this issue. The Jews in Palestine had asserted that they were a people and entitled to exercise the right of self-determination which entailed, in their view, the right to set up an independent state. This had been accepted by the international community through the partition resolution and the acceptance of Israel as a member of the United Nations. This was clear. What was not so clear was the question of which boundaries this new state was entitled to. Many Israelis relied on their 'natural and historic rights' to the land, beyond that which they had been granted in the partition resolution. The Israelis have subsequently given prominence in the international community to the need for recognition of their 'right to exist within secure and recognized boundaries' rather than discussing the question of what their entitlement should be in terms of land. They have also argued that the Arab refugees from Palestine should be treated as refugees and absorbed by other Arab countries. They should not return to their homes nor should they be compensated. Their own acceptance of Jews from other Arab countries should be balanced by the acceptance of Palestinian Arabs into other Arab countries. More recently the 1978/79 Camp David agreements have referred to the 'legitimate rights' of the Palestinians: these do not however rule out the possibility of Israeli annexation of the West Bank and/or the Gaza strip.

The Arabs in Palestine, as the majority indigenous population, considered they had a right to the whole territory and that they were a people entitled to exercise their right of self-determination within it. They looked upon the Jews as new colonizers. The Palestinians have subsequently concentrated on arguing that they are a people with a right to self-determination. They too have been divided on the question of what should constitute the boundaries of the independent state to which they consider they are entitled. Some have argued for the whole of Palestine; some for the borders as laid down in the 1947 partition resolution and, increasingly after the 1967 and 1973 wars, for the borders which have been frequently regarded as implicitly affirmed by Security Council resolution 242 of 1967 which has much support from the international community (i.e., they would take the West Bank and Gaza strip). The problem of Jerusalem would remain. Palestinians consider it should be united and the capital of a Palestinian Arab state.

The conceptual framework against which this debate took place had been highlighted by President Wilson's assertion in January 1917 'that no peace can last ... which does not recognize and accept the principle that governments derive all their just powers from the consent of the governed, and that no right anywhere exists to hand peoples about from sovereignty to sovereignty as if they were property'. This idea was reflected in the 1919 League of Nations Covenant. Palestine was included among the A mandates which comprised (Article 22 paragraph 4) 'Certain communities formerly belonging to the Turkish Empire have reached a stage of development where their existence as independent nations can be provisionally recognized subject to the rendering of administrative advice and assistance by a Mandatory until such time as they are able to stand alone.'

International debate on rights during the inter-war period intensified with the rise of Nazism, and the beginning of World War II. The Atlantic Charter of August 1941, a statement of Anglo-American goals, *inter alia* recognized the principle of self-determination.[5] This aim amongst others was given general endorsement in the Declaration by United Nations in January 1942 and was enshrined in 1945 in Article 1.2 of the UN Charter which described one purpose of the United Nations as being 'To develop friendly relations among nations based on respect for the principle of equal rights and self-determination of peoples ...' It is also mentioned in Article 55. The subsequent Human Rights Declaration passed by the General Assembly in 1948 noted in Article 28: 'Everyone is entitled to a social and international order in which the rights and freedoms set forth in this Declaration can be realised.'

There followed an attempt to put this right and others in a legal framework through the drafting of the two Covenants on Civil and Political, and Economic, Social and Cultural rights. Both covenants contain the same Article 1. These state *inter alia* that 'All peoples have the right of self-determination' and 'By virtue of this right they freely determine their political status.' They also state that all states parties to the covenant shall respect the right of self-determination in conformity with the UN Charter. The origins of these Articles 1 date back to 1950 when the Soviet Union proposed that this right should be added to the draft Covenants. This was rejected but a proposal to study the question by Afghanistan and Saudi Arabia was accepted. Thirteen Arab/Asian delegations proposed the inclusion of such an article during the 1951/2 General Assembly. This was supported by many Latin American states and the Soviet bloc and was eventually accepted by forty-two to seven against (including France, United Kingdom and the United States) and five abstentions (GA Resolution 545 VI). A working party then prepared a new draft in 1955 which with two minor changes became the final article.

The debate on self-determination was carried on through the 1960 General Assembly Declaration on Colonialism and the discussion of the principle of equal rights and self-determination of peoples which was further elucidated in the 1970 General Assembly Declaration on Principles of International Law concerning Friendly Relations and Cooperation among States in accordance with the Charter of the United Nations. The two International Covenants subsequently came into force in 1976. All the main interested parties in the dispute have either ratified or acceded to these Covenants with the exception of Algeria, Israel and the United States which have signed them.

There is intense legal debate about the right of self-determination, what it implies and who can claim it particularly as there is no accepted legal definition of a people. One recent commentator[6] has suggested that the words '"*all* peoples have the right" ... in Article 1 refer to any people irrespective of the international political status of the territory it inhabits'. He suggests that the answer to the question of whether Article 1 confers rights on 'peoples' can be found:

in the general system of the Covenant, but it is also contingent to some extent upon theoretical differences in approaches to international treaties. Under an essentially 'dualist' approach, it would be argued that the Covenant creates duties and confers rights only upon the states parties. The 'peoples' under Article 1, like individuals under other articles of the Covenant, are the beneficiaries of those rights and duties of states. They may have rights under national law if the Covenant is carried out but they do not have rights under the Covenant as a matter of international law. A different view might insist that since the states are bound under international law to grant rights and freedoms to individuals (or, as in Article 1, to peoples) the latter have rights of international character.

This chapter is particularly concerned to show how those concerned have reacted (often by voting for appropriate General Assembly or Security Council resolutions) to the development of the political case for the Palestinian right to self-determination after Israel had achieved recognition in the international community. The first General Assembly resolution asserting this right was passed in 1970.

PALESTINIANS

The initial Palestinian response was mixed and confused; many had been stunned by the traumatic events of the late 1940s and also they lacked a natural leader. They did not push for the setting up of the 'Arab State' called for in the partition resolution which the Arab states at the United Nations had voted against since they hoped with Arab and Muslim help to regain all Palestine. Representatives of the 'Government of all Palestine' attended regional meetings of the Arab League (a regional group of Arab states set up in 1945) and Palestine Arab refugees used the Special Political Committee of the General Assembly to ask for the implementation of the 1948 resolution (GA 194 III) which called *inter alia* for the return of the refugees.

A more positive attitude became apparent by the late 1950s when the Palestinian National Liberation Movement (Fatah) was being set up. Meanwhile Ahmed Shuqairy, a Palestinian and former Saudi Arabian representative at the United Nations became in 1963 the chairman of the Palestinian Arab delegation representing the Arab people of Palestine which addressed the Special Political Committee of the General Assembly at the request of thirteen Arab states. He made Palestinian views clear stating:

> On the refugee question and on the Palestine problem as a whole, the United Nations should address itself to us, the people of Palestine, as the principal party to the Palestine problem. The Arab states are under a national duty to defend our cause by all the means at their disposal, but the final destiny of our people, the people of Palestine and the future of our country shall be determined by our people. It is we who accept, it is we who reject.

At the first Arab League Summit at Cairo in January 1964, Ahmed Shuqairy was asked to prepare the groundwork for the establishment of a Palestinian National Council (PNC). This body representing Palestinian communities throughout the world first met at Jerusalem in May/June 1964 and proclaimed the PLO (Palestine Liberation Organization). Its Executive Committee became its policy arm and a national charter was adopted. It also decided to set up a Palestinian Liberation Army. Following the meeting the PLO sent a message to the UN Secretary-General informing him of the meeting and of the fact that its spokesman would be the only legitimate spokesman on matters concerning the Palestinian people. The first PLO spokesman addressed the Special Political Committee in October 1965 (the year Fatah began guerrilla operations). He noted that the attitudes and feelings of the refugees had led to the establishment of the PLO. The Arab people of Palestine wanted to exercise their inalienable rights, including the right to live in freedom in their homes and not the right offered to them in the resolution 194 III. The establishment of the Palestine Liberation Organization was an expression of the Palestinian Arabs' determination to continue the struggle for those rights which had been taken away from them by invading British colonialists and Zionists and the United Nations, and given to total strangers from all parts of the world. It was also the turning point in the history of the Palestinian Arabs and a repudiation of the claims of those who would have the United Nations believe that the question of Palestine no longer existed and that it was only a refugee problem. He attacked the Balfour Declaration; stated that the partition resolution was contrary to the principle of self-determination proclaimed in the Charter, and pointed to the fact that the General Assembly had unjustly rejected the request to refer the matter to the International Court of Justice.[7] 'Since the UN had failed to remedy the injustice done, the Arab people of Palestine felt free to use all possible means to regain their human dignity and restore their usurped rights.'

The 1967 Arab/Israel war ended with the Israeli occupation of the West Bank, the Gaza strip and the rest of Jerusalem (the final area of the Palestine mandate) plus Egyptian Sinai and part of Syria. Subsequently the Security Council unanimously agreed on a resolution, SC resolution 242. The final resolution's major points were: withdrawal of Israeli armed forces from territories occupied in the recent conflict; termination of all claims or states of belligerency, and respect for and acknowledgement of the sovereignty, territorial integrity and political independence of every state in the area and their right to live in peace within secure and recognized boundaries free from threats or acts of force. It also affirmed the necessity of achieving a just settlement of the refugee problem and guaranteeing the territorial inviolability and political independence of every state in the area.

The immediate response of the PLO to SC resolution 242 was expressed at the United Nations in a speech to the Special Political Committee in December 1967. The PLO representative noted that the resolution had guaranteed a number of rights and privileges to the Israelis and had confined itself to referring to the Palestinian people as refugees deserving pity and a just solution for their plight. Who had given the Security Council the right to give away the birthright of the Palestinian Arabs? Why were 2 million Palestinian Arabs reduced to the status of refugees and exiles? GA resolution 194 III had recognized the right to return. Palestinian refugees claimed for themselves the right to independence, the right to exist and the natural right to be at home in their own country. In March 1968 Fatah forces scored a morale-boosting victory over Israeli troops with the help of Jordanian troops at the Jordanian village of Karameh. The same month an agreement was reached between the PLO, Fatah and the PFLP to give these groups representation on the PNC which also agreed on a Palestinian National Covenant. This emphasized Palestinian Arab rights, including the Palestinian Arab people's legal right to its homeland, and noted that the PLO representing the forces of the Palestinian revolution, was responsible for the movement of the Palestinian Arab people in its struggle to liberate and return to its homeland and exercise within it the right of self-determination. The liberation of Palestine was a defensive act necessitated by the requirements of self-defence. The next session of the PNC held in February 1969 elected Yasser Arafat, the leader of Fatah, as chairman of the PLO's Executive Committee.

After the October 1973 war the debate within the PLO as to whether they might accept a mini-state on the West Bank or whether they should continue to claim all Palestine or accept the partition resolution sharpened. They had become aware that it would be easier to gain more international support if Israel's claim to legitimacy within its 1967 borders, excluding Jerusalem, was accepted. They had also noted as early as 1972 that some major European countries (including France[8] and the United Kingdom) and Latin American countries (including Argentina and Mexico) had for the first time voted for a General Assembly resolution GA 2949 XXVII which *inter alia* reaffirmed SC resolution 242 and recognized 'that respect for the rights of the Palestinians is an indispensable element in the establishment of a just and lasting peace in the Middle East'. They therefore, in June 1974, at the twelfth meeting of the Palestine National Council declared that their new policy was 'to liberate Palestinian soil and to set up on any part of it which is liberated the militant national authority of the people'. This, as David Gilmour[9] has noted, 'clearly indicated that the majority of the PLO leadership was now prepared to accept in the place of the secular, democratic state in all of

Palestine as it was in 1947, an independent country in one quarter of the whole area'.

The qualified endorsement of a mini-state by the mainstream PLO led to the formation of the Rejection Front in October 1974 by radical Palestinian factions supported by Iraq. However it was also followed by a GA resolution, also in October, inviting the PLO to participate in its proceedings by 105 (China, France, Soviet Union) – 4 (United States) – 20 (United Kingdom). The General Assembly is normally supposed only to be addressed by representatives of states. Arafat, in his speech to the General Assembly on 13 November stated he was a revolutionary rather than a terrorist. He was ambiguous as to the extent of the territory the PLO claimed; but did implicitly accept SC resolution 242 by noting that all Security Council decisions and calls by world public opinion for withdrawal from lands occupied in 1967 had been ignored. He discussed Palestine in terms of a secular democratic state including Jews. He noted that the question of Palestine had finally emerged in its true context not merely as a problem of refugees or border disputes but as the question of a people uprooted from its homeland and deprived of its rights as a result of a Zionist plot supported by imperialist powers. He said he had come 'bearing an olive branch and a freedom-fighter's gun' and concluded by saying, 'Do not let the olive branch fall from my hand.'

The speech was followed by the adoption of two major GA resolutions on Palestine, 3236 XXIX and 3237 XXIX. Resolution 3236 adopted by 89 (China, Soviet Union) – 8 (United States) – 37 (France, United Kingdom) consolidated previous GA resolutions besides adding the explicit reference to the right to national independence. It reaffirmed the inalienable rights of the Palestinian people including the right to self-determination and the right to national independence and sovereignty; and reaffirmed the inalienable right of Palestinians to return to their homes and property from which they had been displaced and uprooted. Although the language was deliberately ambiguous, the repeated references in the report on the discussion of this resolution to GA resolution 181 II, as well as acknowledgement of Israel itself, suggested that a Palestinian state along the lines proposed in the partition plan or the 1967 borders was envisaged. Most of the explanations of vote turned on the question of Israel's right to exist and whether the text allowed for this or not. A further historic GA resolution 3237 XXIX admitted the PLO as an observer to the United Nations by 95 (China, Soviet Union) – 17 (United Kingdom, United States) – 19 (France).

By 1974 the PLO had gained much international acceptance (it was to gain more over the next few years). The claims made for the Palestinian people, i.e., self-determination implying national independence, and the right to return to homes and property were clearly laid out, and had been accepted in part, by certain European and Latin American states, and in full by the non-aligned and the Soviet Union and China. The claims had not been accepted by the United States or Israel. Since December 1975 the PLO has been invited to take part in discussions in the Security Council under rule 37 with the same rights as those conferred upon a Member State. This was designed to emphasize the PLO's status as the legitimate representative of a people.

ARAB AND MUSLIM STATES

The Arab and Muslim states have always two major reasons for being involved with the issue of Palestine. The first is their concern for the Palestinians and the land of Palestine. The second is their concern for Jerusalem, the third holiest city of Islam, which contains major mosques sacred to Moslems, notably the Dome of the Rock. They have not, of course, always agreed on aims and tactics and their own interests have, not surprisingly, often come before Palestinian interests.

The UN Charter supports the principle of self-determination but not the right (Articles 1 and 55). The then Arab members of the United Nations, Egypt, Iraq, Lebanon, Saudi Arabia and Syria failed in their attempt to inscribe an additional item on the agenda on, 'The termination of the mandate over Palestine and the declaration of its independence', at the 1947 special session of the General Assembly on Palestine. They also failed in their attempt to seek support for a resolution asking for an advisory opinion of the International Court of Justice on a number of questions including: 'whether the indigenous population of Palestine has not an inherent right to Palestine and to determine its future constitution and government'. And of course they, with a number of mainly Asian states including the Muslim states of Afghanistan, Iran, Pakistan and Turkey, failed to prevent the partition resolution being passed. After this had been passed, they denounced it as being against the UN Charter and declared they regarded it as a recommendation rather than a decision. They also voted against the resolution which called *inter alia* for the Palestine refugees' right to return but subsequently they used this aspect of it to call for the right to return.

Their first major success came in 1951 when ten Arab and Muslim states (Afghanistan, Egypt, Indonesia, Iran, Iraq, Lebanon, Pakistan, Saudi Arabia, Syria, Yemen) plus Burma, India and the Philippines sponsored a General Assembly resolution stating that the right of self-determination should be affirmed in the proposed Covenant or Covenants on civil, political, economic and social rights. This was supported by Latin American states and the Soviet bloc and was eventually accepted by 42–7–5. This resolution showed that more Latin Americans might well be persuaded to support the Palestinian cause: the potential was subsequently exploited.

As the number of Arab states in the United Nations increased (Jordan and Libya joined in 1955 and Sudan and Tunisia in 1956) a new positive attitude appeared among both Arab and Muslim countries towards the problem of Palestine both inside and outside the United Nations. In 1959 the ten Arab states in the United Nations circulated a report on 6 October on the Secretary General's proposals about United Nations assistance to Palestine refugees. This reaffirmed their stand on behalf of the Arab people of Palestine and the right of Arab refugees to return to their homeland, and rejected projects for resettlement. Indonesia and Pakistan then put forward a draft resolution in the General Assembly which gave more emphasis to repatriation and compensation for the refugees than resettlement. An amended version of this draft was eventually approved by 80–0–1. The trend was accentuated in 1960 when a further sixteen African states joined the United Nations. In that year two paragraph votes affirming the 'property rights of the Arab refugees of Palestine' which required a two-thirds majority were just defeated. The Assembly was rounded off by the adoption of the seminal UN Declaration on Colonialism (GA resolution 1514 XV) by 89 (China, Soviet Union) – 0 –7 (France, United Kingdom, United States)). This declared *inter alia* that the subjection of peoples to alien subjugation, domination and exploitation constituted a denial of fundamental human rights and was contrary to the Charter and that all peoples had the right to self-determination.

The Arab League contribution towards the setting up of the PLO has already been noted. Much of the Arab and Muslim efforts after 1961 were devoted to persuading the non-aligned of the justice of the Palestinian case. It is however worth recording their efforts to woo African opinion in the early 1960s. The Organization of African Unity was created in 1963. At the second summit conference of the Arab League at Alexandria in September 1964 the Declaration noted *inter alia* that Arab–African cooperation was a foundation of Arab policy by virtue of historical and geographical association and common interests and objectives.

A further development of note was the establishment of the Organization of the Islamic Conference (OIC) which has also given support to the Palestinian cause. It was formed after an arson attempt against the Al Aqsa mosque in Jerusalem in September 1969, in part because Islamic states considered the United States was ambivalent about the issue of Jerusalem. The United States had abstained on a Security Council resolution 271 that month, which had noted the Council's concern at the damage following the arson attempt and condemned Israel for its failure to comply with the resolutions passed on Jerusalem since the June war. Arab League Foreign

Ministers immediately decided to convene a conference of Islamic Foreign Ministers after the incident at the Al Aqsa mosque. The PLO was present as an observer at its first Summit at Rabat the same month. The OIC (which now has forty-five members) was later (February 1974 or July 1975 – it is not quite clear which date is correct) to accept the PLO as a member, thus giving it head of state status, before both the non-aligned movement (accepted in August 1975) and the Arab League (September 1976).

In 1980 radical Arab states including Algeria, Iran, Democratic Yemen, Libya and Syria for the first time by voting for GA resolution 35/169A reaffirmed GA resolution 181 II the partition plan. This underlined their commitment to a solution which included Israel.

THE NON-ALIGNED

The non-aligned movement, which began in 1961 with 25 members (it now has 101) has been particularly important to those promoting acceptance of the Palestinian people's right to self-determination. The radicals found however that the support had its limits because the movement has since 1969 supported the legitimacy of Israel within the *de facto* boundaries (with the exception of Jerusalem) it had before the June 1967 war (i.e. all the Palestine mandate except Jerusalem, the West Bank and the Gaza strip). The newly decolonised states which joined the United Nations (and often the non-aligned movement) were, as weaker states, often particularly attached to the United Nations, its Charter and its resolutions. They therefore found it difficult to attack the legitimacy of a state which had previously been legitimized by the United Nations.

The first non-aligned Summit in 1961 gave support for the full restoration of all the rights of the Arab people of Palestine in conformity with the Charter and the resolutions of the United Nations. With the addition of seventeen more African states and three more Arab states, in 1964, the second Summit endorsed the fuli restoration of all the rights of the Arab people of Palestine to their homeland and their inalienable right[10] to self-determination and supported the Arab people of Palestine in their struggle for liberation from colonialism and racism. The movement subsequently became less active as the Algerians and Indonesians tried to create a more radical body. Nevertheless the non-aligned produced one of the two draft resolutions (sponsored by India, Mali, and Nigeria) at the beginning of the crucial debate in the Security Council in November 1967 which led to the adoption of SC resolution 242.

Non-aligned support enabled the General Assembly to pass a resolution in 1968 referring to the principle of the right to return as embodied in the Universal Declaration of Human Rights. The movement met once again at a special meeting in 1969. The PLO was represented. The non-aligned reaffirmed the inadmissibility of the acquisition of territory and the withdrawal of all foreign troops from all the Arab territories occupied since June 1967 in accordance with SC resolution 242. This was followed by a General Assembly resolution recognizing that 'the problem of the Palestine Arab refugees has arisen from the denial of their inalienable rights under the Charter of the United Nations and the Universal Declaration of Human Rights'. The resolution also contained a call to the Security Council to take effective measures to implement these resolutions.

The third non-aligned summit at Lusaka in September 1970 (the first since 1964) declared that, 'the full respect for the inalienable rights of the Arab people of Palestine is a prerequisite for peace in the Middle East'. This was followed up by a resolution in the General Assembly declaring that 'full respect for the inalienable rights of the Arab people of Palestine is an indispensable element in the establishment of a just and lasting peace in the Middle East', and acknowledged specifically for the first time their entitlement to equal rights and self-determination in accordance with the UN Charter. A further resolution linked the peoples of Southern Africa and Palestine as peoples being denied the right to self-determination. The right to return, the right to self- determination and the explicit spelling out of the right to an independent state were finally consolidated in the 1974 GA resolution.

Once the non-aligned had been able to ensure that resolutions affirming the basic Palestinian rights could get through the General Assembly as they had in 1969/70, they turned their attention to the Security Council. Here they attempted to get Western countries, in particular the United States, to build on SC resolution 242 by adding to it an affirmation of the rights and legitimate aspirations of the Palestinians. Guinea, India, Indonesia, Kenya, Panama, Peru, Sudan and Yugoslavia put such a draft resolution before the Security Council in July 1973. It was voted for by thirteen countries including France and the United Kingdom but failed to pass because it was vetoed by the United States. Two further resolutions on these lines but using 'inalienable rights' language were also vetoed by the United States in January and June 1976.

The non-aligned had more success in their campaign to ensure global recognition of the PLO which had begun after they had accepted the PLO as the legitimate representative of the Palestinian people at the Algiers Summit of 1973. The PLO was accepted as an observer at the United Nations in the following year and subsequently as a full member of the movement at the Lima Foreign Ministers' Meeting in 1975. In 1980 the European Community declared the PLO would have to be associated with the negotiations for a peace settlement.

LATIN AMERICA

The first Latin American countries to join the non-aligned movement, with the exception of Cuba, which was a founder member in 1961, were the three Caribbean Commonwealth members, Guyana, Jamaica and Trinidad and Tobago[11] in 1970. The first Latin American signs of support for the Palestinian case came about in the vote for GA resolution 2949 XXVII of 1972. This affirmed SC resolution 242 and recognized 'that respect for the rights of the Palestinians is an indispensable element in the establishment of a just and lasting peace in the Middle East'.[12] This was voted for by Argentina, Chile, Cuba, Ecuador, Guyana, Honduras, Jamaica, Mexico, Peru and Trinidad and Tobago. It was followed by the Peruvian and Panamanian sponsorship of the first draft resolution on Palestinian rights in the Security Council in July 1973. Latin American support increased during the 1970s: sixteen Latin American states voted for an important 1980 resolution on Palestine GA resolution 35/169 A; one voted against, ten abstained and three were absent.

THE SOVIET UNION

The Soviet Union voted for the partition resolution, has always supported Israel's right to exist and has also consistently supported resolutions affirming Palestinian rights. One major example of its support was the proposal it made in October 1976 that the Geneva Peace Conference which had met for a few weeks in December 1973/January 1974 should be reconvened with the following agenda:

1 withdrawal of Israeli troops from all the Arab territories occupied in 1967;
2 realization of the inalienable rights of the Palestine Arab people, including their right to self-determination and the establishment of their own state;
3 preservation of the right to an independent existence and to security of all the states directly participating in the conflict – and the granting to them of appropriate international guarantees; and
4 cessation of the state of war between the Arab states concerned and Israel.

The Soviet Union also proposed that the PLO should participate in the work of the conference from the beginning and with equal status. Resolution GA 31/62 which followed by 122 (France, United Kingdom, Soviet Union) – 2 (United States) – 8 called for the early convening of the Peace Conference on the Middle East under the auspices of the United Nations and the co-chairmanship of the Soviet Union and the United States not later than the end of March 1977. It later, on 1 October 1977, issued a joint statement with the United States on the legitimate rights of the Palestinian people.

EUROPE

Positive European support for Palestinian rights began to be expressed about 1970. The British Foreign Secretary made a speech in October 1970 calling for a peace settlement which took into account the legitimate aspirations of the Palestinians. And at the United Nations the French sponsored a clause recognizing 'that respect for the rights of the Palestinians is an indispensable element in the establishment of a just and lasting peace in the Middle East', which was added to a General Assembly resolution affirming SC resolution 242. The final resolution was voted for by France and the Soviet Union. The United States voted against it and the United Kingdom abstained. When an identical clause was added to a similar resolution in 1972, the United Kingdom joined France in voting for it. This was a pointer to the French and United Kingdom vote for the resolution on Palestinian rights in the Security Council in July 1973 which was vetoed by the United States.

The same year the European Community countries put out a joint statement in November recognizing that 'in the establishment of a just and lasting peace account must be taken of the legitimate rights of the Palestinians'. Subsequently EC spokesmen have stated that the right of the Palestinian people to express their national identity had to be recognized (1975), and (1977) that a solution to the conflict would only be possible if the 'legitimate right of the Palestinian people to give effective expression to its national identity is translated into fact. This would of course take into account the need for a homeland for the Palestinian people.' European efforts to promote a dialogue with the PLO followed the Camp David agreements. Yasser Arafat met Willy Brandt, the Chairman of the Socialist International and former West German Chancellor, and Chancellor Kreisky of Austria in Vienna in July 1979. Both claimed afterwards that neither Arafat nor the PLO had any intention of destroying Israel. In February 1980 the Irish government was the first in the EC to recognize the PLO and to call for a Palestinian state. In March, President Giscard d'Estaing declared support for the principle of self-determination for the Palestinians. The most important development during this period occurred on 13 June when the EC countries at their Venice Summit declared that the PLO would 'have to be associated with the negotiations' for a peace settlement. This declaration was reaffirmed in July 1982 following the Israeli invasion of the Lebanon.

UNITED STATES AND ISRAEL

The support of the United States, as a great power and a permanent member of the Security Council, has been crucial to Israel. Despite the fact that it pushed the partition plan through the General Assembly the United States has been extremely reluctant to envisage a two-state solution for the Palestinian problem. They were strong supporters of the idea that a settlement of the subsequent refugee problem could be solved through resettlement rather than repatriation. A small breakthrough was made in June 1967 when President Johnson put forward his ideas about a Middle East settlement which included 'justice for the refugees'. This idea was later incorporated into Security Council Resolution 242 in part because of pressure from non-aligned states in the Security Council. Following this, United States policy moved from the idea that a just settlement 'must take into account the desires and aspirations of the refugees' (Rogers Plan, December 1969) via a veto of a draft in July 1973 calling for a solution based *inter alia* on the rights and legitimate aspirations of the Palestinians to Secretary of State Kissinger's statement at the opening of the Geneva Peace Conference in December 1973 that a peace agreement must include 'a settlement of the legitimate interests of the Palestinians'.

In September 1975 the Israelis extracted a commitment from the United States not to talk directly with the PLO. In 1976 the United States vetoed two further draft Security Council resolutions on inalienable Palestinian rights in the Security Council. But the new Carter administration which came in at the beginning of 1977 brought a more affirmative approach to the question of the Palestinians. This began with a statement by President Carter in March that a homeland had to be provided for Palestinian refugees. This was followed by the State Department's assertion in September that Palestinian participation in a settlement of the Palestinian question was necessary to ensure the successful outcome of the resumed Geneva Peace Conference, and finally, by a joint statement with the Soviet Union of 1 October 1977 which stated that a comprehensive settlement of the Middle East problem must include 'ensuring the legitimate rights of the Palestinian people'.

This high point was followed by retreat under Israeli pressure. The Camp David agreements of 1978/9 carried on the 'legitimate rights' terminology but left the option of Israeli annexation of the occupied territories open. This was followed in April 1980 by a fourth US veto in the Security Council on the question of Palestinian inalienable rights, the first under President Carter. President Reagan's speech of 1 September 1982 made US policy clearer. It referred to the legitimate rights of the Palestinians, and noted that the problem was not a refugee problem. It then went on to state that the United States would not support annexation or permanent control by Israel of the West Bank and Gaza but neither would it support the establishment of an independent Palestinian state in those territories. It would support self-government by the Palestinians on the West Bank in association with Jordan. President Reagan also affirmed that the United States agreed that the withdrawal provision of Security Council resolution 242 applied to all fronts, including the West Bank and Gaza, in return for peace. Jerusalem had to be undivided but its final status should be decided through negotiations.

Assessment

The commitment of the Palestinians and the Arab and Muslim states to the right of self-determination for the Palestinians came primarily from a deep sense of injustice. They were able to communicate this to the non-aligned countries but the radicals among them found that they could not persuade them, as a whole, to deny legitimacy to Israel. They were, as weaker states, more attached to the United Nations, its Charter and its resolutions, and therefore found it difficult to attack the right of a state to exist that had been legitimized through the United Nations. Their norm has been provided by Security Council resolution 242, and since 1969 their goal has been to make sure that the Palestinians could exercise their right of self-determination which in their view (spelled out in the GA resolution of 1974) entails the setting up of an independent state on the West Bank and the Gaza strip.

The position of the Soviet Union is similar to that of the non-aligned. Support for the Palestinians' right of self-determination fits in well with their policy of support for decolonization but they have also been consistent in supporting Israel's legitimacy. They were able with the United States to put out a joint statement in October 1977, part of which is reproduced here:[13]

> The United States and the Soviet Union believe that within the framework of a comprehensive settlement of the Middle East problem, all specific questions of the settlement should be resolved, including such key issues as withdrawal of Israeli Armed Forces from territories occupied in the 1967 conflict; the resolution of the Palestinian question, including insuring the legitimate rights of the Palestinian people; termination of the state of war and establishment of normal peaceful relations on the basis of mutual recognition of the principles of sovereignty, territorial integrity, and political independence.

The United States does not ultimately accept Israeli control of the West Bank but neither does it support the case for a Palestinian state.

The European states' position on Palestinian self-determination has changed during the 1970s. The change began at least three years before the first major oil price rise. The change in response is likely to have occurred both because of the European states' realization of the strength of the Palestinian case and because they perceived the strength of the backing it had obtained. Thus the issue was not likely to die. There is as yet little chance of bringing about Palestinian self-determination unless current minority views gain ascendancy in the United States and Israel. Nevertheless the case has been made.

Notes

1 The best book on the issue in the 1940's is *The British Empire and the Middle East*, W. R. Louis, Clarendon Press, 1984.
2 This was the view of certain United States officials, ibid., pp. 422, 445.
3 Walter Zander, *Is this the Way? A call to Jews* (London, Gollancz, 1948).
4 First Interim Report of the United Nations Economic Survey Mission for the Middle East, A/1106 (November 1949).
5 Louis, *British Empire*, p. 445, n. 12.
6 A. Cassese, 'The Self-determination of Peoples' in Louis Henkin (ed.), *The International Bill of Rights* (New York, Columbia University Press, 1981), p. 108.
7 Official Records of the UN General Assembly, Twentieth Session, 437th meeting of the Special Political Committee, para. 14.
8 France had in fact put this forward in a 1970 resolution and voted for it.
9 'The Creation and Evolution of the PLO' in *Pressure Groups in the Global System*, Peter Willetts (ed.), Francis Pinter, 1982, p. 53.
10 The 1948 Universal Declaration of the Human Rights had used this phrase.
11 Caribbean countries are part of the Latin American group at the UN.
12 This clause is exactly the same as one voted for by the non-aligned and France and the Soviet Union in 1970.
13 *The Search for Peace in the Middle East: Documents and Statements 1969–79*, Report for Committee on Foreign Affairs, US House of Representatives (Washington, DC, US Government Printing Office, 1979), p. 159.

6 Domestic policies and external influences on the human rights debate in Latin America

FRANCISCO ORREGO VICUÑA

The debate regarding the human rights situation in Latin America, particularly with respect to the countries of the Southern Cone, has been intense in recent years. It has focussed primarily on the nature of the policies adopted within each country, on the question of their legitimacy or illegitimacy, and on their scope and effects. These aspects of the debate have produced an extensive body of literature of both a political cast and a humanitarian orientation.[1]

Another dimension of the issue, however, is the relationship that exists between these internal policies and the external influences which have made themselves felt in the region. This aspect of the problem has received comparatively less attention, even though it has very likely been a determining factor in many of the approaches taken at the national level, both in a negative and in a positive sense.[2] It is to the complex interrelationships between these external influences and internal policies, and the various forms in which they are manifested, that this chapter addresses itself.

Problems of transculturization

A distinguished Latin American author has remarked that human rights and their protection are a creation of culture which is associated with certain periods of historical development,[3] particularly in western civilization.[4] Although it can be maintained that today human rights are a universally recognized value, it must also be noted that this is more true in a theoretical sense, since in many areas the degree to which they are respected and observed is far from satisfactory.[5] This is probably a direct consequence of the different cultural levels prevailing in various regions of the world. The various ideologies which exist, when viewed as forms of cultural expression, are another related factor.

As the more advanced contemporary forms of culture become increasingly internationalized, there is likewise a more extensive application of their cultural values. Certainly, it is difficult to identify which expressions of culture are the most developed since in this regard a number of competing concepts exist which, in turn, entail different beliefs as to the role of the individual and his rights. Be that as it may, it can be assumed that Western Christian civilization is one of these advanced cultures by virtue of the fact that it has clearly identified the individual as one of its central values, although the serious difficulties it has encountered in guaranteeing the effective protection of those rights cannot be ignored.

The most difficult problem is determining to what extent these values have actually been embraced in Latin America. As is well known, this region is the cultural product of a complex mixture of civilizations and values which combine the elements of Western Christianity with indigenous values and traditions as well as many other foreign components. Going beyond outward appearances, we might ask ourselves whether the cultural values of Latin America are actually the same as those of the West, or whether they differ in some important respects.[6]

Given the impossibility of arriving at a definite answer, it can at least be stated that although the roots of Western culture are still visible in Latin American society, this society has evolved in accordance with its own realities.[7] So while it is possible and necessary to demand respect for basic human rights as an important value in that culture, the context in which it is placed within Latin America must be taken into consideration, since it differs from that of the European nations and the United States, among others. Hence there are often differences, which have not always been taken into account, as regards the way in which the problem must be approached – at least until the above-mentioned process of transculturization takes on a greater stability and depth. None of this justifies human rights violations or excesses, since it has been demonstrated on many occasions that Latin American nations are as capable as any of respecting human rights. However, it does mean that greater attention must be paid to the causes of the current deterioration in this realm and to the ways in which they can be permanently eliminated. In a broad sense, this is essentially a cultural undertaking.

National security doctrines and their Western origin

The problem of transculturization is even more complex because normally it is supposed that a more highly advanced culture will make positive contributions to the subject which concerns us here – the treatment of human rights. Nevertheless, this has not always been the case. With respect to Latin America, the influence which the concepts prevalent in certain sectors of French, American and, more remotely, German society have had on the development of some extreme versions of the doctrine of national security is well documented.[8]

The policies adopted by France during the Algerian War of Independence, for example – which cannot be described as a model of respect for human rights – have had a strong influence on Latin America both in respect of their simplistic distinction between good and evil, friend and foe, and of the methods of total elimination which were employed. The same is true of the theories relating to counter-insurgency developed by the United States, and of some of the Manichaean concepts which were a product of the Cold War; for several decades, Latin American armies were exposed to these doctrines, just as earlier they had been taught the principles of German geopolitics.

Thus, the process of transculturization has brought its own contradictions along with it, since while jurists, men of the church and common citizens wished Latin America to be the reflection of superior values and ideals, other segments of their own societies projected antagonistic concepts or opposing values. It is not, however, possible to avoid responsibility for the extremes which were reached in Latin America, since there was definitely a receptivity to these negative ideas; neither, however, can the responsibility which these other societies have also had in the generation and development of the problem be disregarded.

It is interesting to observe that after a time during which the influence of unlikeable external political principles was greatest in Latin America – a phase which corresponded precisely with the most difficult stage regarding human rights – a period began in which moderate approaches more in keeping with Latin American tradition have been undertaken.[9] This perhaps marks the starting point of a further separation between Latin American thought and these external influences – a phenomenon which has frequently occurred within Latin America in many other spheres.[10]

Negative international experiences and historical forms of dependency

The problem under consideration should also be viewed within the context of the more general international experience which Latin America has had throughout its historical development ever since independence. This experience has not been a particularly positive one, since its predominant feature has been a marked dependence on the international system and on the dominant world powers in different periods of history. This has resulted in a certain lack of trust of those powers and to some questioning of the real purposes lying behind human rights policies supported by world powers or other countries outside the region.[11]

From an historical perspective, this situation first involved the European countries, which played a leading role in that international system for a good part of the nineteenth century. The numerous economic, political and military conflicts which occurred between European powers and the countries of Latin America were perhaps symptomatic of a relationship which could hardly be described as one of cooperation. Even though it is likely that all of this has been forgotten in Europe, that is not entirely the case in Latin America.

With respect to the United States, these difficulties have been even more severe as a result of the hegemonic role which that country has played in continental relations since the latter part of the last century. What has frequently been defined as a special relationship and a community of interests is in fact more properly a rhetorical formula to conceal what have often been deep-seated and prolonged differences.[12]

Although United States foreign policy has alternated between its well known cycles of isolationism and internationalism, these cycles have not resulted in any fundamental changes in the nature of its relationship with Latin America, even though the means of attempting to achieve those policy objectives may have varied. In consequence, this relationship has basically been perceived by Latin American nations as a manifestation of imperialism.

It must also be borne in mind that, with a certain frequency, US foreign policy has sponsored causes which form a part of that society's traditional morality, thereby taking on a spiritual orientation which on occasion has approached a messianic vision of international policy.[13] While legitimate, this focus has also led to confusion, there being fears that its humanitarian motives might be concealing political purposes of another sort. Unfortunately, historical experience has confirmed these fears.

The imposition of international policies

The points which have been examined above provide the back-drop for an assessment of the different effects on Latin America produced by various forms of international influence regarding human rights which have taken place in recent years. The first was the type carried out by the Carter Administration. Although the problem of human rights had been raised before, the reaction had generally been either slight or non-existent during other administrations.

In this regard it should be borne in mind that, apart from the many historical instances of human rights violations which have occurred in Latin America, serious problems have arisen in contemporary times under popular dictatorships such as those of Perón, Pérez Jiménez and Rojas Pinillas, under

Marxist dictatorships, and under right wing military regimes. Thus the phenomenon was making its appearance fairly regularly in the 1950s and reached its height in the 1970s. This one element alone appears to suggest a profound cultural flaw.

The predominant trait of the methods used by the Carter Administration was that they were founded on an approach based on the imposition of measures consisting primarily of the application of economic and political sanctions. This approach met with three major problems in Latin America. Despite the fact that the US government attempted to give it a positive interpretation, in that the measures did not involve reprisals but were instead directed towards depriving the affected countries of the benefits of a new prosperity, within the Latin American context it could only be understood in its most negative sense. The historical experience discussed above made this inevitable. Worse still, that administration proceeded to apply sanctions to Latin American countries for many other reasons, whether it was a question of Brazil's nuclear policy or Ecuador's fishing policies, among other examples. All of this helped to create a relationship of general antagonism which revived the earlier spectre of imperialism within the region.

A second fundamental difficulty arose out of the fact that this administration introduced a new element into the debate on the subject which created a great deal of conflict: the strategic dimension. Human rights policy was to be less stringent when the country in question represented a political, economic or military strategic interest for the United States. Thus the basic subject entirely lost its humanitarian significance and was converted into a tool for the political advancement of the interests of a world power. This caused the human rights policy to lose a large part of its credibility, even in the United States itself.

As a consequence of these two problems, there was a tendency in Latin America to see this policy as a problem of political confrontation between conflicting national interests rather than as an issue arising out of the need to safeguard vital moral values. Moreover, the application of that policy also failed to make a clear distinction between two basic aspects, thus lending itself to even greater confusion with regard to its scope. The first aspect was the protection of the physical integrity of the individual, while the second related to more general rights of an economic or political nature.[14] While in regard to the former, a definite stringency was admissible in order to ensure that those rights were respected, the latter left room for a greater amount of debate. Since this distinction was not made, it was thought in many circles of government that the entire purpose of this policy was the harassment of military regimes rather than a genuine safeguarding of basic human rights.

There has been an intense debate regarding the effects which this policy has had in Latin America. Two main viewpoints have been expressed on the subject. According to the first, it was a successful effort to correct some particularly serious problems involving the observance of human rights in the region.[15] According to the second point of view, on the other hand, it generated counterproductive effects which, as a result, hardened the position of some Latin American regimes.

Since it is difficult to ascertain the true facts of such a contemporary and recent situation as this, the question as to the effects of these methods might best be approached from two different standpoints. The first relates to the international import which a human rights policy contradictory to the postulates espoused at that time by the United States government could have had. In this context, there seems to be no doubt that the threat of sanctions and the approval of condemnatory decisions had an impact on the region which led many governments to adopt more moderate human rights policies or to initiate various forms of institutional realignment.[16]

Nevertheless, the internal development of the respective political structures must be taken into account. To the extent that they appeared to become consolidated in the national arena, the overall human rights situation tended to improve proportionally, while it also became necessary to proceed with the chosen forms of institutional realignment. If this is the case, then two questions must be asked. The first is whether the same result would not have been achieved in any event as a consequence of this internal development, without these effects being attributed to international pressure. Perhaps the fact that such pressure coincided with this development makes it difficult to attribute the effect to one cause or the other.

The second question posed by this situation is a more important one. Was this greater moderation due to a genuine conviction, or was it merely the product of expediency given the circumstances? In the first case, there would be a positive effect, whether the result of an internal development or international pressure. In the second case, however, its circumstantial nature would mean that the new stance might be abandoned as soon as internal or external conditions changed. Given the fact that coercive methods do not seek conviction or consent but only results, it might be feared that this second alternative would be the most likely. In that case, international pressure would have negative effects, at least in the long run. Nevertheless, no clear answers to these questions were in fact formulated, because the Carter Administration's policies were of short duration and the methods used in this regard underwent a change, as will be discussed later.

One other problem, which stemmed from other aspects of international pressure, was particularly apparent in the policy followed by France and some other countries. It had to do with the economic interests of those states. In this

connection, an inversely proportional relationship exists between the importance ascribed to the issue of human rights and the level of business activity and investment in the country in question. While some Latin American economies were experiencing the boom of the mid-1970s,[17] the pressure diminished considerably. Both before and after this period of prosperity, the interest in human rights was significantly greater. This situation, too, neither lent prestige to those international policies nor strengthened the Latin American governments' conviction as to the merits of the issue.

International policies of deterrence

The international problems encountered by the above methods, which placed the United States in a position of widespread antagonism *vis-à-vis* Latin America and other regions of the world, led to the emergence of an alternative model. The policy developed under this other model, which is based on the same moral values regarding human rights, uses a different technique which is intended to act as a deterrent to excesses of this nature. To that end, discreet steps are taken, while public confrontation is avoided. Thus, both in order to achieve its humanitarian objective and to safeguard the political interests of the United States, this model relies upon avoiding friction with countries which are currently or potentially linked to those interests.

The implementation of this model by the Reagan Administration has not been free from difficulties in Latin America either. Three major problems can be mentioned.

The first problem is that some sectors appeared to interpret the disappearance of public pressure for the protection of human rights as a sign of a lack of concern about the subject on the part of the US government. On this basis, it was thought that once again it was possible to act without fear of reprisal or international sanctions and, in practice, a certain deterioration in the area of human rights was seen in some countries. This situation also sparked a renewed political controversy within the United States itself.

Although there was, in fact, no substantive change in US policy, since it was based on the same humanitarian principles upon which US society is founded, the misunderstanding this caused made it necessary to reiterate its adherence to the principles of human rights. By early 1982 it became evident that the emphasis on the subject had been re-established, after a year of political silence.

The second difficulty is once again related to the link between human rights and strategic considerations. Given the high priority assigned to the latter in regard to both the general policy on the Soviet Union and the situation in Central America in particular, a Latin American government could conclude that its strategic contribution would mean that the human rights situation within that country would be ignored.[18] In a sense, this was in keeping with the same strategic logic which had been employed by the Carter Administration.

This additional misunderstanding had two unfortunate consequences. The first was the deterioration in the human rights picture which has already been mentioned. The second consequence was that one government, believing itself to have achieved a tactical alliance with the United States, set off the conflict in the South Atlantic and sparked a serious international, regional and national crisis.

The third problem area is that this model, as would perhaps be the case with any policy on human rights, encountered dramatic limitations on its effectiveness in situations of civil war or widespread violence such as those which have affected Nicaragua, El Salvador and Guatemala. A new type of phenomenon was thus created which in some senses escaped that policy's area of application. An inevitable consequence is that the policy as a whole could have been damaged by this problem.

It is also interesting to note that the debate as to the effects of this policy has used the same terms as were employed in the debate on the coercive model, but with the difference that the arguments have been reversed. In the view of more conservative groups, it has been a successful effort which has achieved its objectives discreetly and gradually. For those further to the left, the model is a failure which has had counterproductive effects.

Setting partisan arguments aside, it is evident that there have been positive developments in this field recently in Latin America, both with respect to the protection of the individual's physical integrity and in the more general area of the process of a return to democracy. The fact that there are still exceptions does not change the general trend which is evidenced by events in Bolivia and Brazil and, potentially, in Argentina and Uruguay.[19]

Once again, the problem lies in determining whether this is a result of internal developments or a more effective international policy. While that policy may certainly help the process of domestic change along, the current picture seems to leave no doubt that it is mainly the result of internal dynamics – whether they are cooperative in nature, as in Brazil, or conflictive, as has been the case in Argentina. In any event, the limitations of the international model have become apparent.

Selective international policies

While the above models were primarily developed within the framework of inter-governmental relations, a concurrent structuring of some policies took place through the international machinery for the protection of the rights of man, particularly in the United Nations[20] and the Organization of American States.[21] These efforts notwithstanding, other public and private international agencies have also taken action in this area.

Certain forms in which these other policies have been expressed may be grouped together in a model which is characterized by its selectivity. In this model also, political criteria intrude – whether along governmental or partisan policy lines – upon the central humanitarian objectives of the international machinery for protection of such rights. This phenomenon has been especially marked in the United Nations and has also occurred, less intensely, in the actions of the Inter-American Commission on Human Rights.

There are various difficulties associated with this approach. The first is that on many occasions the selectivity has simply been a function of ideological preferences which led to a new form of Manichaeism whereby the human rights violations committed by governments of a certain leaning were to be condemned, while those committed by governments of the opposing orientation were ignored or treated with exceptional deference. This led the operation of this machinery to be perceived as a tool of political harassment rather than as a genuine form of protecting the basic rights of man.

The second major difficulty was that, from the moment that a political interplay of this sort was entered into, the formation of various alliances and understandings began to take place based on the advantages they held for the participants, regardless of their respectability in reference to human rights. The most clear-cut case is perhaps the Argentine–Soviet understanding under which the former was assured of freedom from harassment with regard to certain multilateral mechanisms in exchange for advantages obtained by the latter in other spheres, including trade. Thus this ideological selectivity was further exacerbated by discrimination based on situational strategies.

Another consequence of an approach in which political interests tended to predominate over humanitarian goals was that once again the distinctions between the various categories of human rights were blurred, particularly the distinction between the protection of the individual's physical integrity and other inalienable rights, and the more generic political and social rights. Certainly, the ideal is for all these to be safeguarded, but it is clear that in practice there are some priorities and values which are more important than others. This confusion which arose in this area meant that equal criticism was directed toward an abominable act of torture or the disappearance of an individual as toward the model of liberal economic policy applied in the Southern Cone.

The exaggerations occasioned by this model were wholly counterproductive to the effectiveness of its policies and in large part contributed to the loss of prestige suffered by the international machinery concerned. What should have been a standard of humanitarianism to be strictly applied to all those who violated those rights, whatever their ideology, importance or influence, was transformed into a concomitant political struggle which was taken advantage of for partisan purposes.

It must indeed be pointed out, in no uncertain terms, that international agencies did not always act along these lines; some of them adhered strictly to their humanitarian goals. Some examples are the Intergovernmental Committee for Migration, the International Red Cross, Amnesty International and a number of agencies associated with Christian churches. Even though they often took a tough stance or issued harsh reports which certainly did not please the governments involved, the predominance of humanitarian interests or the great professional impartiality of their directors gave them a stamp of authority which places them outside all political debate. Their influence has undoubtedly grown to the same extent.

The limits of foreign policy

There is yet another international dimension to the problem of human rights which should be analysed. Unlike the above models, it is related to the foreign policies of those countries which have been the object of adverse policies in this sphere or other associated areas.[22] It is a well-documented fact that their foreign policies have met with growing limitations as regards their effectiveness and ability to respond adequately to the needs of the country in question. This situation can be examined on three different levels which are, nevertheless, clearly related.

Firstly, there has been a tendency for bilateral relations and for the relationships between neighbouring countries to deteriorate in those nations affected by the problems under discussion. This seems to be a logical consequence of the predominance in some of these countries of elements linked to extreme nationalism which, just as they may resort to violence against individuals in the domestic sphere, also manifest similar inclinations in foreign affairs. The warlike policy toward Chile which has been supported by some sectors in Argentina, for example, is a manifestation of this problem.

A second area in which this phenomenon can be observed is the regional level, and here too, the same process of deterioration can be seen. The difficulties and crises facing Latin American cooperation and its various regional organizations are a consequence of the existence of antagonistic attitudes which are often related to these nationalistic visions. The separation from the Latin American sphere experienced by a number of countries with military regimes is another expression of the problem. In this same way, the threats to peace and stability created by tense relations between neighbouring countries often spread to all or a large part of a region, which is thereby transformed into a highly conflictive environment.

The third sphere in which the same type of problem occurs is in the broader scope of international relations. Whether it is because bilateral relations are weakened by the presence of important world powers or because the region as a whole becomes less powerful as regards its means of participation in international affairs, the fact is that cooperative relations often turn into ones of conflict. On some occasions, this can reach a point where serious tensions are created for international peace, as is clearly the case in the South Atlantic and Central America.

The limitations on the respective foreign policies which stem from all the above factors are extremely severe. Even when this is often not perceived by the governments affected, or is attributed to other causes, in the medium and long term it is extremely damaging to the national interests involved. To the extent that there is an awareness of this, perhaps the appropriate conclusions can be formulated which will allow human rights policies to be improved and the negative excesses of extreme nationalism to be avoided.

The lessons of experience and the need for a reformulation

The various elements which have been analysed point to a variety of important conclusions in regard to Latin America's recent experiences in this area which could also serve as a basis for the reformulation of those policies which have proven to be in error.

The first conclusion is that there is an obvious need to define objective criteria for the application of international policies on protection of human rights which would provide a clear-cut idea of which conditions and actions would set the respective machinery into motion. The advisability of giving priority to basic human rights and distinguishing between them and other more general rights is also involved. It is not a question of the latter being diminished in importance. However, drawing distinctions among the various categories would prevent any confusion from affecting those fundamental rights, as has occurred in Latin America.

In the same spirit as the preceding section, it is essential that all policies be inspired exclusively by the humanitarian purposes which are properly a part of the issue, while the interference of partisan politics and situational interests should be excluded as much as possible. These criteria may be perfectly legitimate as part of a political struggle, but using them in conjunction with these humanitarian goals inevitably tends to mix the latter up with partisan fights, whereas they should be held above all other considerations. In the Latin American experience, the political use of this humanitarian issue is one of the factors which has most severely damaged the effectiveness of the various international policies which have been instituted.

A third aspect which would also be part of an objective approach is the need to avoid selective and discriminatory applications, above all when this is done for reasons of political expediency, as has occurred in some international organizations. This is not only arbitrary, but is also highly counterproductive to the objectives being pursued, for it definitely tends to rule out the involvement of mechanisms in which those approached have been employed. Special importance should be given in this respect to the universal application of the criteria which are developed, without reference to any ideological considerations.

The experience of Latin America also seems to point to the advisability of putting less emphasis on the repressive aspects and sanctions of these international policies, since they too tend to produce an adverse reaction which is oftentimes related to past memories of imperialism or colonialism. It is more important to give priority to the positive aspects which could be developed, especially those which help to strengthen a genuine conviction as to the need to protect human rights. As was pointed out at the beginning of this article, the problem in question has very deep cultural roots which have been apparent in the history of Latin America for many decades. These cultural problems can only be surmounted by taking a positive approach. Consensualism and non-imposition are also a valid rule in this connection.

Finally, it is also important to remember that the international policies discussed here, particularly the most controversial models, should not lead to the creation of new forms of Latin American dependence on the centers of world power, as has already occurred to some extent. These policies can only be successful if they are designed in a manner which is compatible with the needs and growing trends toward Latin American autonomy *vis-à-vis* the international society.

Unfortunately, this aspect has frequently not been taken sufficiently into account; this has reached the point in some extreme views where it has been suggested that such policies could justify some forms of intervention by international powers in order to safeguard their humanitarian objectives. This point of view indicates a total ignorance of the Latin American tradition and its current needs for autonomy.

If focused correctly, a number of international policies could be conceived and could make a very positive contribution to a greater protection of human rights; this has in fact occurred in some international organizations, where a sense of professionalism and impartiality has prevailed.

Notes

1 In general, see Claudio Orrego Vicuña, *La difícil senda del desarrollo político en América Latina* (CISEC, Santiago, 1983) (particularly the bibliography cited).
2 In 1978 the Institute of International Studies of the University of Chile organized a seminar on the problem of human rights in international relations. The seminar undertook an extensive analysis of the subject, with particular reference to Latin America. See: *Derechos Humanos y Relaciones Internacionales*, Institute of International Studies of the University of Chile, Santiago, 1979; hereinafter referred to as *Derechos Humanos y Relaciones.*
3 Jorge Millas, 'Derechos humanos y diferencias culturales en el mundo', in *Derechos Humanos y Relaciones*, p. 30.
4 Jorje Ivan Hubner, 'Derechos humanos y cultura occidental', in *Derechos Humanos y Relaciones*, p. 30.
5 Antonio Buscuñán and Enrique Barros, 'Hacia una transculturización de los derechos humanos', in *Derechos Humanos y Relaciones*, p. 21.
6 For a more general discussion of the problem, see: Francisco Orrego Vicuña, 'América Latina: ¿clase media de las naciones?' in *Estudios Internacionales*, a journal published by the Institute of International Studies of the University of Chile, no. 40, October–December, 1977.
7 Francisco Orrego Vicuña, 'Europe and South America: Toward a Complementary International Role?', *Western Europe: The Alliance in Transition*, Chicago Council on Foreign Relations, 1981.
8 Genaro Arriagada, 'Seguridad nacional y politica', in *Seguridad Nacional y Bien Común*, CISEC, Santiago, 1976, p. 9.
9 Horacio Toro I., 'Los derechos del individuo y del estado: hacia un esquema de armonización', in *Derechos Humanos y Relaciones*, p. 58.
10 Francisco Orrego Vicuña, 'Democracia, pluralismo y sistema internacional: incidencia en la cooperación regional latino-americana", in Heraldo Muñoz V., *Política exterior latino-americana*, to be published by Westview Press.
11 For an analysis of its historical development, see the article cited in the preceding note, with particular reference to the nineteenth and twentieth centuries.
12 See the paper prepared by the Institute of International Studies of the University of Chile for an Inter-American Dialogue organized by the Wilson Center in Washington, October 15–16, 1982: 'El elusivo entendimiento entre América Latina y los Estados Unidos', in *Estudios Internacionales*, No. 60, October–December, 1982, p. 519.
13 Walter Sánchez, 'Imperialismo e idealismo en la política exterior norteamericana: el debate sobre los derechos humanos', in *Derechos Humanos y Relaciones*, p. 85.
14 For an analysis of this distinction, see the Report of the Inter-American Dialogue organized by The Wilson Center, which is published in the following document: 'The Americas at a Crossroads', *Report of the Inter-American Dialogue*, April 1983, Washington, The Wilson Center, 1983, p. 63.
15 Claudio Orrego Vicuña, 'Permanencia o transitoriedad en la estrategia de la administración Carter: evaluación de dos años y perspectivas', in *Derechos Humanos y Relaciones*, p. 134.
16 Institute of International Studies of the University of Chile, *Ensayos sobre la transición en América Latina*; to be published by the University of Belgrano Press, Buenos Aires.
17 For an analysis of the impact of economic expansion on Chilean foreign policy, see Heraldo Muñoz, 'Las relaciones exteriores del gobierno militar chileno', in *Chile 1973–1982*, Revista Mexicana de Sociología, Facultad Latinoamericana de Ciencias Sociales, 1983, p. 229.
18 Francisco Orrego Vicuña, 'La crisis del atlántico sur y su influencia en el sistema regional', *Estudios Internacionales*, no. 60, October–December, 1982, p. 473.
19 For a recent discussion of the Chilean case, see Hugo Fruhling, Carlos Portales and Augusto Varas, *Estado y Fuerzas Armadas*, Facultad Latinoamericana de Ciencias Sociales, Santiago, 1982. Also see the document cited in n. 16 above.
20 For a general analysis of the United Nations system and its major legal difficulties, see:

Louis B. Sohn, 'The improvement of the United Nations Machinery on Human Rights', in *Derechos Humanos y Relaciones*, p. 171.

21 Edmundo Vargas C., 'El perfeccionamiento de los mecanismos interamericanos a la luz de su experiencia', in *Derechos Humanos y Relaciones*, p. 222.

22 Heraldo Muñoz, see note 17 above.

7 Northern Ireland

CHARLES TOWNSHEND

Analysis of the Northern Ireland problem must begin with recognition of the unique political status of the six north-eastern counties. Between 1921 and 1972 they formed a polity which can best be described as a sub-state, though the term 'state' was frequently used, as was 'semi-state' and, more derogatorily, 'statelet'.[1] No official term was created to describe it, in contrast to the term 'free state' applied to the twenty-six counties of Ireland, or the term 'dominion' applied to self-governing parts of the British Empire. Its powers, framed in the Government of Ireland Act 1920, were consciously modelled on those of the dominions. 'Dominion status' was the prime political bargaining counter employed by Britain in its attempt to reach a compromise with Irish separatism. Nationalists sought sovereign independence, but Ulster loyalists sought the reverse: they accepted 'home rule' with reluctance, to avoid incorporation in an Irish state ruled from Dublin.

Loyalists protested that their own wish was to remain an integral part of the United Kingdom. As a result they made no effort to achieve sovereign powers. Northern Ireland never became a state. It had no foreign policy and neither maintained nor received embassies; its fiscal powers were limited; it had no army or navy. And while it had control of its own internal security through police forces markedly different from those of Great Britain, it did not enjoy full statehood in the Weberian sense of a monopoly of the legitimate exercise of force in the community. This was due not to constitutional limitations but to communal divisions; and represented, as will become clear, the fundamental weakness of the polity.

The term most regularly used to describe the six counties is 'Province' (with, be it noted, a capital P). Prefixed by the inseparable adjective Protestant, it delimited the crucial challenge issued by the Unionist leader Carson in 1911 – 'we must be prepared, the morning Home Rule passes, ourselves to become responsible for the government of the Protestant province of Ulster' – and it has subsequently come to provide the emotional focus of Protestant identity – 'the Province that we love'. Since 1972 it has also been used by Secretaries of State for Northern Ireland, and in recruitment posters for the Ulster Defence Regiment. Its descriptive value is a little doubtful: Northern Ireland of course comprises only two-thirds of the 'historic' province of Ulster. Its analytic value is perhaps greater, as Ulster may be compared with the semi-autonomous provinces, the *pays d'état*, of premodern polities.

Because of its ambiguous status, Northern Ireland forms an issue of foreign and domestic policy simultaneously. Two states, Britain and the Republic of Ireland, claim it as part of their territory. Britain has persistently maintained that there can be no basis for foreign influence or intervention. The claim of the republic is theoretical. Contained in its 1937 constitution (framed at a time when the state was not yet a republic, nor any longer a 'free state', but an unspecified entity named Eire), its actualization has never been the subject of consistent policy. The existence of the claim, however, influences the situation within the six counties, and inhibits the Irish government from handling northern problems as foreign policy issues.[2] Indeed the attitude of nationalists towards the north has remained deeply ambivalent ever since 1921.[3]

This ambivalence has particularly affected their approaches to human rights issues in the north. The question was whether nationalists should pursue the fundamental right of national self-determination, demanding the unification of Ireland and thus refusing to recognize the six-county border. Or should they pursue the cause of justice for the 'nationalist minority' in the six counties (not a minority in their view, but part of the majority of the Irish nation), thus giving tacit recognition to the separate existence of the province? In part this question concerned the definition of human rights. Nationalist logic makes self-determination ('freedom') the fundamental right without which others – even perhaps life itself – are valueless or meaningless. The policy of the nationalist irreconcilables in the Irish Republican Army since the 1920s has reflected this logic, subordinating all other considerations to the struggle for unification.

Irish governments, however, have tended to follow policies based on a less generalized view of rights. Even when hampered by their posture of antagonism towards partition, they have been concerned to secure alleviation of injustices suffered by 'nationalists' within the political, economic and social system of Northern Ireland.[4] Such injustices may be placed in two categories: those suffered at the hands of the loyalist majority, mainly before 1972, and those suffered at the hands of the British government, primarily since the assumption of direct rule in that year.

Domestic responses: Loyalist government

This periodization forces attention back on the origins of the six-county area.[5] The civil disabilities of nationalists under the Northern Ireland political system derived directly from that system's *raison d'être*. The Stormont government existed to defend Protestants against Catholics, to maintain the 'Protestant ascendancy' in Ulster. It resulted from the collective action of Ulster Protestants over the course of a generation. The sudden adoption of Home Rule as the policy of the Liberal party under Gladstone in 1886 catalysed earlier inchoate action of Protestant groups, most notably the Orange Order, into a loyalist mass movement. The muscle for this had been built up in a series of major riots in the preceding half-century.[6] Earlier inter-Protestant sectarian differences dissolved in the polarization of 1886, and even progressive Liberal nonconformists rallied to the loyalist cause, providing vital leadership and political capacity.[7] By the time of the second Home Rule Bill in 1893 a highly effective organization had been created, with direct political influence through the Unionist party at Westminster.

The activity of the loyalist movement was expressed primarily in street-level assertion of Protestant dominance. The celebration of historic victories, in July in Belfast and August in Londonderry (whose very name was an index of polarization), formed the garish centrepiece to this, but the challenge of 'walking' and 'drumming' went on constantly at somewhat lower intensity. Protestant responses were mobilized by forceful slogans, of which 'No Popery', 'Home Rule is Rome rule', and 'No Surrender', were the most ubiquitous. Catholics were simply identified as the enemy at the gates. 'Not an inch' expressed an enduring repudiation of political compromise; 'Ulster will fight, Ulster will be right' validated collective violence.[8]

But Protestant hostility to Home Rule did nothing to dent the nationalist assumption that the island of Ireland formed a natural political unit. Nationalists cheerfully proclaimed the 'invasion of Ulster' when they won the Monaghan by-election in 1883, and crowed when they took a majority of Ulster seats in 1886, heedless of the fact that their attitude triggered a violent defensive reaction (the 'siege reflex'). Liberal statesmen accepted the nationalists' islandism (that is the nationalist assumption that Ireland formed a natural political unit), and dismissed the loyalist reaction with scorn. Islandist assumptions remained dominant as late as 1911, when the third Home Rule Bill was drawn up. This produced a loyalist reaction of unprecedented scope and weight, including the formation of a mass militia, the Ulster Volunteer Force. The charismatic leadership of Carson raised the spectre of civil war, and the tremendous crisis brought the United Kingdom to the point of constitutional paralysis.[9]

Liberal confidence at last buckled under this extreme pressure. By 1914 it was clear that if Home Rule were to be applied, Ulster would have to be given special treatment. The government still hoped that this might be limited to 'home rule within home rule' (making the same arrangement for the north *vis à vis* Dublin as for Dublin *vis à vis* London), or at most temporary exclusion, but Ulster Unionists categorically rejected all compromises. When the last Home Rule Bill, the Government of Ireland Bill 1920, was brought in, it confirmed the curious arrangement whereby the six north-eastern counties received a parliament with powers identical to those exercised by Dublin. A clear trace of islandism survived in the provision for a Council of Ireland, which could assume enlarged powers by the mutual consent of the northern and southern parliaments. This federalism without a federation was stillborn, though it was to be revived much later in ideas of a tripartite arrangement, which reached dramatic fruition in the doomed Sunningdale agreement of 1973. In 1922 the twenty-six counties became a Free State with 'dominion status', leaving the six counties – ironically – as the only part of the British Isles under 'home rule'.[10] Ulster Unionists accepted their parliament as the supreme sacrifice made in order to remain within the United Kingdom.

Once established, however, the Northern Ireland parliament showed no reluctance to exercise semi-sovereign powers. Its transcendent justification was to guarantee the 'security of the state', something which had been identified since the seventeenth century with the Protestant ascendancy. In this sense religious discrimination was built into the very concept 'Northern Ireland'. The British government was uncomfortably aware of this. It had made several unavailing efforts to ensure that the partitioned area would consist of all nine Ulster counties, a better balanced and less nakedly sectarian entity, and one with some historical and geographical credibility.[11] Such an area would of course have all but defeated the loyalists' purpose, while a homogeneously-Protestant four county area would have lost them Londonderry and the borderlands of Fermanagh. British efforts foundered on the loyalist requirement that the Catholic population be as small as possible within an area as large as possible .

The right to which the British government paid most attention in establishing Northern Ireland was that of self-determination. The claim of northern Protestants was seen as analogous to that of the nationalists (an analogy fiercely repudiated then and since by the latter). If they did not have the right to block self-determination for the rest of Ireland – which had been Carson's real aim – they had the right not to be coerced into it. The government believed that British public opinion would not stand for the 'coercion of Ulster', which Unionists represented as driving out loyal citizens into the arms of a hostile power. Concern for the Catholic (presumed nationalist) minority within Northern Ireland could at best be secondary, though steps were taken to guarantee their rights. In particular a dramatic departure from British constitutional tradition was made by basing the electoral system on proportional representation, with the specific aim of protecting minorities.

This recognition of the absence of consensual base was not, however, followed by action to preserve the untried machinery. The first real test of the British government's commitment in this area came early in the sub-state's life. During the negotiations for the Anglo-Irish treaty, and in the early months of the Free State, the Provincial Government leaders made strenuous efforts to prevent partition from becoming permanent. At the same time Michael Collins's political realism led him to face this prospect and to set about securing just treatment for nationalists.[12] An immediate concern was the violent sectarian rioting which engulfed Belfast between 1920 and 1922, and drove many Catholic refugees out of the city. The British government seemed to be on the brink of intervention, but as civil war broke out in the Free State the pressure to intervene relaxed.[13] Unionists in both Ulster and Britain saw their predictions and prejudices confirmed: the Catholic Irish were a violent, anarchic people who could not be trusted with political power.

Subsequently the British left Northern Ireland very much to itself. Civil servants might remain dubious about – or in the case of the Treasury, sharply hostile to – the Unionist state. Politicians preferred to classify it as a sleeping dog. Thus there was no attempt to question the drafting of the Northern Ireland Civil Authorities (Special Powers) Act 1922, which for the next fifty years was to form, in the view of some, a permanent infringement of civil rights.[14] Even more importantly, nothing more than mild disapprobation was registered when proportional representation was abandoned. The question was raised whether abrogation was *ultra vires* the Northern Ireland parliament, and while no clear answer was found (an effect of the Province's uncertain status), officials argued forcefully that abolition 'rightly or wrongly is regarded as an abrogation of the rights of the northern minority', and would 'intensify suspicion and distrust and be a fatal obstacle to conciliatory efforts'.[15]

The Unionist counter to such criticism, repeated at intervals during the following years, was that the nationalist minority had abrogated its own rights by its manifest disloyalty, expressed in its refusal to participate in (and hence accord recognition to) the political process in Northern Ireland. This, substantially, was the response in 1938 when the Eire government presented a formal list of complaints against the treatment of nationalists in the six counties. It alleged discriminatory and oppressive use of the Special Powers Act, discrimination in education and employment, gerrymandering of constituencies for local government and parliamentary elections (Stormont, not Westminster), and the artificial maintenance of partition by British financial subsidy. The nub of the complaint lay in the charges of discrimination and gerrymandering, and these caused a small flurry of official activity. Memoranda bounded about the Dominions and Home Offices. The latter department said that the alleged educational discrimination was due to the fact that whereas the Protestant voluntary schools had transferred themselves to the education authority and were thus supported from public funds, the Catholic schools had refused to compromise their independence and thus received only half their costs.[16] The Dominions Office observed that it was difficult to get statistics for employment discrimination, adding rather lamely that whilst religious discrimination had been prohibited by the Government of Ireland Act and the Treaty, 'in the absence of any means of securing an impartial investigation into the position it is impossible to reach a reliable conclusion as to the facts'.[17] Alongside this feeble argument the Home Office placed the inescapable reality that, 'it is of course obvious that Northern Ireland is, and must be, a Protestant "state", otherwise it would not have come into being and would certainly not continue to exist'.[18] With some justification it accused the 'nationalists' of being largely responsible for perpetuating suspicion of Catholics through their persistent attempts 'to identify nationalism with religion' (in their statistics they always identified Catholic with nationalist).

One minister confidently averred that the influx of Catholics into the north was 'not compatible with allegations about persecution'; the increasing Catholic population had 'seriously alarmed Northern Ireland ministers and others anxious to maintain the Protestant character of the country'. If gerrymandering had occurred, it was 'the fault of the Catholics who boycotted the whole business' (i.e., the setting-up of constituencies after the abolition of proportional representation).[19] This was, historically, quite true; but as a senior civil servant noted, 'it seems doubtful whether any impartial tribunal would regard this as an excuse for a government establishing such a system'.[20] And the minister's view was slightly modified by a conversation with Lord Dufferin, who candidly said that the attitude of the Northern Ireland government towards 'the minority' had been 'illiberal': Catholics had been treated as 'a minority to be kept under rather than as a part of the nation to be incorporated'. Many Protestant Ulstermen, in Dufferin's opinion, were 'uneasy about the attitude of their government which had the effect of perpetuating a division which a more enlightened policy might close'.[21]

Certainly, the Catholic community had not evidenced much desire to be 'incorporated', or reconciled with the sub-state. For a long generation after 1922 its spokesmen relied on the outright removal of the sub-state (that is, reunification), rather than reform within it, as the means of removing discrimination. Such an attitude could only reinforce the legitimacy of discrimination in Protestant eyes.[22] By the time a drift towards integration set in during the 1960s it was perhaps too late for polarized stereotypes to be removed. Hindsight, at least, suggests this. But the significance of this drift was, from the Catholic standpoint, considerable; and it appeared to be matched by a distinct liberalization of Protestant policy.

In spite of a sensational, but ephemeral, vote for Sinn Féin in the elections of 1955, Catholics displayed a steadily diminishing interest in nationalist activism in the postwar years. The failure of the IRA's 'border campaign' between 1956 and 1962 was related to this lack of commitment, and left the republican military movement apparently discredited. The IRA subsequently underwent a radical self-reappraisal. Traditional confrontational politics were modified by a shift towards participation. The process of détente at the higher political level was dramatically symbolized by the meeting between the two Irish prime ministers in 1966. At the institutional level, the most significant development was the emergence of the Northern Ireland Civil Rights Association.[23]

The civil rights campagn raised, to Protestant ears at least, distinct echoes of the Catholic mass movements of the nineteenth century led by Daniel O'Connell. But its more immediate model was American. It had, indeed, an international dimension which offered the prospect of an escape from the prison of atavism.[24] NICRA's demands were political, social-economic, and judicial. The attack on gerrymandering, under the emotive and somewhat misleading slogan 'one man, one vote', spearheaded the civil rights campaign. Discrimination in employment both public and private was the second major target. In the judicial sphere attention was focussed on the law – especially the Special Powers Act – and its enforcers – the police, and in particular the 'B' Special Constabulary.

The substance of these charges could no more be denied in the 1960s than in the 1930s.[25] Gerrymandering was obvious, most glaringly so in Derry city. Discrimination in public employment could scarcely be denied on the basis of publicly available statistics, and was universally believed to prevail in the private sector also. The Special Powers Act lacked the safeguards deemed vital by English legal tradition as well as by the Universal Declaration of Human Rights.[26] The Royal Ulster Constabulary was markedly Protestant in composition, though the initial intention had been that it should be one-third Catholic. (The original Royal Irish Constabulary, its forerunner, had of course been predominantly Catholic.)[27] The Ulster Special Constabulary, initially divided into 'A', 'B', and 'C' categories of which only the second survived as a part-time auxiliary police force, was overwhelmingly Protestant. It was, in effect, the old UVF in a new guise. A former district inspector of the

RUC had predicted in 1922, 'there can never be any possibility of establishing confidence and security so long as the "B" force, the ordinary Protestant countryman and in many cases corner boy, is supplied with arms ... and "authorized" to "get on top", as it were, of his RC neighbour',[28] and this prediction was substantially borne out.

Protestant perceptions remained, in general, the reverse of those manifested in NICRA. Gerrymandering was justified by Catholic disloyalty and political subversion; discrimination was widely viewed as natural; Special Powers were barely used, but were needed to control terrorist violence; the USC was a citizen self-defence militia on which the very lives of Protestants depended.[29] These attitudes underlay the Northern Ireland government's response. Terence O'Neill's conservative liberalism was fiercely attacked by fundamentalists such as Ian Paisley. The reformist wing of Unionism collapsed, as loyalists reacted to a major civil rights march in January 1969 with open violence.

The events of 1969 form a watershed in Ulster history. The near-collapse of RUC discipline in August compelled the British government to provide military forces to stifle communal warfare, and this incomplete intervention left Britain in an illogical position. The ambiguity of Northern Ireland's status once more became critical. Partial responsibility for the maintenance of order led to military demands for the restructuring of the disorganized security apparatus. The report of the Cameron commission sustained NICRA's charges of discrimination, and, together with the Hunt report, led to the hasty disarming of the RUC and the disbandment of the 'B' Specials. The latter were replaced by a reserve battalion, the Ulster Defence Regiment, under full military discipline. The logic of military intervention, escalating in face of a revived IRA (and simultaneously catalysing that revival), exerted its own pressure.[30] The British government was eventually driven to concur with the Northern Ireland ministers' belief – not shared by the British army – in the need for internment without trial as a counter to the early operations of the Provisional IRA.[31] It was already out of its depth, and unprepared for the bitter intensity of the Catholic reaction. At last it was forced to accept that the Stormont government could not remedy a problem of which it was itself a prime cause.

Domestic responses: British government

The reassumption of direct British rule was intended to guarantee the political and other rights of the minority, which devolution had eroded. In the event, however, it served to generate new human rights issues which merely overlaid or replaced the old ones. The Detention of Terrorists Order 1972 and the Emergency Provisions Act 1973 perpetuated internment and 'special powers' under new names. The application of military force inevitably produced grievances, starting with the mass arrests (Operation Demetrius) with which internment was launched on 9 August 1971 and mounting to the affray of 'Bloody Sunday' in January 1972. The struggle against 'terrorists' and 'paramilitaries' extended from the streets into the holding centres where suspects were interrogated 'in depth'.[32] Internees and convicts engaged in violent struggles to secure recognition as political prisoners; hunger-strikes generated widespread sympathy. The process of law was itself revised to make convictions possible. The 1972 Diplock commission was

> driven to the inescapable conclusion that so long as these [terrorists] remain at liberty to operate in Northern Ireland it will not be possible to find witnesses prepared to testify against them in the criminal courts, except those serving in the army or the police ... The dilemma is complete.

By way of the argument that

> the detailed technical rules and practice as to the 'admissibility' of inculpatory statements by the accused as they are currently applied in Northern Ireland are hampering the course of justice in the case of terrorist crimes and compelling the authorities responsible for public order and safety to resort to detention in a significant number of cases which could otherwise be dealt with both effectively and fairly by trial in a court of law

it proceeded to recommend the establishment of non-jury trial and the acceptance of self-inculpatory statements provided that these were not induced by torture or inhuman or degrading treatment.[33]

In the British view the Emergency Provisions were merely a holding operation while a new political 'solution' was devised. A succession of 'initiatives' followed, of which the most far-reaching were the power-sharing assembly of 1974 and the 'rolling' devolution proposal of 1982. These represented real efforts to give effective political rights to the minority. The concept of concurring majority, in particular, involved a departure from Anglo-Saxon tradition in an attempt to meet a circumstance outside the long experience of majoritarian democracy, the existence of a divided community (or, more properly, two communities). It was an exercise in reasonableness and compromise, but its naive realism was as always out of place in an Irish context.[34] In general, British policy suffered for its uncertainty of touch, as in the creation and suspension of 'special category' status. Bipartisanship, hailed as the *sine qua non* of British policy, pointed up the absence of interest or imagination in politicians' approaches. It has been a token of bankruptcy rather than of purpose.

All British 'initiatives', however honourable in the minds of the statesmen who conceived them, have been viewed in Ireland through a prism of 'old coercion, old condescension, old colonialism, and old battles for parity and the rule of ordinary law'.[35] Indeed, the characteristic incoherence of British policy meant that they were actually accompanied by *new* coercion. The unbending determination to restore law and order, to crush terrorism, was a permanent facet of the liberal self-image, and was reinforced in Northern Ireland by the need to reassure Protestants. Since the law could only be enforced, as Diplock said, by extra-legal methods – inevitably viewed as illegal by those unsympathetic to the state – the pursuit of 'public security' could only bolster the propaganda and recruitment of the IRA. Insofar as the security forces were able to restrict the IRA's capacity to act, they impelled it towards a form of terrorism which further alarmed loyalists. This alarm coalesced into mass action when the government appeared to be negotiating with republicans, as at Sunningdale in 1973. The 1974 Unionist workers' strike demonstrated that even the minimum level of compromise needed to work a concurring-majority system – acceptance of a power-sharing polity – did not exist in Ulster. Governing without consensus seemed impossible through democratic political processes, however skilfully rearranged. Henceforth, as a leading analyst of the problem contended, justiciable rights rather than electoral rights offered the only prospect of securing the position of the minority.[36]

Hence the working of the legal system became a central focus of attention. It had been beset by problems since the suspension of habeas corpus in 1971. Interrogation in depth caused public unease. The Compton report on the early interrogations did nothing to still this by finding that although 'physical ill-treatment' and 'some measure of unintended hardship' had been inflicted by such actions as standing prisoners against walls, hooding them and depriving them of sleep, or forcing them to run barefoot on granite chippings, this did not amount to 'brutality', which it defined thus: 'brutality is an inhuman or savage form of cruelty, and ... cruelty implies a disposition to inflict suffering, coupled with indifference to, or pleasure in, the victim's pain. We do not think that happened here.'[37] This common-sense excursion into the psychology of *mens rea* was to be the first in a series of semantic exercises which have highlighted the difficulty of securing human rights amid anti-terrorist operations.[38] It was quickly superseded by the reports of the Parker committee, set up to consider 'authorized procedures for the interrogation of persons suspected of terrorism', in relation to the Joint Directive on Military Interrogation in Internal Security Operations Overseas.[39]

Parker examined interrogation by the 'five techniques' – wall-standing, hooding, continuous noise, sleep deprivation, and bread and water diet – developed during counter-insurgency campaigns from Palestine and Malaya in the late 1940s to Aden in the 1960s.[40] The majority report dismissed the view expressed by some witnesses that, even though innocent lives had been saved through use of the techniques, a civilized society should eschew them – 'that, once methods of this character were employed on people in detention in order to obtain information, the society which employed them was morally on a slippery slope leading to the deliberate infliction of torture'.[41] It accepted that techniques which had succeeded in World War II were 'unlikely' to work in counter-revolutionary operations, in particular urban guerrilla warfare.[42] It laid great stress on the fact that the five techniques had produced results, and on the argument that:

> Whether or not what is done is in conformity with the Directive falls in our view to be judged by how a dispassionate observer would view the operation if he saw the techniques being applied. Further ... such expressions as 'humane', 'inhuman', 'humiliating' and 'degrading' fall to be judged by such an observer in the light of the circumstances in which the techniques are to be applied, for example, that the operation is taking place in the course of urban guerilla warfare in which completely innocent lives are at risk; that there is a degree of urgency; and that the security and safety of the interrogation centre, of its staff and of the detainees are important considerations.[43]

Amidst all this relativism, it made no effort to define the problematic concepts of 'urban guerrilla' and 'counter-revolutionary' warfare, and specifically rejected the possibility of forming precise terminology for 'the spectrum between discomfort and hardship at the one end and physical or mental torture at the other end'.[44]

The report of the minority, Lord Gardiner's report, was radically different, condemning the five techniques as illegal by domestic and (less certainly) international law. Thus it was meaningless to speak of them as 'authorized procedures'; the authorization, the Joint Directive, was invalid.[45] It pointed out that if the IRA's campaign of 'brutal murders, arson, the use of explosives against innocent men, women, and children' was to be regarded as 'virtually a war', it followed that 'the position of the forces of law and order depends very much on how far they have the sympathy of the local population against the guerrillas'.[46] The implication of Gardiner's argument was that short-term successes, even measured in the saving of lives, were less important than the reputation of the legal system. He put the 'slippery slope' problem very acutely:

> If it is to be made legal to employ methods not now legal against a man whom the police believe to have ... information ..., [I am] unable to find, either in logic or in morals, any limit to the degree of ill-treatment to be legalised. The only logical limit ... would appear to be whatever degree of ill-treatment proves to be necessary to get the information out of him, which would include, if necessary, extreme torture.[47]

He castigated the development of secret and illegal methods, alien to the British democratic tradition, in 'emergency conditions in colonial-type situations', and their transfer by the army to Northern Ireland without any thought about their legality or their public effect.[48]

Although the Parker report upheld the use of the five techniques – with adequate 'safeguards' – as being in accord with the Directive and thus the 1949 Geneva Convention[49] – Gardiner's indictment produced a rapid political adjustment. The prime minister announced, on 2 March 1972, that the techniques would cease to be used. Shortly afterwards a further committee was set up, this time under Gardiner himself, to consider 'in the context of civil liberties and human rights, measures to deal with terrorism in Northern Ireland'. Its report confronted the root problems of preserving civil liberties amidst endemic intimidation. Focussing primarily on the double issue of internment without trial and trial without jury, it reviewed the arguments for and against these measures.

> Those in favour of detention argue that, when times are relatively normal, the needs of an ordered society may be met by the criminal courts functioning with a high regard for the common law's presumption of innocence and a strict observance of the rules of evidence and the standard of proof. But when normal conditions give way to grave disorder and lawlessness, with extensive terrorism causing widespread loss of life and limb and the wholesale destruction of property, the courts cannot be expected to maintain peace and order in the community if they have to act alone. The very safeguards of the law then become the means by which it may be circumvented. Terrorism means widespread intimidation in all sections of the community. Material witnesses refuse to testify on peril of their lives, and the law will not accept hearsay evidence; furthermore police officers who have knowledge and belief about the commission of certain offences may find their conclusions inadmissible in court, because they cannot satisfy the law's necessarily stringent requirements.[50]

Against this persuasive reasoning, others contended that detention 'brought the law into contempt', operating in 'an atmosphere of secrecy which undermines sound community life':

> Although the quasi-judicial system of Commissioners' hearings and reviews operates with a scrupulous regard for the principles of justice, and produces just decisions in the majority of cases, it is not perceived as being just by members of the general public.[51]

Some witnesses even argued that internment facilitated the growth of terrorist networks rather than weakening them.[52]

Gardiner approached the issue of terrorism itself head-on, proposing that it should be made an offence *per se*. But his definition of terrorism – 'the use of violence for political or sectarian ends . . . for the purpose of putting the public or any section of the public into fear' – was unsatisfactory, and revealed the same problems of conceptualization as British governments had faced long before in trying to legislate against social ostracism ('boycotting') and intimidation.[53] This weakness rendered some of the report's general pronouncements problematic. On the issue of human rights, it made the inescapable point that 'while there are policies which contribute to the maintenance of order at the expense of individual freedom, the maintenance without restriction of that freedom may involve a heavy toll in death and destruction'.

> While the liberty of the subject is a human right to be preserved under all possible conditions, it is not, and cannot be, an absolute right, because one may use his liberty to take away the liberty of another and must be restrained from doing so. Where freedoms conflict, the state has a duty to protect those in need of protection.[54]

But how is it to do this if a terrorized community will not assist it? Gardiner seemed to think that the suspension of legal safeguards could lead to the successful imposition of order,[55] though emergency powers could 'if prolonged, damage the fabric of the community, and they do not provide lasting solutions'.[56] These solutions could only be political, and must include 'further measures to promote social justice between classes and communities'. Such equivocation and conventional piety was reflected in the report's conclusion that detention must be abolished at some time, but that 'the present level of violence' made it 'impossible to put forward a precise recommendation on the timing'.[57]

Nonetheless the Compton, Parker and Gardiner reports, taken together, represent a real, if not quite open-minded, effort to come to terms with the impact of terror and counter-terrorist operations. The prohibition of the five techniques, and the ending of internment shortly after the Gardiner report, indicated an attempt to meet criticism – though it could also be said that internment had become irrelevant when 'Diplock courts' proved successful in locking up terrorists 'by what appeared to be, and was certainly loudly proclaimed to be, due process of law'.[58] After 1975 attention centred on the functioning of these courts and of the police. The level of social confidence in the legal system as a whole was held by some to have dropped, perhaps fatally.[59] The use of violence appeared to be a continuing feature of police interrogation methods.[60] (This, as will be seen, was the prime concern of an Amnesty International mission to Northern Ireland in late 1977.) A further domestic inquiry produced the Bennett report, the bulkiest and most detailed so far;[61] but this was not altogether successful in dispelling an unease which was often aggravated by the attitude of the head of the RUC. Newman's declaration that 'there is no policy or toleration of ill treatment in this force. Quite the contrary. And this force is vitally concerned with human rights. In fact, it is very concerned with the most fundamental right of all, the right to live,'[62] had to be set alongside evident disquiet of police surgeons about the treatment of detainees in Gough and Castlereagh interrogation centres.[63]

Complaints of assault during interview (ADI) were roundly dismissed by police as terrorist propaganda fabrications; and while some were no doubt such, it appeared that the police might be using these emotive labels to suggest that if suspected terrorists were roughly treated, they probably deserved it. Such blurring of the presumption of innocence may have seemed natural and even necessary to the police and some of the public. To others they were ominous.

Bennett's complex recommendations – over fifty in all – were designed to counteract public apprehension by increasing the mechanical controls and the safeguards built into the regulations on interrogation. One investigator of the ADI rate reported that RUC detectives greeted the suggestion that they should master the contents of the Bennett report with derision. A more recent official report, however, holds that while the police were initially hostile to the Bennett procedures, they subsequently found that they 'had indeed helped them in their work'.[64] This issue remains inseparable from the wider question of public confidence in the police in the United Kingdom as a whole.

International responses

British insistence on the domestic status of the Northern Ireland problem has denied the possibility of external mediation or any other international remedy for the multiform difficulties which make up the problem. This denial remained as absolute in 1983, when the European parliament sought to investigate political and economic aspects of the Province (on the ground that EEC funds were disbursed in regional aid), as it had been in 1919 when Sinn Féin sought to bring the case for Irish self-determination before the Versailles conference. The jealous defence of British sovereignty has been a nonparty principle. No direct or indirect intervention has been brooked, even as part of the special relationship with the United States.

The United States has been inescapably involved in Anglo-Irish affairs since the mid nineteenth century through the fact of its large and vociferous Irish–American community. This ethnic group was amongst the first to organize for self-help and political influence within the United States, and more sporadically for intervention in Ireland. The Fenian Brotherhood and Clan na Gael were formidable organizations whose tradition of financial assistance to armed revolutionary movements in Ireland has persisted to the present.[65] Irish–Americans have provided the most ecstatic audiences for advanced nationalist speakers, though direct action has been rare. Attempts to mount a Fenian invasion of Ireland in the wake of the American Civil War proved abortive, and the nearest approach to a military campaign was the brief invasion of Canada in 1870. The object of this, to provoke a rupture in

Anglo-American relations, remained a primary aim of Irish–American organizations, though there were also occasional forays into direct attacks like the dynamite bombing of the 1880s.[66] A more feasible alternative was the idea that political pressure might induce the US administration to exert diplomatic pressure on Britain in the nationalist interest. This hope reached a peak in 1919, but the response of US policy at that point established the subsequent pattern.[67] Britain's sovereign rights were meticulously respected, and great care taken not to offend its delicate sensibilities. Since 1969 the official silence of the United States, apart from bland assertions of a desire to see a just solution to the problems of Northern Ireland, has been striking – in contrast to the outspokenness of a few individual politicians.[68] Any covert pressure on Britain has been disavowed by both parties.

Britain has been traditionally sensitive to American views, and perhaps still more to those of the Dominions. These seem, however, not to have amounted to much more than Britain's own: a pious desire to reach a fair settlement. This has of course been precisely the root of the present political problem – it has been impossible to be fair to all, if being 'fair' to loyalists meant allowing them freedom to be unfair to nationalists. A specific concern for justiciable rather than political rights might have offered a concrete way forward, but was not officially evidenced. Foreign policy, outside the special case of the Irish Republic, has therefore not been an element in the Northern Ireland question. Real concern with human rights issues has been manifested not amongst governments so much as international agencies, both autonomous and quasi-autonomous. The Amnesty mission, already referred to, seems to have exercised a measurable influence, at the time, on the behaviour of the security forces.[69] Its ritual condemnation of 'the use of political murder by the para-military groups involved, and their practice of deliberate maiming of persons in their temporary custody as a device of deliberate intimidation and control,'[70] had, by contrast, no effect at all. It concentrated on the issue of police interrogation of suspected terrorists, obtaining direct testimony from fifty-two people and considering reports of a further twenty-six cases. It reached the conclusion that 'maltreatment' had occurred with sufficient frequency to warrant a public inquiry.[71] It observed also that the erosion of civil liberties[72] had helped to create the circumstances in which maltreatment occurred, and was particularly disturbed by the judgement delivered by Justice McGonigal in May 1977.[73]

Considering Section 6 of the Emergency Provisions Act of 1973, McGonigal had reached the view that Article 3 of the European Convention on Human Rights had superseded the English judges' rules on the admissibility of evidence. As a result, by declaring inadmissible only evidence obtained by 'torture, or inhuman or degrading treatment', it 'appears to accept a degree of physical violence which could never be tolerated by the courts under the common law test, and ... it leaves it open to an interviewer to use a moderate degree of physical maltreatment for the purpose of inducing a person to make a statement'.[74] The idea that the European Convention had weakened legal safeguards was rejected by Amnesty, which argued that McGonigal had failed to note that 'fundamental ... difference between the tests applied in national and international law. In order to generate international concern a much greater infringement of a person's rights ... is necessary than would warrant interference by a judge upholding the rule of law on a national level'.[75]

The response of the British government to Amnesty's conclusions was characteristic. With some aplomb the Secretary of State for Northern Ireland, Roy Mason, accused Amnesty of a breach of natural justice by its refusal to publish the names of its twenty-eight respondents.[76] The demand for a public inquiry was rejected with the familiar argument that it would merely create a platform for terrorist propaganda (the argument deployed later against the European Parliament).[77] The same tone of injured innocence marked the government's reaction to the most remarkable international intervention so far: the case brought by the Irish government before the European Commission on Human Rights in 1971–2.

The Irish action in alleging breaches of the European Convention by another state was almost unprecedented. It was only the sixth inter-state case to be brought before the Commission (as compared with 5,960 individual petitions, of which 100 had been accepted as admissible), and perhaps the first to be widely interpreted as an act of foreign policy.[78] It may certainly be seen as the only positive result of Taoiseach Lynch's *défi* 'we won't stand idly by'. The Irish government's most serious allegations were that (a) methods of custody and interrogation constituted an administrative practice in violation of Article 3; (b) internment violated Articles 5 and 6, and in addition Article 14, since detention was applied with discrimination on grounds of political opinion.

The Commission decided the admissibility of the Irish application in September 1972.[79] Between then and March 1975 the merits of the allegations were examined, a period protracted partly by the mechanism of the Commission itself, and partly by the conduct of the British defence, which, it has been suggested, 'indicated an attitude consistent with the most cynical interpretations' placed by opponents on its own official inquiries.[80] The eventual finding of the Commission, in January 1976, was that the five techniques had constituted a practice of inhuman treatment and torture, and that other violations of Article 3 had occurred during the autumn of 1971.[81] Since, however, the allegations only concerned that period, and since the British government had publicly abandoned the five techniques, it was effectively cleared.[82] Still more significantly, the charges under Articles 5 and 6 were not upheld. Britain was permitted to derogate from these articles under Article 15, on grounds of 'public emergency threatening the life of the nation'. The Irish contention that, notwithstanding the acknowledged existence of an emergency, the British security measures were not 'strictly required by the exigencies of the situation', was not accepted.[83]

The issue of derogation is clearly central to the problem of upholding rights during civil conflicts. Britain, like most states, is hypersensitive to challenges to its sovereignty, external or internal. In such circumstances the rights of individuals are traditionally subordinated to those of the society, in effect the state. If the ordinary law is paralysed or superseded, the public safety can only be interpreted by the state itself. This prerogative was if anything reinforced by the decision of the European Court of Human Rights in 1978. The Irish government, apparently hoping for a clearer and less politically-inhibited verdict than it had obtained from the Commission, exercised its right to take the case to the court in March 1976. The judgement delivered there in January 1978 was unexpected. The court not only weakened the impact of the Commission's verdict on the five techniques by finding that 'although [they] undoubtedly amounted to inhuman and degrading treatment, although their object was the extraction of confessions ... and although they were used systematically, they did not occasion suffering of the particular intensity and cruelty implied by the word torture as so understood'.[84] But it emphasized the British government's 'margin of appreciation' in determining the measures to adopt in an emergency 'threatening the life of the nation'. It appeared not to consider the point that the emergency could only be threatening the life of the whole nation if Northern Ireland was a separate political unit and not, as the British claimed, an integral part of the UK state.[85] It found it sufficient to say that the British government's justification was the need to 'combat an organization which had played a considerable subversive role throughout the recent history of Ireland and which was creating a ... particularly far-reaching and acute danger for the territorial integrity of the United Kingdom, the institutions of the six counties and the lives of the province's inhabitants'.[86] This view clearly favoured the state's interpretation. The court further underlined the Commission's rejection of the Irish argument that internment had been unjustified by the strict exigencies of the situation, by saying that it was not its place to 'substitute for the British government's assessment any other assessment of what might be the most prudent or most expedient policy to combat terrorism'.[87] (Yet if it could not do this, it is not clear how it could determine, as it might in theory be obliged to, the 'limits of the margin of appreciation', and whether the British government had 'overstepped' them.[88])

It is not possible to conclude that internationalization of even these restricted aspects of the Northern Ireland problem has brought a solution in prospect, or indeed substantially modified the position of any of the protagonists. Advocates of formal international intervention have been denounced for their naivety on all sides of the 'Irish triangle'.[89] International opinion doubtless has effects, at least on the rhetoric of a state that cultivates a liberal image, and maybe to a limited extent on policy as well. (For instance, the system of exclusion operated under the Prevention of Terrorism Act was called in question partly because it had 'led to criticism of the United Kingdom in the international fora on human rights'.[90]) However, the limit of these effects is evident, where the state's vital interests are involved. In the delicate matter of justification for encroachment on civil liberties, like the concept of 'operational necessity [in] the interest of saving lives' used in the Compton report, it remains open to the state to plead, as the United Kingdom did to the European Court of Human Rights, that 'when there is . . . a terrorist campaign, it is, unfortunately, probably inevitable that on occasions a member, or members, of the security forces, acting under the influence of anger and stress, will ill-treat a suspected terrorist'.[91]

This placing of primary blame on the side of the state's opponents is scarcely unjust, yet it remains true that, as the Inter-American Commission on Human Rights declared, 'Each government that confronts a subversive threat must choose, on the one hand, the path of respect for the rule of law, or, on the other hand, the descent into state terrorism'.[92] The path of law, if it is not crudely construed as the imposition of order, is an exacting one to follow. The protection of life and property, however important, is not the sole duty of the state. The values placed on life and property are part of the system of values of the community as a whole, and it is to defend this whole system that the state exists. The sacrifice of civil liberties to provide powers which may help to save lives is a complex and possibly unbalanced equation. If liberal democracies are in an obvious sense vulnerable to terrorism – in that terrorists can operate more easily in them than in repressive states – it does not appear that this vulnerability is fatal; whereas the crushing of democracy by governments is a phenomenon only too well attested by history.

In the last analysis there are things beyond the control of international agencies and governments alike. One of the most powerful influences in Ireland, the Papacy, has consistently failed to dent the legitimacy or conviction of the movement dedicated to the use of physical violence to 'liberate' Ireland.[93] The visit of John Paul II to Ireland in 1979 constituted a resounding external intercession in favour of human rights as interpreted by the Roman Catholic church. But his pronouncement that 'violence is the enemy of justice' was brushed aside by the IRA on the grounds that the

British 'presence' was a greater evil.[94] The fact is that political and communal 'rights', like self-determination, can conflict in a way that juridical rights cannot. Guarantees of human rights generally apply to individuals, and do not easily make provision for communal discrimination. While Britain remains hostile to the idea of a Bill of Rights, the fate of its successive attempts at constitutional reconstruction in Northern Ireland indicates that economic and social rights cannot be sustained by government fiat.

Notes

1 The most neutral term is 'six counties'; the most hostile nationalist title was 'Carsonia'.

2 Cf. P. Keatinge, *A Place Among the Nations. Issues of Irish Foreign Policy* (Dublin, 1978), pp. 100–25.

3 J. Bowman, *De Valera and the Ulster Question 1917–73* (Oxford, 1982).

4 The problem of defining human rights violations in the Northern Ireland context may be seen in W.C. Ewing's worthy but woolly 'Human Rights in Northern Ireland', in W.A. Veenhoven (ed.), *Case Studies on Human Rights and Fundamental Freedoms* (The Hague, 1976), vol. 5, pp. 35–68. The Cobden Trust's writers, T. Hadden and P. Hillyard, cautiously suggest that the term 'civil rights cannot be precisely defined', *Justice in Northern Ireland. A Study in Social Confidence* (London, 1973), p. 8.

5 To put it another way, 'what history is and means becomes the very stuff of the conflict'. J.B. Bell, 'The Chroniclers of Violence in Northern Ireland: the First Wave Interpreted', *Review of Politics*, 34 (1972), 148. For a more elegant analysis of 'the elision of time' in Irish historical perception see O. MacDonagh, 'Time's Revenges and Revenge's Time: A View of Anglo-Irish Relations', *Anglo-Irish Studies*, 4 (1979), 3, 6.

6 Especially 1857, 1864, and 1872. S.E. Baker, 'Orange and Green: Belfast 1832–1912', in H. Dyos and M. Wolff (eds.), *The Victorian City: Images and Realities*, vol. 2 (London, 1973); I. Budge and C. O'Leary, *Belfast: Approach to Crisis. A Study of Belfast Politics 1613–1970* (London, 1973), pp. 73–95.

7 P. Gibbon, *The Origins of Ulster Unionism: The Formation of Protestant Politics and Ideology in Nineteenth-century Ireland* (Manchester, 1975); H. Patterson, *Class Conflict and Sectarianism. The Protestant Working Class and the Belfast Labour Movement 1868–1920* (Belfast, 1980), pp. 1–18.

8 The outstandingly sensitive 'Unionist' analysis of these developments is A.T.Q. Stewart, *The Narrow Ground. Aspects of Ulster 1609–1969* (London, 1977).

9 A.T.Q. Stewart, *The Ulster Crisis* (London, 1967); P. Jalland, *The Liberals and Ireland. The Ulster Question in British Politics to 1914* (Brighton, 1980).

10 D.W. Harkness, *The Restless Dominion. The Irish Free State and the British Commonwealth of Nations 1921–31* (London, 1969), pp. 21–24; P. Buckland, *The Factory of Grievances. Devolved Government in Northern Ireland 1920–1939* (Dublin, 1979).

11 Cabinet, 19 December 1919; Cabinet Committee on Ireland, report, 17 February 1920. Public Record Office, London, CAB. 23 18, CAB. 24 98 (C.P.664).

12 Beginning with Collins' argument for 'local option' for 'solid blocks who are against partition in the north of Antrim, through a part of Derry and part of Armagh ... If we are not going to coerce the N.E. Corner, the N.E. Corner must not be allowed to coerce'. Conference, 4th session, 14 October 1921. T. Jones, *Whitehall Diary*, (London, 1971) vol. 3, p. 131; culminating in the Craig–Collins Pact of 30 March 1922.

13 K. Boyle, 'The Tallents Report on the Craig–Collins Pact of 30 March 1922', *Irish Jurist*, 12 (1977), 148–75; P. Bew, P. Gibbon and H. Patterson, *The State in Northern Ireland 1921–72. Political Forces and Social Classes* (Manchester, 1979), pp. 57–62.

14 National Council for Civil Liberties, *Report of a Commission of Inquiry appointed to examine the purpose and effect of the Civil Authorities (Special Powers) Acts 1922 and 1933* (London, 1936).

15 Opinion of Sir F. Liddell, Sir F. Greer, Sir J. Risley, and Sir J. Anderson, 24 July 1922. Cabinet, 31 July 1922, App. C. CAB. 43 2.

16 Notes in PRO, D.O.35 893 X.II/251.

17 Memo. by Stephenson, 7 March 1938, D.O.35 893 X.II/123.

18 Markbreiter to Home Secretary (27 March 1938), ibid.

19 Note by Lord Hartington, 10 March 1938. ibid.
20 Note by Sir H. Batterbee, 18 November 1938. D.O.35 893 X.II/251.
21 Additional note, 19 March 1938. D.O.35 893 X.II/123.
22 This is well analysed in S. Nelson, 'Discrimination in Northern Ireland: the Protestant Response', in W.A. Veenhoven (ed.), *Case Studies on Human Rights*, vol.4 (The Hague, 1976), pp. 405–30. See also the penetrating study by F. Wright, 'Protestant Ideology and Politics in Ulster', *European Journal of Sociology*, 14 (1973), 213–80.
23 L. de Paor, *Divided Ulster* (Harmondsworth, 1970), pp. 141–50; T.W. Moody, *The Ulster Question 1603–1973* (Cork, 1974), pp. 25–42.
24 R.B. Rose, 'On the Priorities of Citizenship in the Deep South and Northern Ireland', *Journal of Politics*, 38 (1976).
25 Cf. Buckland, op. cit.; de Paor, op. cit., pp. 152–8.
26 Arts. 7–11; cf. European Convention for the Protection of Human Rights and Fundamental Freedoms, Art. 5 (4); Claire Palley, 'Internment: The Need For Proper Safeguards', *The Times*, 23 November 1971.
27 It was noted in 1938 that 'nothing like' the required number of Catholics had come forward – about 500 in a force of 2,700. Home Office notes, D.O.35 893 X.II/251.
28 Notes in Tallents MSS, PRO C.O.906 27.
29 The 'state of siege' as a synonym for emergency powers was less metaphorical in Ulster than in most of the modern world. On the Special Constabulary, see W. Clark, *Guns in Ulster* (Belfast, 1967), a semi-official RUC publication.
30 J. Darby, *Conflict in Northern Ireland: the Development of a Polarised Community* (Dublin, 1976), pp. 188–9.
31 B. Faulkner (ed. J. Houston), *Memoirs of a Statesman* (London, 1978), pp. 114–7.
32 For an early indication of public reaction, The *Sunday Times* Insight Team, *Ulster* (Harmondsworth, 1972), p. 289.
33 *Report of the Commission to consider legal procedures to deal with terrorist activities in Northern Ireland*, Cmnd.5185 (1972), paras. 27, 87; Northern Ireland (Emergency Provisions) Act 1973 c.53, Sec.6.
34 Cf. MacDonagh, 'Time's Revenges', 16, on the exaltation of 'the moral as against the actual'.
35 Ibid. 15.
36 Rose, 'Priorities of Citizenship', 289–91. On the problem of public 'security' there is a slapdash but suggestive approach in C.H. Enloe, 'Police and Military in Ulster: Peacekeeping or Peace-subverting Forces?' *Journal of Peace Research* (1978), 243–55; and *Ethnic Soldiers: State Security in Divided Societies* (Harmondsworth, 1980), pp. 106–8.
37 *Report of the Enquiry into Allegations against the Security Forces of physical brutality in Northern Ireland arising out of events on 9 August 1971*, Cmnd. 4823 (November 1971), para. 105.
38 For early criticisms, I. Brownlie, 'Interrogation in Depth: the Compton and Parker Reports', *Modern Law Review*, 35 (1972), 501–7; D. Lowry, 'Ill-treatment, brutality and torture: some thoughts upon the "treatment" of Irish political prisoners', *DePaul Law Review*, 23 (1973), 553–81.
39 The Directive, incorporating Art.3 of the Geneva Convention 1949 Relative to the Treatment of Prisoners of War (but quoting 'the wrong Geneva Convention', as Lord Gardiner pointed out), was printed as an Appendix to the report.
40 *Report of the Committee of Privy Counsellors appointed to consider authorized procedures for the interrogation of persons suspected of terrorism*, Cmnd. 4901 (1972), para. 10. In *The Guineapigs* (Harmondsworth, 1974), pp. 34–5, J. McGuffin held this ancestry to be 'totally inaccurate', insofar as sensory-deprivation techniques as such had not been used earlier.
41 Cmnd 4901, para. 8.
42 Ibid., para. 26.
43 Ibid., para. 30.
44 'Whatever words of definition are used, opinions will inevitably differ as to whether the action under consideration falls within one or the other definition'. Ibid., para. 9.
45 Ibid., Minority Report, para. 8.
46 Ibid., paras. 12, 15.
47 Ibid., para. 20(2). For a discussion of the 'consequentialist' (utilitarian) morality of Parker as against Gardiner's intrinsic morality, Lowry, 'Ill-treatment', 573–5.
48 Minority Report, para. 21.
49 See note 39 above.

50 *Report of a Committee to consider, in the context of civil liberties and human rights, measures to deal with terrorism in Northern Ireland*, Cmnd. 5847 (Jan. 1975), para. 140.
51 Ibid., para. 145.
52 Ibid., para. 147.
53 Cf. the definition used in Parker's opening sentence: 'Terrorism no doubt connotes violence, and violence for political ends', and that in the Emergency Provisions Act 1973, the same as Gardiner's but without 'sectarian'. These are in effect definitions of war in general. On the nineteenth century problem, Sir J. Stephen, 'On the Suppression of Boycotting', *The Nineteenth Century* 118 (1886); Criminal Law and Procedure (Ireland) Act 1887, 50 and 51 Vict.c.20, Sec. 2.
54 Cmnd. 5847, para. 15.
55 Ibid., para. 17, 19.
56 Ibid., para. 21.
57 Ibid., para. 148.
58 P. Taylor, *Beating the Terrorists? Interrogation in Omagh, Gough and Castlereagh* (Harmondsworth, 1980), p. 37.
59 See the impressionistic if plausible assertions in Hadden and Hillyard, *Justice in Northern Ireland*, and K. Boyle et al., *Law and the State. The Case of Northern Ireland* (Oxford, 1975), pp. 78ff.
60 R. Fisk, 'The Effect of Social and Political Crime on the Police and British Army in Northern Ireland', in M.H. Livingston (ed.), *International Terrorism in the Contemporary World* (London, 1978), pp. 89–90.
61 *Report of the Committee of Inquiry into Police Interrogation Procedures in Northern Ireland*, Cmnd. 7497 (March 1979).
62 Taylor, op. cit., 222.
63 Ibid., 271–9, 287–90, 304–23.
64 By reducing the potential for the making of false complaints – and presumably thereby improving public confidence in the force. *Review of the Operation of the Prevention of Terrorism (Temporary Provisions) Act 1976*, by the Rt Hon. Earl Jellicoe, Cmnd. 8803 (February 1983), para. 86.
65 W. D'Arcy, *The Fenian Movement in the United States* (Washington, DC, 1947); T.N. Brown, *Irish–American Nationalism 1870–1890* (Philadelphia, 1966).
66 K.R.M. Short, *The Dynamite War. Irish–American Bombers in Victorian Britain* (Dublin, 1979).
67 A.J. Ward, *Ireland and Anglo-American Relations 1899–1921* (London, 1969), pp. 189–213.
68 Keatinge, *A Place Among the Nations*, p. 119.
69 Taylor, *Beating the Terrorists?*, pp. 217–85.
70 *Report of an Amnesty International Mission to Northern Ireland (28 November – 6 December 1977)* (June 1978), p. 1.
71 Ibid., p. 9. It also concluded that the machinery for investigating complaints against the police, though elaborate, was 'deficient in practice'. Ibid., pp. 64–7, 70.
72 'legal provisions, which have eroded the rights of suspects held in connection with terrorist offences'. Ibid., p. 70.
73 R. v. McCormick and others (1977), N.I.4.
74 McGonigal added that while judges might use their discretion to exclude statements obtained by moderate maltreatment, they should not use it to 'defeat the will of parliament' as apparently expressed in Section 6 of the EPA.
75 *Amnesty Report*, p. 63.
76 Taylor, op. cit., 291. Amnesty's view, that to name the respondents would, in the circumstances, be to expose them to considerable danger, is persuasive.
77 *House of Commons debates*, 951 (15 June 1978), cc.1167–8.
78 The Irish government, however, pointed to its long record as a pioneer of human rights guarantees. Keatinge, op. cit., p. 187.
79 Additional allegations under Art. 2 concerning the deaths of certain persons in Northern Ireland were declared inadmissible, as were a number of other complaints. A.H. Robertson, *Human Rights in Europe* (Manchester, 1977), pp. 42–3.
80 M. McKinley, The Ulster Question in International Politics 1968–78 (Ph.D. thesis, Australian National University, 1981), 358–61. On the machinery H. Hannum and K. Boyle, 'Ireland in Strasbourg: an Analysis of Northern Irish Proceedings before the European Commission on Human Rights', *Irish Jurist*, 2 (1972), 329–46.

81 Council of Europe, Commission on Human Rights, *Application No.5310/71, Ireland v. United Kingdom: Report of the Commission* (25 January 1976).
82 Cf. R.B. Lillich and F.C. Newman, *International Human Rights: Problems of Law and Policy* (Boston, 1979), pp. 614–6.
83 Ibid., pp. 603–5. The charge of discrimination (Art. 14) was not upheld.
84 I.e. in Art.3 of the European Convention and Art. 1 of Resolution 3452 (XXX) of the United Nations, 9 December 1975. European Court of Human Rights, *Ireland v. United Kingdom: Judgment* (18 January 1978). For a critique, B.M. Klayman, 'The Definition of Torture in International Law', *Temple Law Quarterly*, 51 (1978), 497–500.
85 Cf. R. Higgins, 'Derogations under Human Rights Treaties', *British Yearbook of International Law* (1976–7), 302.
86 *Ireland v. U.K.: Judgment*, para. 212.
87 Ibid., para. 214.
88 Cf. Higgins, op. cit., 296–301. Technically, Britain appears to have been in breach of the requirement that it keep the Commission informed of its continuing derogation from Art. 15.
89 In particular R.H. Hull, *The Irish Triangle. Conflict in Northern Ireland* (Princeton, 1976), pp. 237–55.
90 Cmnd. 8803, para. 175. Cf. also the guardedly optimistic argument in D. Freestone, 'Legal Responses to Terrorism: Towards European Cooperation?', in J. Lodge (ed.), *Terrorism: A Challenge to the State* (Oxford, 1982), p. 199.
91 Final submission, 20 April 1977.
92 Quoted in S. Hoffmann, *Duties Beyond Borders* (Syracuse, 1981), pp. 108–9.
93 Cf. D. McCartney, 'The Churches and Secret Societies.', in T.D. Williams (ed.), *Secret Societies in Ireland* (Dublin, 1973), pp. 68–78.
94 'IRA defies Pope as Atkins promises initiative', *Guardian*, 3 October 1979.

8 The United Nations, UNESCO and the debate on information rights

CLARE WELLS

Introduction

The setting of legal norms and standards, including the codification of human rights, constitutes part of the mandate of several agencies of the United Nations system, but has never been among their least controversial activities.

As is generally conceded, the world order envisaged in the constitutional texts of the UN Specialized Agencies, and the human rights it embodied, broadly reflected the policy preferences of the leaders of the post-war era and notably of the United States. It was thus within a liberal framework of economies based upon private enterprise, and of rights understood in individualistic terms, that public welfare and 'freedom from want and fear' were to be ensured.

But a liberal if not *laissez-faire* world order and liberal conceptions of rights never went entirely unchallenged. With the accession of the Third World to the status of a large majority in the UN system, and with increased coordination among Third World ranks, the challenge has taken the form of organized calls for a new international order based on a number of new rights.

The rights asserted may be seen as new in terms of substance, since they focus on the material basis for fulfilment of rights rather than upon freedoms of a more narrowly civil and political nature.

They may also be considered new in terms of proposed beneficiaries, insofar as they deal explicitly with groups (notably nations). More specifically, where liberal rights treated individuals atomistically, the new rights are designed to take explicit account of structured inequalities within and between societies. Thus the doctrine of the rights of individuals freely to produce and exchange goods and services is alleged by the new majority to have worked mostly to the advantage of monopolistic enterprises operating globally. The countervailing rights advocated are those of users, be they individuals, nations or international society as a whole, and whether as consumers, potential participants, or would-be sharers of control over relevant resources. The rights at issue are held also to involve concomitant duties incumbent upon enterprises and/or states.

In asserting such rights and duties, the new majority in the UN system has, more or less directly, challenged powerful interests, which in turn have organized resistance to international endorsement of the proposed new norms. In the case of information rights within the United Nations Educational, Scientific and Cultural Organization (UNESCO), to be discussed here, the new majority has not only challenged liberal concepts of the press; they have also taken on the Western 'knowledge industry', that is the world's leading producers of communications hardware and software (news, newsfilms, newspapers, films, television programming, records, cassettes, books, and so forth).

This chapter will consider the evolution of the debate on information rights within the United Nations and UNESCO, setting out the broad positions put forward by the West (i.e., the advanced industrial market economies), the Soviet bloc and the Third World, and will analyse the outcome of debate to date. First, it will sketch liberal democratic theory as it bears on information and the press, to which the various positions tend to refer in one way or another.

Information and liberal democratic theory

The liberal model of democracy as classically expounded by J. S. Mill[1] is based on a concept of developing rationality: democracy is seen as self-government through reasoned choice as opposed to guidance by authority or custom, and applies equally to the individual, to the group and to society as a whole. It is also essentially dynamic, in that it builds in the potential of a minority to become a majority by virtue of rational persuasion.

Truth in this model is approached by means of a self-righting process based on competition between interpretations of reality. The central requirements are continuing entry of new information with which to correct prevailing misconceptions; and roughly equal competition or 'fair play to all sides of the truth'. Further conditions are the need for each interest to speak on its own behalf so that a case may be heard 'in its most plausible and persuasive form'; and especial tolerance of minority views as representing 'the neglected interests, the side of human well-being which is in danger of obtaining less than its share'.

The liberal model of reasoned self-guidance may thus be said to assume not only bias, but also effectively competing bias. Monopoly of information by any single set of interests is considered to act as a restriction on rational choice and thus on both individual and social development. As such it is seen as inefficient and damaging to the general interest of the community.

The role of the press in this model is that of a public intelligence service, keeping the citizenry fully supplied with information on matters of public relevance and identifying the range of options available at any given time. In the process, it acts as 'watchdog' on the state, understood as autocratic ruler. The traditional claim for special status of the press before the law is based on this quasi-constitutional or 'fourth-estate' role.

The post-war debate on information rights in the United Nations: 'free flow' as controlling frame of reference

The question of information rights was first raised in the United Nations and UNESCO at the initiative or with the backing of the United States.[2] Introduced in the wake of World War II and as the Cold War intensified, the debate reached a peak of intensity in 1949 but was soon after to be deadlocked.[3]

Within the UN system, information rights tended to be handled in the context of 'peace', the primary goal of both the United Nations and UNESCO: as will be seen, the various approaches discussed below are couched in terms of their contribution to that goal.

THE WESTERN POSITION[4]

The United States, backed by certain Western delegates, advanced the following set of arguments: peace, the supreme goal of the United Nations and UNESCO, was to be seen as a function of international understanding, which in turn depended upon the free flow of information between peoples. Obstruction of information flows by totalitarian regimes had recently, and could again shortly, lead to misunderstanding and ultimately to war. State monopolies of information, and state intervention in information processes more generally, were thus identified as the major evil in the field of information rights. The best checks on possible abuse of freedom did not lie so much at the level of media structure, let alone in mobilizing the media in support of truth as defined by the state. Rather they lay, on the one hand, in respect of the practitioner's right to 'tell the truth as he sees it' and in the operation of practitioner ethics; and, on the other hand, in the reasoning abilities and sovereignty of the consumer. In short, freedom of information, nationally and internationally, was seen as the surest guarantee of mutual understanding and peace.

The United States and its supporters were duly to seek extension of the principle of freedom of information to the global sphere through endorsement of the concept as a norm of international law.

The rights and freedoms advocated by these states could be seen to apply in practice at two levels. On the one hand, information was handled as an individual right. This approach is reflected in an early General Assembly resolution proclaiming freedom of information to be 'a fundamental human right' and 'the touchstone of all the freedoms to which the United Nations is consecrated'.[5] It was also reflected in the relevant article of the Universal Declaration of Human Rights of 1948, according to which: 'Everyone has the right to freedom of opinion and expression; this right includes freedom to hold opinions without interference and to seek, receive and impart information and ideas through any media and regardless of frontiers'.[6]

On the other hand, information rights were treated as applying at the corporate level of the mass media. Although the concept of corporate information rights was never made explicit, the United States was from the start to stress within UNESCO the part which could be played by the media of mass communication (press, radio and cinema), if free of political control, in achieving that Agency's goal of peace. Similarly, early debates in the United Nations focussed largely on the conditions governing international collection, transmission and dissemination of information by these media.

At a more tactical level, and when it appeared in the course of debate that some restrictions might have to be countenanced, Western delegates advocated that these be kept to a strict minimum and be based on concepts of sufficient legal precision to prevent abusive interpretation. Equally, they preferred that instruments dealing with restrictions be permissive rather than binding, and that wordings be 'positive' rather than 'prohibitive'. They also pressed, among other things, for insertion of safeguard clauses based on domestic constitutional provisions with respect to professional autonomy. Meanwhile, the drafting and adoption of ethical codes were seen as falling within the jurisdiction of the profession and not that of intergovernmental agencies.

OPPOSITION TO 'FREE FLOW' PROPOSALS

Although American delegates in the post-war era could generally count on the support of the Scandinavian countries, certain West European states and the White Dominions, opposition to their proposals for *laissez-faire* norms of international information law were in fact to be registered from the outset by a majority of member states comprising the Soviet bloc, the then independent developing countries and a number of West European states.

Soviet bloc opposition

The most vigorous opposition during the middle to late 1940s came from the Soviet bloc and Yugoslavia.[7]

While also working from the perspective of 'peace', Soviet bloc spokesmen arrived at opposite policy prescriptions. As against individual rights of a civil and political character, delegates from these countries stressed a collective right to peace as the condition for the exercise of all other rights. War in their view resulted not – or at least not solely – from subjective factors but rather from conflict of objective interests, notably competition between capitalist concerns and the states which served them. The state, in their view, had an ethical role to play in ensuring the conditions necessary to peace; and to the extent that, as Western delegates claimed, information was instrumental to peace, the ethical role of the state in peace maintenance also extended to the sphere of information.

By the same token, UNESCO's primary constitutional commitment to peace required that member states take all measures necessary to prevent use of the means of communication for other than peaceful purposes.

Beyond the right to peace, in the Soviet view, the individual as citizen had a right to the 'objective truth' and to protection from the 'misinformation' spread by leading Western news organs. Hence only 'correct' information should be permitted to flow freely between states.

But the cardinal principles affirmed by Soviet bloc states in the debate on free flow were those of national sovereignty and self-determination. As they saw it, the activities of certain Western media, notably organs such as the Voice of America, aimed at subverting the peoples' democracies and consequently violated these fundamental principles of international law.

Similarly, the delegates of Eastern Europe claimed that US instigation of the debate on freedom of information within the UN was designed to serve the interests of American business and press monopolies, that the latter were already engaged in 'war-mongering' and in slandering the USSR, and that the debate should itself be regarded as part of an anti-Soviet campaign led by US cold warriors.

In pressing the case for restrictions on 'war propaganda' and 'incorrect' information, Soviet bloc spokesmen pointed out that information was subject to some degree of regulation in every country, and had even been regulated under League of Nations auspices.

Reacting at first to US moves, but later more often acting as initiators, Soviet bloc countries have worked in the UN system for condemnation of private press monopolies and for binding restriction of certain types of expression, either by 'prevention' and 'suppression' (understood by others as censorship) or by legal prohibition. As a last resort, they have sought support for statements in positive form of the goals to whose achievement they consider that mass media should contribute. Among these, peace and disarmament have been constant; but the list has been adjusted at different times to include 'peaceful coexistence' and (in potential conflict with the goal of peace understood as order, but no doubt with an eye to Third World support) the elimination of colonialism, racism and related phenomena.

Moral codes and individual conscience, meanwhile, have tended to be seen by Soviet bloc delegates as ineffectual checks on abuse of freedom, and indeed as largely irrelevant in contexts where the production of information is predominantly corporate.

However, ill-placed as they were in the post-war era to influence the outcomes of standard-setting activities, the preference of Soviet bloc states at the time was for technical rather than normative approaches to information problems (e.g., reconstruction of war-damaged communications facilities). The best gauge of Soviet reactions to Western policy in this sphere may perhaps be found in the failure of the USSR to take up membership in UNESCO until the mid-1950s, for it was in UNESCO's constitution that the Western view of the relationship between free flow and peace found clearest expression.[8]

Non-Soviet opposition

Reservations about US proposals were also aired by several of the then independent developing and Latin American countries, as well as by certain West European states. Few of the states in question challenged prevailing liberal values as such. Rather, they justified calls for regulation by reference to the powerful impact of mass media, to the weakness (or declining strength) of their own information capabilities, to fears that the better-endowed might abuse their freedom, and/or to the requirements of a 'just peace'.[9]

In particular, it was felt that a policy of free flow would work to American commercial advantage, especially at a time when American news agencies were rivalling British and French agencies seriously as leading world suppliers of news, and might also result in US global cultural domination.[10]

Thus France and the United Kingdom, whose post-war governments were in addition left-of-centre, emphasized the risks of private censorship and the rights of journalists *vis-à-vis* centres of political and economic power (including media institutions). British delegates asserted the priority of local production over free flow and, backed by Latin American spokesmen, stressed the virtues of cultural pluralism. Similarly, countries with newly-launched news agencies, notably India and China, pleaded the case for protection of infant industries, while those with none argued for protection against swamping by foreign and/or commercial information and cultural products.

The UNESCO Secretariat, at the time largely Western-run, for its part argued forcefully that freedom of information required concrete means to make it effective. Recalling the principle of mutual respect for cultures, and contending that free flow was a 'two-way proposition', they stressed the need for 'a just equalization' of the material and technical means of communication and urged the importance of not allowing such means to be concentrated in monopolies, whether instituted for political purposes or for private gain. In addition, they held that freedom of information entailed responsibility in proportion to the power to communicate, especially at the international level.[11]

The American press, it may be noted, was to prove somewhat unreceptive to these views. As a French staff member (later Director-General of UNESCO for thirteen years) was to report, coverage by leading US newspapers of an important early UN conference portrayed UNESCO positions as advanced by the senior officials representing the agency as inclining towards the Soviet attitude.[12]

Meanwhile, for spokesmen from developing countries in particular, the major threat to peace lay in inequality and injustice generally, and in racial discrimination more especially. Nazism having been in their eyes but an extreme manifestation of prejudices endemic in Western society, it was necessary to rehabilitate all mankind and to work for a 'just peace'. To this end, it was also necessary to distinguish the concept of a 'free press' from licence to direct propaganda against other peoples and racial groups, and to take measures against the latter phenomenon.[13]

The countries concerned called for an international right of reply or correction and for restriction of certain types of expression. Among the specific categories of material considered offending, singly or in some combination, were those damaging to 'friendly relations between peoples', or to 'national prestige', or inciting to racial, ethnic, religious or other forms of violence, discrimination, hatred or intolerance. Also considered undesirable were 'Soviet propaganda', or 'Western propaganda', or 'rival superpower propaganda'; partisan reporting of local conflicts; etc. Meanwhile, the forms of regulation envisaged ranged from mandatory prohibition, through permissive legal controls, to codes of professional ethics.

OUTCOMES OF POST-WAR DEBATE

However, in the post-war era such reservations were not clearly articulated as a set of rights competing with those of individuals or of the media. The information policy of states adhering to neither the US nor the Soviet positions was still largely uncoordinated, and no decisive majority emerged on either the content or the mode of regulation. As a result, while able – jointly with the Soviet bloc – to prevent adoption of any legally-binding instrument codifying freedom of information in *laissez-faire* terms, the states in question were unable to present a coherent alternative. As far as adoption of formal norms with respect to information rights was concerned, the outcome amounted in the event to a stalemate, and thus to frustration of US initiatives.[14]

On the other hand, the principles of freedom of information and free flow were to be written not only into the (technically non-binding) Universal Declaration of Human Rights but also into the mandates of various bodies set up under UN or UNESCO auspices, and into the latter's constitution. As a result, freedom of information was to remain the controlling frame of reference for subsequent debate on information rights within the UN system. At this not insignificant level, post-war US policy could thus be considered to have been successful.

The contemporary debate: UNESCO and the challenge of participatory information rights

For most of the 1950s and 1960s, debate on information rights within the United Nations was sporadic, information being treated during this period more as a technical adjunct to development than as a policy area in its own right.

But during these two decades, the global information environment underwent major technological change, most dramatically illustrated by the appearance of communications satellites and computerized information systems. The unprecedented potential power of satellites in particular was to lead to an enhanced sense on the part of many in the West of the relationship between the means and the ends of communication. This heightened awareness was to be registered more especially within UNESCO as the agency which, during the standard-setting moratorium, had been responsible for administering UN technical assistance in the communications field.[15]

Attention was in fact first to be drawn to the implications of the new technologies from the late 1960s by observers in Western countries with fewer or less advanced communications resources, notably Canada, France, the Nordic countries and the Netherlands.[16]

The Non-Aligned Movement, for its part, did not formally concern itself with the problem until a series of meetings from 1973 onward, when it began to build on research conducted in other arenas and to develop earlier questioning of the doctrine of 'free flow' into a more thoroughgoing critique. Presented in the mid-1970s as a set of new rights, and accompanied by calls for structural change, this was to become the official Third World information platform.[17] But, as will be seen, the major change lay less in substance than in the new scale of support for Third World positions: although more polished in style, these were still based at heart upon a shared condition of communications-poverty.

CRITICISM OF 'FREE FLOW'

The Third World analysis holds in essence that, given existing global communications structures, traditional rights and freedoms in this sphere have served primarily the interests of a few well-endowed countries and groups, but are virtually meaningless for the larger part of the world's population.

First, it is argued, present information relationships are structurally imbalanced. The West, and especially the United States, spearhead technological advance in the communications sector and produce the bulk of the hardware traded internationally. Global flows of software or 'messages' (a term used to overcome what are seen as overdrawn distinctions between news, entertainment and advertising) are also held to be dominated by the West. This is held to result, in part, from the resources available to the 'Big Four' news agencies based in the West, and from the 'packages' of programming and commercial sponsorship by which poorer countries finance acquisition of the hardware. In addition, tariff structures are seen to discriminate against smaller countries on the periphery and against non-bulk producers, so that South–South and South–North communications tend to cost more than those from North to South. To the communications-poor, therefore, the doctrine of 'free flow' appears to have promoted not so much a balanced exchange as a 'one-way flow' of messages moving vertically from dominating to dominated.

Secondly, imbalance in structure is considered to have produced imbalance in content, in that information tailored primarily to Western markets is seen intentionally or unintentionally to reflect particular (Western) rather than universal relevance and values. This is held to be best evidenced in the selection of items (insufficient and sensationalist coverage of the Third World) and in the definition of problems (e.g., the time-honoured 'freedom fighter'/'terrorist' dichotomy).

The existing information order has also come in for more radical criticism which is held to apply not only at the global level but also within Western society, and which in fact echoes long-standing domestic critiques of the 'free press'.[18]

The arguments of radical critics run broadly as follows. Technological advance in the communications sphere has been largely controlled by a few private enterprises including some of the most powerful corporations in the world (AT and T, Philips, Siemens, General Electric, AEG-Telefunken, Standard Telephones and Cable, Plessey, Sony and Marconi, among others), often moreover supported by the defence sector of the state. Ownership and control of the media have become increasingly concentrated and linked to big business, including the communications industry, while big business as advertiser and thus as major source of media finance has in practice largely usurped the sovereignty of the consumer. Such trends are held to be reinforced by the nature of contemporary news gathering and recruitment processes.

In terms of content, this structural situation is seen by radical critics as generating not only a commercial bias but a bias towards the 'maintenance of consensus' on an order based on private profit and thus inherently unequal. These biases (seen as differing in content rather than kind from what Western observers have dubbed 'committed', 'mobilizing' or 'developmental' journalism) are held to be reflected in a focus on the sensational and the trivial, as well as in propagation of values supportive of the private enterprise system; and in avoidance of attention to long-term trends in concentration of power. As a result, it is alleged, information media increasingly assume the format of entertainment rather than of a public intelligence service as conceived in the liberal model: people are supplied with the information they are assumed to 'want' rather than that which they may be deemed to 'need'.

Whatever their ideological perspective, the less well-endowed agree that the existing information order represents a third dimension of colonialism (after the political and economic) and that it is unfavourable to them at more than one level.

At the level of communications as such, Third World countries view present arrangements as a threat to survival of traditional forms of communication and culture, and as discouraging local creativity.

At a deeper level, they regard the present order as inimical to achievement of a 'just peace'. As they see it, peace cannot be stable where based on order alone (armed peace) but only where also based on justice as envisaged in their calls for a New International Economic Order. Establishment of a juster world order is seen to depend upon the consent of Western publics, which in turn is seen as a function of Western perceptions of Third World realities. But Western perceptions of remote and unfamiliar societies, where the individual cannot 'test reality' directly, are held to be shaped chiefly by Western media. As Third World spokesmen see it, so long as they are unable to reach Western publics directly and to correct what they view as misconceptions regarding Third World realities, they will be unable to recruit support for fundamental change.

On the contrary, they contend, incoming flows to their own peoples create expectations which cannot be fulfilled and which may thus prove destabilizing. Present arrangements are seen as not even catering adequately for exchanges of experience on matters of shared Southern relevance, but rather as helping to perpetuate the old atomization of the South, with further adverse consequences for peace.

The less well-endowed hold, in short, that the present information order precludes new entry at international and/or national levels, and that it fails to deliver the 'effectively competing biases' required by the liberal model, not least at the level of Western audiences.

THE NEW WORLD INFORMATION AND COMMUNICATION ORDER

The challenge to the existing state of affairs has been expressed as a call for a 'new world information and communication order' (NWICO).[19] The new order is framed as a participatory model of communication, the latter term being harnessed to underline the ideally two- or multi-way nature of the process.

The NWICO is based on a number of new rights. Chief among these is the 'right to communicate' (a term coined by a French commentator[20]) which incorporates among others the 'right to inform' (i.e., the right of self-interpretation to others); the 'right to be heard'; the right to a 'balanced flow' of news and cultural products; and the right to preserve a way of life (cultural integrity). These are seen as involving, among other things, creation of Third World news agencies, adjustment of international tariff rates, and improved access to relevant resources.

The 'right to communicate' and related rights may be seen as new in that they are held to have relevance at the societal as well as at the individual level and to constitute a dimension of national sovereignty and self-determination. Western critics tend to regard the assertion of 'national information rights' and the call for democratisation of information structures at the international level as a cloak for reinforcement of actual or would-be state control, not least through exclusion of Western journalists. But Third World spokesmen see them as complementing rather than supplanting existing channels and as necessary conditions for domestic information democracy.

Seen from this perspective, the rights in question might perhaps be viewed not so much as collective rights but rather as the rights of individuals-as-members-of-groups. The distinction between individual and collective rights might also appear less clear-cut if the 'corporate' press rights defended by the

United States in the post-war era were borne in mind: the dichotomy then would be not so much between individual and group rights, but rather between the rights of different groups.

The rights at issue may also be regarded as new insofar as they deal less with freedom from political control than with the material conditions for communication. Indeed, so far from proscribing state intervention in information processes, the information rights asserted by the new majority require that states intervene actively at local, national, regional and global levels to rectify market distortions and ensure some measure of balance in the allocation of relevant resources.

State intervention with respect to structure is thus seen as necessary to guarantee the liberal requirement of 'new entry' and 'effectively competing bias' at the various levels.

At the level of content, efforts have also been renewed to codify what are seen as the responsibilities of communicators (understood as those who purvey information on a large scale and professionally) towards users and those about whom they communicate. In this connection, post-war proposals for regulation of the goals of communication under intergovernmental auspices have been revived.

Such moves, being more or less explicitly directed towards Western mass media, tend to be perceived by Western critics as involving a double standard on the part of the Third World with respect to national sovereignty. But for Third World spokesmen, the superior power of Western media, and the likely persistence of major differentials in capability for the foreseeable future, entail correspondingly greater accountability. To the extent that they are affected by the kind of coverage devoted (or not devoted) to them in Western media, Third World states consider themselves justified in pronouncing on the latters' standards of conduct.

RESPONSES TO THE CHALLENGE

The normative challenge of the Third World has encountered resistance on the part of Western states and media interests. The strongest opposition has been registered by the United States as well as by other Western countries with important communications industries (West Germany, United Kingdom, Japan . . .) and by the mass media. On the whole, leading Western media have continued to present more extreme views of the debate than Western statesmen in that they have tended, with some exceptions, to present Third World positions as broadly compatible with those of the Soviet bloc.[21]

Although Western delegates initially showed a somewhat similar inclination, more recently they have identified distinctions. Moreover, while denying any suggestion of Western intent either to distort reality or to dominate world information structures, they have declared that Third World claims of imbalance in the existing information order with respect to both structure and content are far from ungrounded. Indeed, representatives not only of smaller Western countries but also of the United States have expressed sympathy with the Third World plight in this field.[22]

However, Western delegates have also voiced anxiety that any attempt by states to 'balance' or 'democratise' the situation at the level of structure, let alone by seeking to codify the proper 'use' or 'duties' of the media, is likely to result sooner or later in direct state control over content.[23]

The approach to the problem favoured in the contemporary debate by Western states, now reduced to about one-fifth of the membership of the United Nations and UNESCO, is technical rather than normative. As against codification of new rights or duties, Western spokesmen have instead held out the prospect of enhanced programmes of aid in the communications field.[24]

Meanwhile, the Soviet bloc, still primarily concerned to promote binding regulation of the world's leading media of communication and to diminish Western dominance in this field, has shown relatively little enthusiasm for a NWICO as envisaged by the Third World.

OUTCOMES OF THE CONTEMPORARY DEBATE[25]

The debates which have best served to test the relative strengths of the established and challenging positions within UNESCO have been those dealing with conventional forms of communication and handled by full-membership organs. Cases in point have been the Media Declaration and debates on the work of the MacBride Commission.

*UNESCO Media Declaration**

The Media Declaration originated in 1970 with a Soviet bloc motion aimed at ensuring that mass media were not used for purposes of 'war propaganda', racialism or hatred among nations, but were instead used to strengthen peace and international understanding. As such, it was directly concerned with the goals or content of communication.[26]

Press attention was not devoted to the draft on any scale until the nineteenth session of the General Conference in 1976. By that time, press interest in UNESCO involvement in the communications field had been

* Full title: Declaration on Fundamental Principles concerning the Contribution of the Mass Media to Strengthening Peace and International Understanding, to the Promotion of Human Rights and to Countering Racialism, Apartheid and Incitement to War.

aroused (with the help of a Western UNESCO official) by developments related to a conference held in Latin America shortly before.[27] Thus at the nineteenth session opposition to the draft was to be registered unequivocally by Western states and mass media.

Up to this point Third World countries as a group, although interested in the race aspects of the proposal, had taken a strong stand neither for nor against the draft. On the other hand, the circumstances of the nineteenth session were such as to render the new majority vulnerable to Western pressure. African states in particular had an interest in the smooth running of the General Conference which was meeting in Africa for the first time, under the stewardship of the first African Director-General (Amadou-Mahtar M'Bow of Senegal). The agency had also by this time experienced two years' exposure to reprisals by Western members (notably US budgetary withholding) consequent upon decisions taken in connection with Israel at the eighteenth session, as well as media coverage which seemed to some designed to discredit the organization.[28]

The opening of the conference was attended by widespread publicity. Focussed mainly upon the draft Declaration, coverage was generally unfavourable not only to the new majority but also to the Secretariat which it tended to criticize as having given an interventionist and/or Marxist lead in the communications sphere.[29] A despatch from Agence-France Presse suggested that the presence of numerous American journalists and representatives of private media interests had contributed to the level of tension, and recorded the view of many Third World and Soviet bloc delegates that the pressure thus brought to bear upon them before debate had even begun was intolerable.[30]

In due course, it was decided by a comfortable majority to refer the subject to the Drafting and Negotiation Group.[31]

The Drafting and Negotiation Group (DNG) was a new institutional feature of UNESCO, set up at the initiative of the Director-General in response to confrontation over Israel at the previous session. It consisted of twenty-five members, meeting at plenipotentiary level and off the record, with a mandate to achieve 'consensus' on subjects deemed sensitive by the steering committee of the General Conference. The Third World majority, although reflected on the DNG, was diminished relative to its numerical advantage in full-membership organs. In the event, Western preference for postponement of debate and reworking of the draft was to prevail both in the DNG and in plenary.

At the twentieth session of the General Conference in 1978, a minority of those consulted in the intervening two years, comprising a few Western states and private media interests, continued to oppose both the principle of a Media Declaration and the draft as revised.[32] United States intimations of renewed budgetary withholding and possible withdrawal from membership were reported[33] and, as on previous occasions, several Western delegates questioned the value of UNESCO's standard-setting role, not only in the communications field but more generally.[34]

As at the previous session, the opening of the conference was surrounded by large-scale publicity, mostly predicting confrontation over the declaration.[35] Journalists complete with visual and sound recording equipment were also to attend debates on the subject in strength.[36] A leading French commentator was to refer to the 'big battalions' of journalists and writers unleashed upon UNESCO[37] while a number of Western delegates were to appeal for objectivity in reporting on the debates.[38]

This time, the new draft was not referred to the DNG, but was instead considered by an informal group of five delegates meeting around the Peruvian chairman of the relevant Programme Commission. The group consisted of representatives of the United States, the Soviet Union, Italy (for the EEC), Sri Lanka (for the Group of 77) and Tunisia (elected coordinator for the Non-Aligned Movement on information questions).[39]

In the declaration as reworked by the group and adopted by the conference, all references to the 'use' of the media, to the 'duties' or 'responsibilities' of media owners or practitioners, and to those of the state in relation to mass media were deleted, along with the prescriptive mode.[40]

Clearly, adoption of a declaration on media content by an intergovernmental agency could of itself be seen as a defeat for the West, and was to be claimed as a victory by the Soviet bloc and many Non-Aligned states.[41] Nevertheless, the fact that the text in final form was devoid of all prescription may be assumed to have deprived such a victory of much of its force. In the event, Western states declared the text acceptable and, in the opinion of several Western journalists, Western views had prevailed.[42]

The MacBride Commission, the NWICO and the IPDC

Non-Aligned calls since the mid-1970s for a NWICO may be seen as more significant than Soviet bloc moves for regulation of the media not only because they are concerned as much with structure as with content but because they enjoy clear majority backing.

At the nineteenth session of the General Conference in 1976, Western members secured support for a review of 'the totality of the problems of communication in modern society' which subsumed and effectively postponed decisions on proposals for a NWICO. The review was entrusted to an international commission of sixteen experts sitting in a personal capacity and chaired by Sean MacBride, after whom the Commission was to be known.

Membership of the MacBride Commission on balance reflected Non-Aligned positions, but the Commission's final report in 1980[43] was fully satisfactory to none. The Soviet member of the Commission held that the report was 'too westernized', over-emphasized the 'right to communicate' and played down the role of international law, while the Non-Aligned spokesman on information regretted that the Commission had failed to propose the text of a declaration and draft charter on a NWICO.[44] Western members of the Commission, meanwhile, had formally dissented from certain recommendations, notably those calling for decreased commercialization of communication; less concentration of control over relevant technology; regulation of advertising content and influence; codification of the responsibilities of journalists; and the contribution of mass media to certain goals.[45] Similarly, Western delegates were to express unease at what they regarded as the report's basically normative approach to communications problems, urging more 'practical' remedies.[46]

The report as such was not in fact submitted to the General Conference. Instead the Director-General, to whom the Commission reported directly, presented an account of the latter's findings which was to set the tone of debate, and which – perhaps not fortuitously – anticipated the position of Western states and media. The latter were revealed in studies of press coverage by Western observers, including the National News Council of the United States, to have been almost unanimous in expressing apprehension at Third World proposals for a NWICO.[47] The Director-General concluded that the report constituted a 'valuable contribution to the continuing international debate' and should be widely circulated, but sought no endorsement of its findings by the Conference. In addition, M'Bow counselled that no firm decisions on the principle of a NWICO be taken at that stage.[48] On all these points, he was warmly backed by Western delegates.

The Director-General's proposals on the MacBride report itself were endorsed in the resolution adopted by the General Conference;[49] the outcome of the debate could thus reasonably be seen as a diplomatic shelving of the report, in line with Western preferences.

But at Third World initiative, the relevant resolution also called for further steps to be taken towards establishment of a NWICO, and set out considerations on which the latter 'could be based'.[50] As a result, several Western states declared that they had joined in adoption of the resolution by consensus only with the greatest reluctance.[51] At this level, the outcome could thus be considered an achievement for the Third World. But even so, given the tentative wording of the section on the NWICO, and given also that the text in question was only a programme resolution, the achievement could not easily be regarded as commanding a strong consensus. The concept of a NWICO has not in fact been endorsed in any binding standard-setting text within the UN system to date.

Meanwhile, the Western preference for technical solutions was to be reflected in 1980 in the establishment under UNESCO auspices of the International Programme for Development of Communication (IPDC). The IPDC has the essentially operational task of coordinating international aid for development of communication facilities in the Third World, and is financed mainly by voluntary contributions.

However, Western contributions to date have been of a meagreness[52] which the Norwegian chairman of the Intergovernmental Council of the IPDC was to pronounce himself at some loss to explain.[53] Meanwhile, the United States and the United Kingdom under the Reagan and Thatcher administrations have explicitly declared their intention not to contribute to the programme but to work on a more bilateral basis by channelling funds directly to selected projects submitted to the IPDC.[54] This response is generally attributed to fears that aid not so tied might be used to strengthen government information agencies,[55] but might also conceivably be interpreted as a system for rewarding 'good behaviour' in the rule-making sphere.

Less ambiguously, the US Congress was to adopt an amendment in 1982 whereby the American contribution to UNESCO's budget would cease 'if any UNESCO program restricts the free press'.[56]

Summary and conclusions

In this paper, we have traced the shift in debates on information rights within the UN system from a post-war focus on freedom from political control to contemporary advocacy of a participatory information order at national and global levels.

Setting the debate in historical context, we have shown that changes in the debate over time lie less in substance than in the presentation of and increased scale of support for Third World positions.

We have also shown that the West was led in the sphere of information rights in the 1940s by the United States, but that the latter was never all-powerful and in particular that it consistently faced some degree of opposition within the Western camp. But although the United States failed to secure endorsement of 'free flow' as a principle of international law, it could be seen as largely the result of US efforts that free flow was to remain the dominant frame of reference for subsequent debate on information rights within the UN system.

As the new minority, however, Western states have abandoned an earlier preference for normative approaches to information issues in favour of more technical solutions.

Meanwhile, as we have seen, the new majority has so far failed to secure international endorsement of binding proposals for a substantial reordering of global information relationships and for a concomitant set of new rights and duties. On the contrary, Western states have tended to secure outcomes broadly acceptable in terms of their own policy orientations by means of referral to recently-created, minority-based arenas of semi-official or unofficial character where they are better able to control proceedings. They have also increasingly begun to cast doubt on the legitimacy of UNESCO's standard-setting role.

These trends have been encouraged by press attention of a scale and kind which, as certain Western delegates and observers have hinted, might be considered somewhat less than wholly objective.

In the circumstances, it might seem to Third World delegates excluded from the stages of close bargaining that not only have they been effectively disenfranchised, but the Western media have, in a sense, been enfranchised in their place. Of late, a number of Third World spokesmen have cautioned against what they regard as an undue tendency to usurp the sovereign authority of the General Conference.

Similar revisionist patterns are visible throughout the UN system, both in the same field but in other agencies (e.g., the International Telecommunications Union) and in other fields altogether. Parallel responses, and notably the bypassing of majority-based procedures, are also visible as for instance in the much-observed Law of the Sea Conference.

But in one important respect, which has tended to escape Western comment, the debate on information rights within the UN system is untypical: in this instance, mass media act as judges not in another party's cause but in their own. It would seem only reasonable to assume in the circumstances that reporting might almost inevitably lean towards the media view of the debate. If such were indeed the case, the consequences would not be insignificant. At the best of times, the overcoming of established interests and concepts is liable to meet resistance; but the virtually unique position in which mass media stand, as arbiters of proposals for reform in the communications sector, would seem to render agreement within UNESCO on any new rights and duties in this field more than usually hard to achieve.

At the broader level, the disparity of approaches to human rights represented within UN agencies raises questions as to the latters' value as arenas for debate on the subject.

On the one hand, representativeness and enriched debate may be seen as maximizing opportunities for enhanced understanding and accommodation of contending positions. The UNESCO debates on information rights, for instance, may be assumed to have helped raise awareness of Third World problems on the part of many Western delegates and individual journalists.

On the other hand, if established interests consider themselves unfairly challenged, such debates may simply help confrontation to escalate, as witnessed not only in retreat to minority-run organs but in threats of budgetary sanctions or withdrawal from membership. Such measures will tend to succeed in containing challenge within certain limits, since the purposes of Third World states cannot be achieved if the latter are left talking to themselves. But where the legitimacy of majority-based procedures is thus called into question, the risk arises both that the new majority becomes embittered and that the new minority becomes vulnerable to charges of double standards.

The value of the UN system as an arena for any given human rights debate is thus likely to depend on the relative strength of the challenged and challenging interests, and on the receptiveness of the various parties to persuasion.

Notes

1 J. S. Mill, 'On Liberty of Thought and Discussion', in *On Liberty* (Harmondsworth, Penguin Books, 1978).

2 See United Nations, 1st session, *Official Records* (1 *GAOR*), Part I, Gen. Ctee, pp. 19–20, 32–3 (1946); and Plen. (26th meeting), p. 365 (1946); and Part II, C.3 (28th meeting), pp. 163–8 (1946). See also UNESCO, Preparatory Commission, *Conference for the Establishment of UNESCO*, London, June 1946, pp. 40–1, 68–9 (1945); 1 UNESCO Gen. Conf. *Records*, Proceedings, esp. pp. 64, 157–61 (1946); and 2 UNESCO Gen. Conf. *Records*, Proceedings, pp. 75–6 (1947).

3 For the major debates on the subject in the General Assembly between 1947 and 1952, see: 2 UN *GAOR*, C.1, 79–86th meetings (22–7 October 1947), pp. 179–247; C.3, 68th–72nd meetings (24–9 October 1947), pp. 126–59; Plen. 115th meeting (15 November 1947), pp. 956–9; 3 UN *GAOR* (II), C.3, 181st-226th meetings (6 April–11 May 1949); 5 UN *GAOR*, C.3, 320–4th meetings (20–2 November 1950) and Plen., 325th meeting (14 December 1950); 7 UN *GAOR*, C.3, 421st–428th meetings (22–8 October 1952) and Plen. 403rd meeting (16 December 1952). See also UN Conference on Freedom of Information, Geneva, March–April 1948, *Final Act*, UN Doc. E/CONF.6/79 (1948) and Confidential report on the proceedings by R. Maheu, an official representing UNESCO at the Conference, dated 3 May 1948, UNESCO Central Registry File 001 A 3/82 '66', Part I. For briefer parallel debates within UNESCO, see esp. 1 UNESCO Gen. Conf. *Records*, Proceedings, pp. 157–61 (1946); and 2 UNESCO Gen. Conf. *Records*, Proceedings, pp. 96–100, 127–36, 142–50 (1947).

4 This summary of the Western position is based on the above debates.

5 UN GA Res. 59(I) of 14 December 1946 (UN 1 *GAOR* Part II).

6 Universal Declaration of Human Rights, adopted by UN GA Res. 217A(III) on 10 December 1948 (UN 3 *GAOR* Part I).

7 See statements by Soviet bloc and Yugoslav delegates in debates cited above. For a contemporary statement, see Y. N. Zasursky and Y. I. Kashlev, 'The Mass Media and Society: A Soviet Viewpoint', *The UNESCO Courier*, April 1977.

8 *Constitution* of the United Nations Educational, Scientific and Cultural Organization, adopted on 16 November 1945, 4 *U.N.T.S.* at 275. On Soviet non-participation in UNESCO during this period, see e.g., John Armstrong, 'The Soviet Attitude Toward UNESCO', *International Organisation*, 8: 2 (May 1954) esp. pp. 232–3.

9 For the following discussion, see e.g., statements in debates cited in note 3 above by delegates of Argentina, China, France, Egypt, India, Lebanon, Mexico, Pakistan, Saudi Arabia and Syria. See also debates and votes on UNESCO agreements to promote free flow of educational, scientific and cultural materials: 1 UNESCO Gen. Conf. *Records*, Proceedings, pp. 157–60 (1946); 3 UNESCO Gen. Conf. *Records*, Proceedings, pp. 174–80, 295, 301–8 (1948); and 4 UNESCO Gen. Conf. *Records*, Proceedings, p. 310 (1949), esp. statements by Austria, Canada, France, Iraq, Italy, Mexico, Norway and Pakistan. For an account of these and related debates within UNESCO, see also James Sewell, *UNESCO and World Politics* (Princeton NJ, Princeton University Press, 1977).

10 For contending interpretations of US policy and the role of the American Society of Newspaper Editors at this time, see C. Binder, 'Freedom of Information and the United Nations', *International Organisation*, 6: 2 (May 1952); and H. Schiller, 'Libre Circulation de l'information et domination mondiale', *Le Monde Diplomatique*, September 1975. See also Sewell, *UNESCO and World Politics*, cited note 9 above.

11 See, e.g., speech by Julian Huxley, Director-General of UNESCO, reproduced as annex to report by Maheu, cited in note 3 above; Introduction to UNESCO Doc. 2C/83 (1947); and discussion at 2nd session of General Conference in UNESCO Docs 2C/G/SR.1 and SR.2 (1947) and 2C *Journal*, pp. 72–3, 90–118, 135–6 (1947).

12 Report by Maheu, cited in note 3 above, pp. 18–23 (1948).

13 See UNESCO Preparatory Commission, *Conference for the Establishment of UNESCO*, op. cit., pp. 32–4, 50–99 (1946), esp. statements by India, Ecuador, Mexico and Poland; also 2 UNESCO Gen. Conf. *Records*, Proceedings, pp. 104–6 and 347 (1947); and 3 UNESCO Gen. Conf. *Records*, Proceedings, p. 59 (1948).

14 For a fuller account of the outcomes of the post-war debate, see C. Wells, *The 'Politicisation' of United Nations Specialised Agencies? The UN, UNESCO and the Politics of Knowledge* (London, the Macmillan Press, forthcoming), chapter 4.

15 Ibid., chapter 3 for a discussion of reasons for the shift in the policy debate from the United Nations to UNESCO.

16 See, e.g., Jean d'Arcy, 'Direct Broadcast Satellites and the Right to Communicate', *EBU Review*, 118 (1969); Herbert Schiller, *Mass Communications and American Empire* (NY: Augustus M. Kelly, 1969); *Reports* series of the Institute of Journalism and Mass Communication at the University of Tampere, Finland, etc. See also D. Stairs, 'The Press and Foreign Policy in Canada' and other articles in *International Journal*, 31: 2 (Spring 1976).

17 The classic statement of Non-Aligned policy is to be found in Mustapha Masmoudi, *The New World Order for Information*, Tunis, Secretariat of State for Information, 1976. See also the *The New World Order for Information* reproduced as UN Doc. A/SPC/33/L.5 and Annex (1978).

18 For radical critiques by Third World academics, see esp. *Development Dialogue*, 1976: 2 and 1977:1; and Report of the Dag Hammerskjøld Institute for 1975, *What Now? Another Development*. For recent Western critiques of the free press, see e.g., F. Hirsch and D. Gordon, *Newspaper Money* (London, Hutchinson, 1975), and R. Miliband, *The State in Capitalist Society* (London, Quartet Books, 1973) esp. chapter 8. For an earlier critique, see Upton Sinclair, *Brass Check*, 1919.

19 As note 17.

20 Jean d'Arcy, cited in note 16 above. On the concept of the right to communicate, see e.g., L. S. Harms and J. Richstad (eds.), *Evolving Perspectives on the Right to Communicate* (Honolulu, East–West Center, 1977) with foreword by Jean d'Arcy.

21 See e.g., 'UNESCO Head Backs Media-Control Draft', *International Herald Tribune*, 27 October 1978 (quoting UPI); 'The Way to a Captive Press', *The Times*, 30 October 1978; 'To Bar State Control in Third World, US Offers to Help in Creating Media', *International Herald Tribune*, 4 November 1978; 'UNESCO Relief Over Achievement', *The Scotsman*, 29 November 1978; etc. See also UNESCO *Press Reviews*, nos. 203–41 of 20 October 1978 to 13 December 1978. For more dispassionate coverage, see e.g., J. Power, 'The Unesco Debate on Role of Press', *International Herald Tribune*, in UNESCO *Press Review*, no. 207 of 26 October 1978; 'Unesco damming the flow?', *The Guardian*, 23 October 1978; P. Webster, 'Unesco Plan Not Meant to Gag Press', *The Guardian*, 27 October 1978; R. Cans, 'Le Rééquilibrage des Moyens d'Information', *Le Monde*, 24 October 1978; F. Giroud, Décoloniser l'information, *Le Monde*, 9 November 1978; etc. For a critical account of press coverage of various contemporary UNESCO debates on communications policy, see Roger Heacock, 'UNESCO and the Media', *Etudes et Travaux*, no. 15, (Geneva, Institut Universitaire de Hautes Etudes Internationales, 1977).

22 See, e.g., 20 UNESCO Gen. Conf. *Records*, Proceedings, esp. statements by United States pp. 648–53; United Kingdom, pp. 496–9; Norway, pp. 361–2; and Sweden, pp. 519–20 (1978).

23 See 20 UNESCO Gen. Conf. *Records*, Proceedings, esp. statements by United States, pp. 648–53; Canada, p. 769; West Germany, pp. 528–9; Netherlands, pp. 578–9; Switzerland, p. 750; Australia, p. 555; Denmark, p. 449; and Ireland, p. 415 (1978).

24 Ibid.

25 For fuller discussion of the outcomes of the contemporary debate, see Wells, *The 'Politicisation' of United Nations Specialised Agencies?*, chapter 5.

26 For drafting history, see UNESCO Doc. 20 C/20 (1978). For an account by a *Sunday Times* journalist of the debate on this instrument up to 1976 and on related texts, see R. Righter, *Whose News? Politics, The Press and the Third World* (London. Burnett Books, 1978).

27 On this point, see 20 UNESCO Gen. Conf. *Records*, Proceedings, pp. 294–5 (1978); R. Righter, *Whose News?*, cited in note 26 above, p. 142; and R. Heacock, 'UNESCO and the Media', cited in note 21 above, p. 31 and chapter 4.

28 For coverage during this period, see e.g., UNESCO *Press Reviews* of September 1974 to October 1976; see also comment by Director-General, 20 UNESCO Gen. Conf. *Records*, Proceedings, pp. 294–5 (1978).

29 On this theme, see esp. UNESCO *Press Reviews* nos. 187–215 (25 October 1976 onward); and R. Righter, *Whose News?*, cited in note 26 above, esp. chapter 4.

30 Jean Mauriac, AFP despatch reproduced in UNESCO *Press Review* no. 189 of 27 October 1976.

31 For discussion of the draft at the 19th session of the General Conference, see esp. General Policy Debate: 19 UNESCO Gen. Conf. *Records*, Proceedings Part I (1976), and Summary of statements on the subject in Programme Commission III in UNESCO Doc. CC/77/WS/21 (1977).

32 For summary analysis of replies, see UNESCO Doc. 104 EX/28 (1978); for full text of replies, UNESCO Central Registry file 659.3:323:1 INT.

33 See O. Todd, 'Le tiers monde et l'information', *L'Express*, 4 November 1978; and J. Nielsen and S. Sullivan, 'Pressure on the Press', *Newsweek*, 6 November 1978.

34 See e.g., 19 UNESCO Gen. Conf. *Records*, Proceedings Part 1, statements by United Kingdom, Switzerland, Italy, Canada and the Netherlands, pp. 478, 499, 579, 594–5 and 631 (1976); UNESCO Doc. 104 EX/SR. 1–35, statements by Norway, United States, Switzerland and France, pp. 213–5, 226–7 (1978); and 20 UNESCO Gen. Conf. *Records*, Proceedings, statements by United States, United Kingdom, Canada, West Germany, Netherlands, Switzerland, Australia, Denmark, Iceland and non-governmental organizations, pp. 648–53, 496–9, 769–70, 528–9, 750, 555, 449, 415, 834–5, 867–8 and 876 (1978).

35 See e.g., AP despatches in UNESCO *Press Reviews* nos. 203 and 206 of 20 October 1978 and 25 October 1978; Reuters despatch of 21 October 1978; AFP despatch in UNESCO *Press Review* no. 203 of 20 October 1978; Ian Murray, 'Clashes over Press Freedom and Israel Likely to Dominate Unesco Meeting in Paris', *The Times*, 24 October 1978; etc.

36 See press accreditation registers held by Press Office, UNESCO Headquarters, Paris.

37 Jean d'Ormesson, 'La chronique du temps qui passe', *Le Figaro* Magazine, 10 November 1978.

38 See e.g., 20 UNESCO Gen. Conf. *Records*, Proceedings, pp. 257, 497 (1978).

39 On this point, see AFP despatches of 3 and 6 November 1978 (UNESCO *Press Reviews* nos. 213 and 215) and article in *International Herald Tribune*, 27 October 1978. 'West offers Unesco Panel Softer Proposal on Media', *International Herald Tribune*, 8 November 1978; letter from P. Galliner, 'Unesco and the World's Press', *The Times*, 3 November 1978; R. Smyth, 'Bid for Unesco Harmony', *The Observer*, 5 November 1978; etc.

40 For text as adopted, see Declaration on Fundamental Principles concerning the Contribution of the Mass Media to Strengthening Peace and International Understanding, to the Promotion of Human Rights and to Countering Racialism, Apartheid and Incitement to War, adopted by UNESCO 20 C/Res. 4/9.3/2 of 28 November 1978 (20 UNESCO Gen. Conf. *Records*, Resolutions, p. 100).

41 See, e.g., statements by the USSR, other East European States and Third World delegates, 20 UNESCO Gen. Conf. *Records*, Proceedings, pp. 1097–117 (1978).

42 See statements by Western states in UNESCO Doc. 20 C/135 App. (1978). See also e.g., R. Righter, 'Unesco's Close Shave for Press Freedom', *The Sunday Times*, 26 November

1978; 'Truce in Paris', *Time Magazine*, 4 November 1978; 'Pious Promises', *The Economist*, 25 November 1978; AP dispatch in UNESCO *Press Review* no. 229 of 27 November 1978; Reuters despatch of 22 November 1978; etc.; and R. Righter, 'Newsflow International', *The Political Quarterly*, 50:3 (July–September 1979) p. 310.

43 UNESCO, *Many Voices, One World* (Paris, UNESCO 1980), subtitled 'Towards a new, more just and more efficient world information and communication order'.

44 Ibid., pp. 280–1.

45 Ibid., e.g., Recommendations 31–2, 17 and 165–7.

46 See 21 UNESCO Gen. Conf. *Records*, Proceedings, esp. statements by United Kingdom, pp. 719–22; Netherlands, pp. 500–1; West Germany, p. 838; Australia, p. 849; United States, pp. 1353–4; also Reports, pp. 178, 182 (1980).

47 A. H. Raskin, *Report on News Coverage of Belgrade UNESCO Conference* (New York, The National News Council, March 1981).

48 See UNESCO Doc. 21 C/85 (1980).

49 UNESCO 21 C/Res. 4/19 of 27 October 1980 (21 UNESCO Gen. Conf. *Records*, Resolutions, at 68).

50 Ibid., Section VI.

51 21 UNESCO Gen. Conf. *Records*, Proceedings, esp. statements by West Germany, United Kingdom and Canada, pp. 1358–60; and Reports, pp. 182–3 (1980).

52 For statement of contributions, see UNESCO Doc. COM-82/CONF.213/2 (1982) and Intergovernmental Council of the International Programme for the Development of Communication (2nd Session), *Final Report*, UNESCO Doc. COM/MD/1 (1982), esp. pp. 6–7.

53 Intergovernmental Council of the IPDC, 3rd Session, December 1982, *Final Report*, para. 11 (1982).

54 See, e.g., J. Friendly, 'Unesco Shifts Approach on Press in Third World', *New York Times*, 30 November 1981; A. Riding, 'US Offers to Aid Journalism in Third World', *New York Times*, 22 January 1982; A. Riding, '"New Information order": Debating pragmatics', *New York Times*, 24 January 1982; and House of Lords, *Parliamentary Debates*, vol. 426, February 1982.

55 Ibid.

56 See 'UNESCO Should Not Ignore the West', *Newsweek*, 17 January 1983, p. 53.

Part Two: Responses

9 The United States

JAMES MAYALL

If such a thing as a normal country exists the United States is not it. Its peculiarity has been regularly remarked upon by Americans themselves since the debate that accompanied the drafting of the Declaration of Independence, and by outsiders, who, at least from the time of de Tocqueville, have tended to see America as the blue-print for the future of mankind, reacting variously with enthusiasm or horror at the prospect.

Two aspects of the peculiarity of the United States' experience are relevant to a discussion of the role of human rights in American foreign policy. The first is the central place that the language of rights occupies in American political life at all levels; the second the habitual search for a legitimating framework of ideas to justify the projection of American power beyond the frontiers of the state. Typically, Jeane Kirkpatrick opened her now celebrated assault on the human rights policies of the Carter Administration with a statement with which few of her adversaries could quarrel. It covered both points.

> The fact that Americans do not share a common history, race, language, religion gives added centrality to American values, beliefs and goals, making them the key element of our national identity. The American people are defined by the American creed. The vision of the public good which defines us is and always has been a commitment to individual freedom and a conviction that government exists, above all for the purpose of protecting individual rights ... *Defending these rights or extending them to other peoples is the only legitimate purpose of American foreign policy*. [My italics][1]

With so elevated a definition of the national purpose, it is hardly surprising that the consensus does not extend from ends to means. Nor is it to be wondered at that public policy in the United States is presented with as much hypocrisy as in other 'open societies'. Whether public life is *more* hypocritical than elsewhere, as is often claimed, is a more dubious proposition. Nonetheless, insofar as concern with human rights at some level is more unavoidable in the United States than in many other countries the formulation of specific policies to protect and extend these rights is complicated by the intellectual ambiguities in the American ideology and the institutional tension between the executive and the legislative branches in the making of American foreign policy. Before turning to the US record on various human rights issues, therefore, it will be useful to look at the way in which these complicating factors influence the American debate on human rights, both directly and in more covert fashion.

Human rights and American political culture

By the American ideology, what Jeane Kirkpatrick refers to as the American creed, I mean simply those assumptions and preconceptions about the nature of society and the purposes that government exists to promote which appear to be widely diffused amongst Americans of all political persuasions and social classes. In caricature, the typical exponent of this ideology is a free market, free world individualist, suspicious of any encroachment by government on his rights at home and confident that individual freedom, i.e., being left alone to pursue his own interests, is what men everywhere want.

What the American government should do to universalize American values, however, is a hotly disputed question, even among the ideologically faithful. There are two main idealized positions. The first, isolation, is the view of the United States as a city set upon a hill to shine forth its light amongst all nations, the light being shed however by example rather than intervention. The second position, the crusade, reflects the belief that the United States is not only the one country to be based on genuinely universal rather than ethnocentric principles, but that as a consequence of its twentieth-century primacy it is also the one country with the power and the responsibility to protect freedom and democratic values within international society.

There are not many pure versions of these cartoon figures in contemporary America if only because the crusaders have been forced to acknowledge, however reluctantly, that the possession of nuclear weapons imposes some constraints even on the virtuous, while the isolationists have been forced to acknowledge the inevitability of intervention, a permanent standing intervention as it were, in an interdependent world. But the features which the cartoon exaggerates are familiar enough.

Behind such caricatures moreover, there are, I believe, two intellectual strands which contribute to the American ideology. Since the two strands are in a state of permanent tension, if not blatant contradiction, together they are also largely responsible for the inconsistency and incoherence which is such a feature of American human rights policy. I shall attempt to identify them under the headings of libertarianism and egalitarianism.

LIBERTARIANISM

The libertarian tradition in the American ideology is the original position. The inalienable rights of the Declaration of Independence are derived, through Locke, from natural law theory in its protosecular version. It is this tradition to which Jeane Kirkpatrick referred in the passage which I quoted earlier. The rights, life, liberty and the pursuit of happiness, for the protection of which, in the words of the Declaration, 'Governments are instituted amongst men' are, of course, negative rights; there is on this view no positive commitment by the government to provide welfare beyond that implied by the provision of defence from external attack and the essential structure of law and order. (It is perhaps worth noting in passing that as with the other great modern revolutions, the seeds of betrayal were planted very early in the American Revolution: while Jefferson worried about slavery, but concluded that the issue must be traded off in order to consolidate the American Republic, there is so far as I know no record that the rights of American Indians were considered at all, even though there is some evidence that ideas for the collective organization of the thirteen colonies were influenced by the example of the Iroquois Confederacy).[2] There is nothing so far in the original libertarian position which would suggest a very active foreign policy in support of human rights or anything else for that matter.

Two other aspects of the libertarian inheritance, however, have a more direct bearing on contemporary American foreign policy. The first is the theory of just rebellion which is implanted in the Declaration along with the inalienable rights; the second the map of international society which the Founding Fathers envisaged. If the United States has not been notable for active support of oppressed peoples in rebellion against central authority, this is no doubt largely because American governments have perceived that their economic, political and strategic interests are best served by the status quo, but it is also because they inherited from the natural law tradition a profound distaste for rebellion itself, except as a last and desperate resort.

In the view of the Founding Fathers, the right to self-determination (not that it was referred to as such) was not something which just any people could indulge at any time they chose. 'Prudence', they insisted, 'will dictate that governments long-established should not be changed for light and transient causes', and they went on to note approvingly that 'mankind are more disposed to suffer, while evils are sufferable, than to right themselves by abolishing the forms to which they are accustomed'. Here at the outset we have not only the lineaments of the Conservative revolution but, it is perhaps not too fanciful to suggest the intellectual origins of much American intervention in the Third World; for a belief in the natural conservatism of people everywhere can plausibly be extended in one of two directions, towards a policy of support for the status quo in defence of established interests or towards an instrumental social engineering to prevent 'light and transient causes' revealing their subversive and radical potential.

In any event one may note how often American governments have supported authoritarian regimes, often regardless of the evils which they perpetuate, presumably on the grounds that the tolerance of the population had not been stretched to breaking point, while support for the established order was necessary to protect vital American or western interests; or how when reform has been urged it has been to forestall a popular reaction which would be uncontrollable and inevitably anti-American. The poor 'track record' of both these tactics has led conservative liberals like George Kennan to advocate a return to a minimum foreign policy wherever possible: the peoples of Latin America and Southern Africa, he has argued, should be left to work out their own salvation, or damnation, free from either help or hindrance from Washington.[3]

That few American governments, least of all the present one, have shown any tendency to heed his advice has much to do with the view of international society which the Founding Fathers developed, drawing heavily on the ideas of the French *philosophes*, and bequeathed to their successors. Much as they may have aspired to live in isolation from the old world they needed an alliance with France. The relevance of this unfortunate contingency for the present discussion is the way in which they sought to confine this alliance in accordance with the *philosophes*' project for a new international society. Like them the Americans believed that 'relations among nations should follow moral law. There should be no difference between the "moral principles" which rule the relations among "individuals" and "moral principles" which rule relations among states.' What this meant in practice, as Felix Gilbert argued thirty years ago in a celebrated article on 'The New Diplomacy',[4] was that the customary system of power politics was to be transformed into a new and peaceful world by a 'total emancipation of commerce'. And they really did mean total. In the draft treaty which John Adams took to France it was proposed to go beyond the conventional most favoured nation clause; the French it was suggested, 'should treat the inhabitants of the United States with regard to duties and imports like natives of France and vice versa; moreover they shall enjoy all other Rights, Liberties, Privileges, Immunities and Exemptions in Trade, Navigation and Commerce, in passing from one port thereof to another, and in going to and from the same, from and to any part of the world which the said natives or companies enjoy'.

It would be wrong, I believe, to suggest that this view of international society in which the market is emancipated from political control, leaving the state to protect the right of the citizen to pursue his (and latterly her) interests within it, is not still deeply entrenched in American foreign policy attitudes. When the United States finally accepted the leadership of the Grand Alliance during World War II, Cordell Hull resurrected the vision of a cosmopolitan commercial society and placed it at the centre of America's war aims. Even before the crusaders began to whip up anti-communism after the war it was clear that collectivism was viewed as the major impediment to a rational and harmonious world order. No wonder then that in the range of human rights issues, American governments have always placed the Soviet denial of political and civil rights to its own citizens and those of Eastern Europe at the top of the list.

The question which arises for any government which is heir to the libertarian tradition is what it should do about other governments which deny civil and political rights to their opponents, which deny them freedom of speech and association and which resort to torture, arbitrary arrest and political assassination. The original libertarian answer to this question was nothing, i.e., non-intervention – a people's salvation lay in their own hands; otherwise each must go to hell in his own way. However, at least since Woodrow Wilson, a liberal president who intervened more times in Central America than any other president before or since, this has been very much an eccentric position. What in practice American administrations have done is to intervene, directly or indirectly, positively or negatively, either on the side of offending governments or on behalf of the victims and human rights activists, but always in the name of free institutions.

I shall return in more detail to the reasons for this inconsistency in the next section. The point to note here is that when American governments get exercised about Soviet and East European dissidents and impose economic sanctions on communist countries while they habitually refuse to impose them on South Africa or in Latin America, intellectually they are not being as inconsistent as their critics maintain. More fundamental than the fashionable distinction between authoritarian and totalitarian regimes is the distinction between market and command economies; within the libertarian tradition the one enjoys a privileged immunity since it belongs in theory to the private realm, the other is fair game.

EGALITARIANISM

The view that libertarianism is the original and natural basis of the American ideology has not gone unchallenged. One historian, indeed, has argued eloquently that it was the Scottish Enlightenment rather than Locke that inspired the Declaration and that on the issue of property there was a crucial and deliberate departure from Locke's teachings.[5] Property, on this view, was deliberately omitted from the list of inalienable rights in the Declaration since it was believed that a constant transferral of property was necessary to prevent the emergence of a hereditary aristocracy on the European pattern and for the health and happiness of society. At the time the issue was, of course, land, not central government transfer payments to disadvantaged groups. It may not be altogether fanciful, however, to trace the tension between the libertarian and egalitarian positions on the issue of rights to the origins of the republic.

But if there is no insuperable intellectual obstacle within the American ideology to property transfers in the interests of equality it remains true that the version of egalitarianism in which political claims are advanced on the basis of a theory of positive, and often discriminatory, rights is a more recent, and theoretically less coherent intrusion into American political culture than the libertarian version described above. Its implications for foreign policy are also more equivocal and open-ended. This is because, where the whole thrust of libertarian thought is to limit the discretionary power of government in interfering in the market order at home and abroad, modern egalitarianism relies on the exercise of discretionary power. Thus, depending on circumstances, it may require the government to abstain from interference at home but to intervene abroad on humanitarian grounds, or as Henry Shue has argued,[6] to intervene to provide for basic human needs without discrimination between citizens and foreigners, or to intervene at home, for example, through affirmative action programmes, while withholding support from regimes which abuse human rights abroad.

The theoretical incoherence of the new egalitarianism, as libertarians never tire of pointing out, is the extreme difficulty of specifying in advance what criteria should be used in taking these decisions. Coherence, however, may not be a necessary precondition for a successful political movement. It is true that President Johnson's pledge to work for 'not just equality as a right but equality as a fact and a result' has led the American courts into very unfamiliar territory, into prescribing positive rights rather than the redress of grievances. As a result, it has also opened the courts to charges of incompetence and illegitimacy from the libertarian opposition. This is a long-standing and inconclusive battle going back at least to the New Deal in which both sides have won victories and suffered defeats. But few would deny that the extensive legal involvement in what has been called 'structural litigation' (i.e., where the focus is on the operation of public policies to influence institutional structures rather than on the settlement of private disputes) constitutes a major change in American political culture in general and in the relationship between state and citizen in particular.

If the new egalitarianism is not yet secured at home it is not surprising that it does not fit into the established pattern of American foreign policy. Neo-conservatives such as Professor Robert Tucker maintain that it does not fit at all and that the attempt to fashion a foreign policy based on its principles is simply a mistake;[7] the alliance between American liberals and Third World governments, he suggests, is an alliance between two groups who are interested in quite separate things, rights on the one side and power on the other. Foreign policy, in this view, occupies a largely autonomous realm and will sometimes require the projection of American power in defence of American interests. In such cases there is neither time nor necessity for agonizing over the human rights of foreigners; foreign policy is not and cannot be about making people over whom the United States has no jurisdiction into better human beings.

Although this position probably accords fairly closely with the official view under most administrations, whether this is represented by the State Department or the National Security Council, it is offensive to the heirs of both the libertarian and egalitarian traditions. Henry Kissinger's frequent complaint that the American people have a deep antipathy to the concept of a politically managed equilibrium is not unfounded: the new egalitarians, like the Founding Fathers themselves, refused to accept the idea of a new morality in international affairs, or rather the idea that morality stops at the border. But where the original libertarians held that state power should only be used to defend the country from direct attack, and generally favoured an isolationist stance in foreign affairs, the new egalitarians have generally favoured an active human rights policy in which the United States relies on a combination of negative and positive sanctions to persuade governments to improve their performance. In this context economic sanctions, such as those regularly demanded by 'the human rights community' against South Africa or Pinochet's Chile are viewed essentially as expressions of solidarity with the victims of oppression while foreign aid is seen as a means of entrenching and supporting the political gains made by the disadvantaged in Third World countries, a rough analogue of the welfare and affirmative action programmes which are seen as the major achievements of the new egalitarianism in the United States itself. Certainly many of the human rights activists of the Carter Administration, above all Andrew Young, believed that the experience they had gained in the civil rights movement in the United States was directly relevant to the pursuit of human rights abroad, indeed, that it was essentially the continuation of the civil rights movement by other means and in a different context.

ETHNIC POLITICS AND THE NATIONAL INTEREST

Two other aspects of American political culture have a bearing on US human rights policy. The first concerns the definition and protection of the national interest, the second the successful mobilization of ethnic constituencies in the political arena.

The concept of the national interest is alien to both libertarianism and egalitarianism, at least in their pure forms. This is because libertarians regard the community interest as an automatic outcome of competition and pursuit of private ends, while egalitarians believe that respect for individual and group rights should take precedence over any conception of the national interest where the two are in conflict. But in practice libertarians and egalitarians have never lived in the pure world; consequently they have to present their arguments in terms of the national interest whose defence is ultimately the responsibility of the president and whose formulation has increasingly resulted from an often ferocious competition between the multiple agencies which make up the executive branch.

The traditional libertarian distrust of all bureaucracy, and by extension of an active foreign policy in peace time, is well-illustrated by reference to the annual Congressional Hearings on the Aid Bill. The one legitimate use of public revenues abroad is to ensure the security of the state. As a result, once the security of the United States had been identified with a world wide struggle against communism, administrations never had the same difficulty in securing appropriations for military aid as they have all had with persuading a reluctant Congress that the national interest required development aid. Indeed, whatever the intentions of their authors, development programmes have always had to be publicly justified in terms of their contribution to free world security, with the result that development has been presented as much as a strategy for fighting communism as a means of relieving poverty and/or fighting social and economic injustice. And wherever the two aims came in conflict it was inevitably the latter which was sacrificed. This was as true for President Kennedy's Alliance for Progress, a programme which was designed at least in part to appeal to the egalitarian sentiment within the Democratic Party as in President Reagan's Caribbean Basin Initiative, designed to provide help for those who help themselves. The experience of both programmes, as Gordon Connell-Smith has pointed out, 'demonstrates the incompatibility of an anti-communist policy, which strengthens right-wing authoritarian governments, with one of encouraging reforms and democracy in Latin America'.[8]

If libertarians have been willing to grant the executive extensive freedom of action provided the national interest was defined, however broadly, in security terms, egalitarians have found themselves forced to argue their case for a strong human rights policy in a similarly instrumental fashion. In other words they have urged the United States to base its relations with foreign countries on their human rights record not merely on moral grounds but because failure to do so is likely to have an adverse effect on US interests.

The reason for this tactic no doubt has much to do with the traditional resistance of the foreign policy establishment to encroachments on its preserve and to arguments, other than those which deal with anti-communism, which are not firmly grounded on a conception of the United States' material interests. Thus Secretary of State Vance explained the Carter human rights policy to the Senate Committee on Foreign Relations: 'The advancement of human rights is more than an ideal. It, too, is an interest. Peaceful gains for freedom and also steps towards stability abroad, and greater security for America.'[9]

In Latin America the argument that the Monroe doctrine is breached everytime a left wing government comes to power and that, despite its undisputed economic and military hegemony, the United States itself is therefore at risk, appears to be so deeply embedded in American political psychology that a purely moral appeal will make little impact. The prospect that Cuba rather than the United States might provide the model for Latin America is profoundly distasteful to both the main political parties. In El Salvador, Carter gradually renewed the traditional US policy of support for the military when the success of the left raised this spectre.[10] And what is seen as a particular problem in the United States' own backyard is often converted into a general problem throughout the Third World.

In such circumstances it seems reasonable for egalitarians to point out that cooperation with tyrannies may produce precisely the effect it is designed to avert. Thus, for example, at the time of the Falkland Islands crisis in February 1982, it was argued that the Reagan Administration had miscalculated its interests by supporting the Argentine junta: a regime with such an appalling human rights record could not be relied on to behave rationally in any context. Similar reasoning was applied in other cases: Iran it was said was 'lost' to the United States because the government continued to arm the Shah despite his systematic abuse of human rights. When the people finally turned against him the United States found its Middle Eastern policy irretrievably ruined. If the argument holds for Iran, why should it be different for Central America. And so on. The logic of the argument, a kind of mirror image domino theory, is plausible if question-begging.

Such arguments have seldom penetrated official foreign policy attitudes very deeply unless supported by a powerful political constituency within the country (and arguably even then their impact on traditional formulations of the US interest has always been transient). Nevertheless the fact that the domestic debate about rights has coincided with the emergence of ethnic politics and indeed has often been the central issue in the political mobilization of ethnic communities, has undoubtedly forced American governments into taking positions on human rights issues in foreign policy about which in other circumstances they might have preferred to have remained silent. Ethnic politics are possible because of the refusal of large numbers of Americans to melt their original identitites beyond recognition. It is tempting to see their political mobilization as simply a tactic adopted by egalitarians to offset the handicap from which they suffer in terms of economic and political power. But in so far as foreign policy is concerned, this view misses the essential point, namely that by definition ethnic communities have ties, real or idealized, with the nationals of their original homelands.

Ethnic pluralism, in other words, reinforces the traditional American preoccupation with rights on both sides of the debate. In foreign affairs it consequently complicates the problem of achieving a coherent or consistent human rights policy. Very roughly it is no doubt true that the Jewish or Polish communities often take the traditional view of negative human rights while the political leaders of the black community support the egalitarian view of positive social and economic rights as a necessary precondition for the enjoyment of life, liberty and the pursuit of happiness. But political doctrine is nowhere closely correlated with ethnic identity. A major objective of ethnic Americans is to mobilize support for those with whom they are allied in their countries of origins, often on the basis of sentimental allegiance rather than right. Although what is at stake will often be perceived and presented as a denial of rights, the success or failure of a particular ethnic foreign policy invariably depends on domestic political considerations, which may have very little to do with the question of rights, and on the ability of the group in question to make its case fit with the prevailing ideological consensus on the nature of American strategic and economic interests.

The American response to international demand for human rights

Against this background how has the United States reacted to the internationalization of human rights in general and to the demands for international action on the issues discussed in the earlier chapters of this book in particular?

In broad terms the answer to this question falls under three heads. First, successive American administrations have reacted with scepticism to the attempts to universalize human rights standards through the United Nations. This scepticism was modified during the Presidency of Jimmy Carter but not abandoned and it has since been strengthened. Secondly, all American administrations have insisted with varying degrees of emphasis (less during détente, more before and since) that the main barrier to the universalization of human rights standards has been constructed by Soviet expansionism. Thirdly, where American governments have reacted strongly to the abuse of human rights by particular regimes this has been either because it was deemed necessary in the context of the East–West conflict or because a domestic constituency succeeded for a time in keeping the issue highly visible in American political life. Let us now consider each of these reactions in more detail, although in practice of course they are seldom mutually exclusive.

THE UNITED STATES AND INTERNATIONAL ORGANIZATION

The United States government played a prominent part in the conception and drafting of the original United Nations Declaration on Human Rights but has generally viewed subsequent UN activities in this field with deep scepticism. In 1978 President Carter proposed that the United States should ratify the two United Nations Conventions on human rights and so associate the United States with the international attempt to establish universal standards in the economic and social as well as the political field.[11] But although US involvement in the work of the United Nations Commission on human rights became more active during his presidency – and by some accounts more effective – like other aspects of his foreign policy this proposal fell victim to the disastrous relationship between his Administration and the Congress. Not only have the United States still not ratified the two 1966 Conventions but of the forty-two treaties and agreements drafted by the United Nations, the ILO and the Organization of American States which deal with human rights issues, they are only a party to twelve. At the United Nations itself, apart from agreements relating to the law of war, the United States is only a party to three agreements – the Supplementary Convention on Slavery, the Protocol relating to the status of refugees, and the Convention on the Political Rights of Women.[12]

There would appear to be three reasons for the scepticism with which American governments habitually view UN activity in the field of human rights. The first reason is the strongly entrenched view that it is impossible to define positive economic and social rights clearly enough to translate them into legal obligations. As we have already noted, in recent years this view has been reinforced by the difficulties which the courts are having in dealing with litigation arising from welfare legislation in the domestic context. Secondly, scepticism, or more accurately opposition arises from the traditional American unwillingness to have US law-making subordinated to international interests, a position which originally led to strong opposition to all foreign entanglements and treaties and which effectively kept the United States out of international organizations until 1945.

It is the third reason, however, which has probably been decisive in recent years. This is the American conviction that the United Nations has been effectively subverted by a Soviet bloc–Third World coalition and turned into a propaganda forum for denouncing US imperialism. This view was powerfully articulated by Daniel Moynihan during his time as UN Ambassador in the mid-1970s. Thus, in the view of one commentator,[13] when Moynihan described President Amin of Uganda as a 'racist murderer' the Afro-Asian states were outraged on the grounds that such an extension of the use of racism beyond its usual context both detracted from and diluted their own attack on white supremacy in South Africa. Their revenge was swift if indirect; it took the form of the General Assembly resolution which denounced Zionism as racism and therefore by implication labelled the United States as a proxy racist for its support of Israel as well as of South Africa.[14] Since the UN Human Rights Commission is dominated by Third World and communist countries (of its thirty-two members only seven are Western 'liberal' states: Austria, Canada, West Germany, United Kingdom, Italy, France and the United States), attempts by the United States to raise issues in which the majority and their allies are implicated, such as the imprisonment of Soviet dissidents or the murder of Ugandan churchmen, are doomed. It is certainly true that the Commission has in the past been used for propaganda purposes: its 1976 Report, for example, cited specific violations in only four countries, Palestine, Chile, South Africa and Cyprus, and although the Carter Administration claimed briefly to have injected more realism and balance into its work, the Reagan Administration is if anything more distrustful of the United Nations than were its predecessors.

There is one ambiguous exception to this record of American disassociation from the UN campaign for human rights. It concerns South Africa. Long before Carter attempted to 'tilt' US policy back towards black Africa, the United States had accepted, somewhat ahead of its Western allies, that the South African policy of apartheid was unique in using the full apparatus of the law to maintain a system of racial discrimination, that this was contrary to the UN Charter and that consequently South Africa could not reasonably shelter from international criticism of its domestic policies behind Article 2 (7). Since the Sharpeville massacre in 1960, moreover, the United States has always either voted in the General Assembly with the majority for resolutions condemning apartheid, or, when it has abstained because it disapproved of particular policy recommendations in the resolution, the US representative has explained that this does not affect his government's solidarity with the majority on the objective of abolishing the racist system within South Africa.

The ambiguity in the US position on South Africa arises therefore over means not ends. From the beginning the Afro-Asian states have demanded the imposition of mandatory economic sanctions against South Africa. Except in one case – the imposition of a mandatory arms embargo in 1977 – all US governments, like their Western allies, have refused to accept that South Africa's denial of rights to the majority of its citizens constitutes a threat to international peace and security which would justify action under Chapter 7 of the Charter; and when necessary they have vetoed these demands in the Security Council. The obvious explanation is that US economic interests, like those of the United Kingdom although to a lesser extent, are deeply involved in the South African economy and therefore, in the final analysis, opposed to the overthrow of the system from which they derive their profits.

This view is no doubt substantially correct. In any case it certainly explains why the campaign against South Africa at the United Nations has been directed as much at the Western powers as at South Africa itself. It is not the case, however, that the United States has done nothing in response to international demands for direct action against South Africa (and probably more important in response to domestic demands supporting the international campaign).

Three aspects of their response have relevance for the debate about US human rights policy in general. First, once persuaded of the necessity for action, it is easier for American governments to impose military than economic sanctions if only because, as we have seen, defence is the one sphere which legitimately belongs to the state within the classical libertarian system. Thus, when President Kennedy sought to woo the newly formed Organization of African Unity in 1963 he instituted an arms embargo against South Africa. Although it was announced by Adlai Stephenson in the Security Council the embargo was a unilateral decision taken prior to the Council's meeting. Since the United States went along with a Security Council Resolution which described the South African situation as seriously disturbing international peace and security, the Africans concluded that this represented a half-way position between Chapter 6 and 7 of the Charter and would be followed in due course by American and Western agreement to mandatory sanctions.[15]

In this view they were mistaken on two counts. The fact that it was a unilateral decision meant that the United States was not being dictated to by the United Nations. More importantly the arms embargo could be justified, at a pinch, as designed to limit the capability of the South African regime to inflict harm on the black population in South Africa and neighbouring countries; it did not imply any willingness on the part of the American authorities to extend sanctions to the economic field which indeed they believed could inflict more harm on black than on white South Africans.

The second aspect of the US response is an extension of the first: although the United States supported the first ever imposition of UN mandatory sanctions in 1977, following the death in detention of the black consciousness leader, Steve Biko, the same logic applied. In this unique case the Charter could be stretched to include action against South African human rights violations – the arms embargo was imposed for reasons which were avowedly to do with the increasingly repressive nature of the South African regime rather than with any threat to international peace and security in the traditional sense – but action could not be taken against the South African economy.

The mandatory arms embargo allowed the Carter Administration to close some loopholes which had always existed in the original unilateral embargo and had widened in the years since its imposition, and even to go beyond it, for example by banning the export of spare parts such as tyres for police vehicles, but in economic relations the Administration had to rely on exhortation and cooperation with the private sector.

In the event, the Americans warned Pretoria of what they saw as the inevitable consequences of a failure to reform. For this purpose, in certain respects the market served them well: after the Soweto riots commercial banks were for a time reluctant to provide new funds on account of the political risk. Then, following the British and EEC lead, the major corporations agreed to a set of principles on employment practices drawn up by the Reverend Sullivan, a prominent black American who was on the Board of General Motors. Finally, the Administration did not oppose, although it did not itself propose, the passage of legislation, which would have denied EXIM bank cover to American exports to South Africa, had it been sought, which it was not.

Finally, it is worth recalling that the United States always paid attention to African demands for changes in its Southern African policies primarily as a result of broad strategic calculations rather than out of concern for specific human rights abuses. Thus the original decision to impose an arms embargo on South Africa was quite self-consciously taken as part of Kennedy's general policy towards the non-aligned world; it was in this sense of a piece with his support for, and in crucial respects takeover of, the UN peace keeping operation in the Congo, a deliberate attempt to keep the Cold War out of Africa and neutralize Soviet attempts to establish a bridgehead of influence on the continent. Similarly, when Henry Kissinger finally 'discovered' Africa after the Angolan civil war, his energetic pursuit of a negotiated settlement in

Zimbabwe had much more to do with his perception that there was now a danger that the local balance of power would be tilted against Western interests than with any sudden conversion to the principles of majority rule.[16] Moreover, it was an important part of his diplomatic effort to secure South African support for Western diplomacy by tacitly acknowledging South Africa's importance to the Western powers over the long run, an objective diametrically opposed to the Afro-Asian majority at the United Nations.

The Carter Administration attempted to distance itself from Kissinger's realpolitik in Southern Africa. Cyrus Vance explained the policy to the NAACP Convention in July 1977 in the following terms:[17]

> Some have argued that apartheid in South Africa should be ignored for the time being in order to concentrate or achieve progress on Rhodesia and Namibia. Such a policy would be wrong and would not work ... it could mislead the South Africans about our real concerns ... we will welcome and recognise purposive action by South Africa on each of the three issues. But the need is real for progress on all of them. ... If there is no progress our relations will inevitably suffer. We cannot defend a government which is based on a system of racial discrimination and remain true to ourselves.

This attempt to follow a three-barrelled policy failed both in the region and at the United Nations where it was vigorously advanced by Ambassador Andrew Young. In the Zimbabwe negotiations the initiative reverted back to the United Kingdom in 1979, much to the relief of the US Administration which was by then under attack over a wide front of foreign policy issues from an increasingly hostile Congress; and on South Africa the human rights activists within the Administration had to content themselves with the arms embargo and the largely rhetorical gains they had chalked up in the early days of the Administration. The resignation of Andrew Young in July 1979 effectively marked the end of Carter's human rights offensive at the United Nations.

ANTI-COMMUNISM

There is little dispute about the primacy of anti-communism in official American attitudes on human rights. Although amongst recent presidents only Ronald Reagan has gone so far as to challenge the legitimacy of the Yalta settlement (and even then only rhetorically), Americans have generally given bipartisan support to Soviet and East European dissidents and have been prepared, when requested, to offer them political asylum. As we have seen, however, human rights activists have increasingly challenged the way in which anti-communism has been used by the authorities to justify support for dictatorial regimes within the Nato Alliance, in Central and Southern America and indeed throughout the Third World. The accusation is that they habitually adopt double standards. As one radical critic of Reagan's human rights policy has put it: 'The Administration failed to understand that dissidents imprisoned in Romanian psychiatric wards are no different from and are joined to Indian peasants massacred in Guatemala.'[18]

This kind of criticism (where the target is not the Administration's disregard of positive welfare rights but the failure of the government to base its policy consistently on the securing of those rights to life and liberty which Americans themselves take for granted) raises two questions. The first is why it is that the United States governments find it easier to act in the one kind of case than in the other. The second, given that this is so, is what can or should the United States do in relation to human rights abuse in the Third World?

The answer to the first question is no doubt largely that few Americans, even on the right of the Republican Party, seriously believe that the United States can itself change the nature of socialist societies, whereas its influence is still widely (and probably wrongly) held to be decisive over much of the Third World. The paradoxical outcome of this view is to free the government from restraint in dealing with communist regimes, with most of which in any case their ties are fairly restricted, while making it more difficult for them to act coherently in many Third World countries where American interests are often heavily involved and where previous administrations have often compromised their freedom of action by cooperating with the authorities.

The most obvious form of pressure which can be applied against governments which abuse the fundamental human rights of their populations is economic, and it is easier doctrinally and in terms of material interest and popular support to take such measures against communist bloc countries than others as the examples of the sanctions imposed, against the Soviet Union after the invasion of Afghanistan, and Poland after the suppression of Solidarity, illustrate.[19] Such constraints as US governments face in this regard do not derive from domestic opinion, which is generally enthusiastic, but from America's allies who do not share the current US enthusiasm for economic warfare, and from residual considerations of prudence and self-interest within the balance of terror. But, as a rule, human rights agitation in the East–West context can be subsumed within a conception of the national interest which is dominated by security; in other words it becomes merely another instrument in the ideological confrontation of the blocs.

The answer to the second question is more complicated. This is partly because most Third World economies occupy a peripheral position within the 'open' world economy and there is, therefore, always likely to be a domestic lobby against economic sanctions, partly because bipartisan support for a strong human rights policy towards countries about which the American public knows little is seldom available and partly because in the wider strategic context anti-communism rather than respect for human rights is generally held to be the better guarantee of stability where the two are in conflict.

Occasionally, a strong human rights policy will prove to be compatible with anti-communism. In Uganda under Idi Amin, for example, the Carter Administration was able to impose economic sanctions partly because the Ugandan dictator had committed the tactical error not only of massacring his opponents but also of forging a close diplomatic relationship with Moscow.[20] Such cases, however, are relatively rare. President Mobutu of Zaire may not have committed crimes on the scale of Amin but his human rights record is far from clean. But from the beginning he has been Washington's man, and while from time to time he may have flirted with defection to enlarge his own freedom of manoeuvre, he has never exposed himself by committing that ultimate indiscretion. The IMF may attempt to check his notorious mismanagement of Zaire's economy, but this public act of humiliation – the Fund representative is effectively in charge of the Ministry of Finance – is clearly directed at keeping Zaire within the Western sphere of influence; it does not constitute a threat that the West will withdraw support if the regime does not improve its human rights record.

There is, in any case, relatively little that any US government can do, even if it is so disposed, which is likely to make much impact on a determined Third World tyrant. Once the use of sanctions against open market economies has been ruled out the options are seriously narrowed. EXIM bank cover can be withdrawn for businesses which trade with countries whose governments have a bad record; and aid and military cooperation can be either withdrawn or reduced. But those who rule by diktat or arbitrary terror are unlikely to be deterred by rationalistic calculations of marginal advantages. Thus, by placing human rights at the centre of his foreign policy in 1977 without first assessing the weakness of the instruments of influence available to him, President Carter was courting disaster.

The most serious charge that can be levelled at the Carter human rights policy is that it trivialized the fundamental values of Western society. The charge is not that it is pointless to be concerned about the way that foreign governments treat their own citizens, nor even that intervention on behalf of the victims must under all circumstances be ruled out in advance out of respect for the principle of non-interference in the domestic affairs of other states, but that it is counter-productive to preach a universal policy which cannot be implemented consistently. Carter did not invent this policy – he inherited legislation under which the State Department is required to report annually on the status of human rights in countries receiving US aid – but he greatly strengthened it, for example, by appointing an Assistant Secretary of State for Human Rights. Inevitably, since strategic and political commitments in countries such as Saudi Arabia or South Korea could not lightly be set aside, their human rights record received scant attention while the abuses of other unattractive but less important regimes, primarily those in Central and South America, felt the full weight of American disapproval.[21] In these circumstances it was easy for the president's critics at home and abroad to portray the whole human rights policy as humbug.

In support of the policy it may perhaps be argued that it was necessary to overshoot the target in order to sensitize a reluctant executive into taking international demands for human rights, particularly in Latin America, more seriously and as a check to the automatic institutional reflex under which the question of human rights is almost invariably subordinated to anti-communism. But in a region where reform has always been anathema to the ruling oligarchies and where proximity ensures that a policy pursued in relation to one country will inevitably have demonstration effects on its neighbours, the risks were enormous. Indeed, it is possible that even sympathetic historians will conclude that Carter's inconsistencies in the field of human rights contributed as much, if not more, to the current Central American crisis than Reagan's more old-fashioned and one-sided intervention.

Like any other President, Carter was constrained not only by the legacy of the past but by the pressure of events beyond his control and for which he was not prepared. The key event in this regard was the revolution in Nicaragua. By negotiating the Panama Canal Treaties in 1977, and taking the first tentative steps towards normalizing relations with Cuba, he attempted to establish a new basis for US policy in Latin America, without abandoning anti-communism altogether – a move which he was never in a position to contemplate. The unintended consequences of his human rights policy, however, inexorably undermined his efforts. Thus, by successfully forcing a measure of reform on the Guatemalan oligarchy (as the price for continued military assistance) while simultaneously adopting a more equivocal attitude towards the hated Somoza regime in Nicaragua, Carter effectively alienated the political centre in that country forcing it into an accommodation with the Sandinistas. After their successful revolution Carter concentrated his Central American policy on the search for a centrist solution in El Salvador by combining continued pressure for reform with increased support for the military in their repression of left-wing elements.[22] The Guatemalans for their part were anxious not to be caught in the same fork and took their own swift and bloody revenge on their political opponents.

It would be absurd to hold Carter solely responsible for the vicious cycle of political repression and human misery in which the countries of Central America are now caught as a result of these events; but it seems clear also that, like his successor, he must bear a measure of that responsibility.

Reagan has 'tilted' American policy back towards anti-communist regimes in Chile, Guatemala, and before the Falklands War, in Argentina, for example by removing military-related vehicles from the list of munitions whose export to rights-violating countries is forbidden by the Congress, and has intervened actively against left-wing regimes in Nicaragua and Grenada; but he has not abolished the office of the Assistant Secretary of State and he has been forced by public opinion to challenge the means adopted by his predecessor rather than the basic objective of using foreign policy in pursuit of human rights. In relations with right-wing governments, the emphasis has accordingly been on quiet diplomacy and positive engagement although it is far from obvious that this had had any great effect.

The problem with positive engagement – i.e., establishing new ties and continuing existing ones as a basis for influence – is that it is a mirror image of the sanctions policy to which it is preferred. And as with sanctions it is very often a policy designed essentially for home consumption: if the target government refuses to be influenced in the direction of domestic reform there is nothing that the United States can do about it. More generally the problem for any strong human rights policy, whether it is pursued in the full glare of publicity or by quiet diplomacy is that it must combat the strong ties which have developed as a result of military training programmes and the military related trade which tends to follow in their wake. In Latin America such links with the military have a long history but during the 1960s the general policy of favouring the military was reinforced by the widespread perception of them as anti-communist modernizers, a view which has been attributed amongst others to such influential political figures as MacNamara and Rostow. From the evidence accumulated since 1977 it is apparent that, even discounting the CIA, whose activities are predicated on the primacy of anti-communism, cooperation with the military is clearly a difficult habit to break.

THE DOMESTIC SOURCES OF THE AMERICAN HUMAN RIGHTS POLICY

Where the strategic consensus on the primacy of anti-communism has been breached by human rights activists (or at least where they have succeeded in establishing a temporary parity between the two concerns) it has generally been because particular ethnic groups have been able to use the domestic political arena to champion the interests of those with whom they are identified by ties of sentiment abroad. This linking of pressure for *universal* rights with the claims of particular groups for equal treatment is one of the major ironies of US policy in the human rights field.

The reasons for this phenomenon have already been discussed earlier in this chapter; in conclusion, therefore, it is only necessary to re-state the main argument in more specific terms. The underlying explanation for the marriage between universalism and particularism lies in the social composition and broad ideological egalitarianism of the civil rights movement within the United States itself. Carter was the first American president to owe a political debt to black voters. As we have seen this debt was initially discharged, although without any great effect, by his refusal of positive engagement with South Africa. But the blacks, whose new political militancy was now supported by the active caucus of black congressmen in Washington, were only the most numerous of the heterogeneous liberal alliance of civil rights activists and sympathizers. And their debut in the foreign policy debate did not alter the traditional ideological complexion of that debate: egalitarians and libertarians alike have always been reluctant to accept a division between domestic and foreign policy.

Indeed, Henry Kissinger has argued that it was a fortuitous alliance between the representatives of the two ideological traditions in American political life which was largely responsible for frustrating his attempt to fashion what he regarded as a more appropriate foreign policy for a contemporary super power. Once again it was a particular group which struck the fatal blow. The Jewish lobby has not only been spectacularly successful in nurturing the US–Israeli alliance, even where it appeared to operate against other US interests in the Middle East, but in extending it to cover the rights of oppressed Jews everywhere. The Jackson–Vanik amendment to the 1974 Trade Bill which made the granting of most-favoured nation status to the Soviet Union dependent on Soviet agreement to allow the free emigration of Soviet Jews, was the result of a temporary alliance between conservatives and liberals who for different reasons were determined to challenge the imperial presidency. The amendment aimed a deadly blow at Kissinger's 'linkage' policy and not only undermined his conception of détente but set the stage for the successful Congressional onslaught on US policy in Chile, Argentina and Iran as well.[23]

By re-asserting the central role of the ideological debate in the formation of US foreign policy, however, the libertarian anti-communists were bound to win. Carter's policies scarcely survived the war in the Horn of Africa in 1977/8 in which Soviet and Cuban military support to the Ethiopian revolution was of decisive importance, and they crumbled away after the Soviet invasion of Afghanistan in 1979. Anti-communism was now firmly in the ascendant. It is indeed a final irony of US human rights policy that despite the steady flow of Hispanic immigrants across the Rio Grande and despite the fact that it was an Irish–American president who was the first to respond positively to the civil rights movement, neither the Irish–Americans nor the

Latinos have succeeded in breaching the strategic consensus on the primacy of anti-communism. In the former case Irish–American groups have been a thorn in the side of successive British governments, since they represent a major conduit for the financing and arming of the Provisional IRA, but they have never succeeded in persuading the American government to exert significant pressure on their British ally to modify its policies in Ulster; in the latter, President Reagan has been able to head-off liberal opposition to his policies by reasserting the traditional American 'right' to dominate its own immediate neighbourhood in order to contain the Cuban threat, and by playing on the fears of Hispanic as well as other Americans that an uncontrollable influx (he has spoken of the need to stop the potential tide of 'feet' people at its source) would follow a communist takeover of Central America.

One conclusion seems clear from the argument advanced in this chapter. While it is inherently unlikely that American governments will refrain from conceiving of foreign policy in terms divorced from any concern for human rights, it seems equally unlikely that they can either formulate or sustain for long a policy which is both internally coherent and effective. Logically, a strong human rights policy (under which certain standards have an absolute status) could be pursued by either isolationist or imperialist means; it cannot be pursued in a world where trade-offs between competing objectives and interests are the normal coinage of diplomatic life. In practice, however, no modern American government has a choice between either isolation or full-blooded imperialism.

In Africa, Zaire illustrates the general dilemma for American human rights policy which stems from the traditional priority given to anti-communism. The abuse of human rights in that country is only one amongst many signs, material as well as moral, of a bankrupt regime. Yet given the original premise of US support for Mobutu – i.e., as a buffer against radicalism – what is the United States to do? If the Administration does not in the end have the means to enforce reform, and if it cannot get out without inviting a radical anti-American takeover of power, it has only two choices: to look the other way leaving things much as they are or to intervene positively in support of a contender. It is of some interest that the French, whose foreign policy has never been greatly influenced by liberal ideology, have periodically accepted the need for choice which this dilemma poses, for example in Central Africa where they finally deposed their own client Bokassa as a result of his grotesque and persistent violations of human rights. The United States whose foreign policy has never been successfully divorced from its liberal foundations, remains firmly impaled on the horns of this same dilemma.

Notes

1 Jeane Kirkpatrick, 'Human Rights and American Foreign Policy', *Commentary*, November 1981, p. 42.

2 On 20 March 1751 Benjamin Franklin wrote to James Parker that

> it would be a very strange Thing if six Nations of ignorant Savages should be capable of forging a Scheme for such a union, and be able to execute it in such a Manner, as that it has subsisted Aegis, and appears indissoluble; and yet that a like Union should be impracticable for ten or a Dozen English Colonies, to whom it is more necessary, and must be more advantageous; and who cannot be supposed to want an equal Understanding of their Interests.

Quoted in Robert W. Venables, 'Iroquois Environments and "We the people of the United States"', *Gemeinschaft and Gesellschaft in the Apposition of Iroquois, Federal and New York State Sovereignties, American Indian Environments, Ecological Issues in Native American History* (Syracuse University Press, 1980) pp. 81–127.

3 George F. Kennan, *The Cloud of Danger: some current problems of American Foreign Policy* (London, Hutchinson, 1977), chapters 3 and 4.

4 Felix Gilbert, 'The New Diplomacy of the 18th Century', *World Politics*, vol. 4, 1951, pp. 1–38.

5 Garry Wills, *Inventing America, Jefferson's Declaration of Independence* (Doubleday, New York, 1978), chapter 16.

6 Henry Shue, *Basic Rights, Subsistence, Affluence and US Foreign Policy* (Princeton, Princeton University Press, 1980), chapter 6, 'Nationality and Responsibility'.

7 Robert Tucker, *The Inequality of Nations* (New York, 1977).

8 Gordon Connell-Smith, 'The Crisis in Central America, President Reagan's Options', *The World Today*, October 1983, pp. 385–92. See also Tom J. Farer, 'Manage the Revolution?', *Foreign Policy*, Fall 1983, pp. 96–117.

9 US Foreign Policy Objectives, Hearings Before the Committee on Foreign Relations, US Senate, 96th Congress, Second Session (27 March 1980).

10 See Stewart W. Fisher, 'Human Rights in El Salvador and US Foreign Policy', *Human Rights Quarterly*, vol. 4, no. 1, Spring 1982, pp. 1–38.

11 On 23 February 1978, President Carter transmitted to the Senate for its advice and consent four human rights treaties. For a discussion of this initiative, see Richard B. Lillich (ed.), *US Ratification of the Human Rights Treaties With or Without Reservations* (Charlottesville, University of Virginia Press) 1981.

12 See Richard B. Lillich, *International Human Rights – Instruments, a compilation of Treaties, Agreements and Documents of Especial Interest to the United States* (William S. Hein Co., Buffalo, New York, 1983).

13 Quoted in Abraham Yeselson and Anthony Gaglione, 'US Foreign Policy and the United Nations' in Seymour Maxwell Finger (ed.), *US Policy in International Institutions? Defining Reasonable Options in an Unreasonable World* (Boulder, Colorado, Westview Press, 1978), p. 438.

14 GA Resolution 3379 (XXX).

15 For a more detailed discussion of this episode see James Mayall, *Africa, the Cold War and After* (London, Elek, 1971), pp. 177–85.

16 Our efforts have been founded upon one fundamental reality: peace requires a sense of security and security depends upon some form of equilibrium between the great powers. And that equilibrium is impossible unless the United States remains both strong and determined to use its strength when required. This is our historic responsibility, for no other nation has the capacity to act in this way. While constantly seeking opportunities for reconciliation, we need to demonstrate to potential adversaries that co-operation is the only rational alternative. Any other course will encourage the trends it seeks to accommodate; a challenge not met today will tempt far more dangerous crises tomorrow.

Angola, Hearings Before the Subcommittee on African Affairs of the Committee on Foreign Relations, United States Senate, Second Session on US involvement in the Civil War in Angola, January 20, February 3, 4 and 6, 1976. (US Government Printing Office, Washington, DC, 1976.)

17 Excerpts from his speech are reprinted in Finger and Harbert, op. cit., pp. 93–9.

18 Cindy M. Buhl, 'A Disappearing Policy: Human Rights and the Reagan Administration', *Policy Analysis* (Coalition for a New Foreign and Military Policy, October 1981).
19 On US attitudes to economic sanctions see Christopher Hill and James Mayall, *The Sanctions Problem: European and International Perspectives*, EUI Working Paper, No. 59, July 1983.
20 See Judith Miller, 'When Sanctions Worked', *Foreign Policy*, 39, Summer 1980.
21 See Linda B. Millar, 'Morality and Foreign Policy: a Failed Consensus?', *Daedalus*, vol. 109, no. 3, Summer 1980.
22 Fisher, 'Human Rights in El Salvador and US Foreign Policy'.
23 Henry Kissinger, *Years of Upheaval* (New York, 1982).

10 Europe

CHRISTOPHER BREWIN

Within Europe the reception of human rights has two aspects. The more important is the recognition of the duty of governments to secure such rights. Interpretation of that duty is bound to vary widely among countries as different as Sweden and Turkey, East Germany and West Germany, Russia and Spain. The more novel is the attempt by international pressure to protect individuals against abuse by their own governments. There are precedents for the provision of international remedies – the reporting procedures of the International Labour Organization, the protection of minorities in Central Europe, the abolition of the slave trade – but the present development of collective remedies amounts to a new direction in international law, whose implementation has gone furthest in Western Europe.

In diplomatic relations between the states of Western Europe and the Eastern bloc on the one hand and the less industrialized states of the South on the other, the reception of human rights has also led to far-reaching claims of which the following quotation is typical. 'The quality of our relations with others depends on the extent to which Europe is ready to make a serious and concrete effort to integrate the prescriptions of the rights of man and of humanity into the political, military, economic and other relations with the whole international community.'[1]

In terms of East–West relations I shall argue that human rights in post-war Europe fulfils much the same role as the principle of toleration which followed the Thirty Years War in Germany. The Final Act of Helsinki has been well compared with the Treaty of Osnabruck which provided for the protection of the rights of individuals against princes of another belief.[2] Secondly, in regard to what may loosely be categorized as North–South relations, I argue that calls for the protection of others' rights have not led to serious commitments. With a few spectacular exceptions, the states of Western Europe have sheltered behind the argument that sanctions are an ineffective or counter-productive form of leverage in improving or weakening oppressive regimes with which they have commercial, sporting or special diplomatic links.

In contrast with the United States, human rights has been basic but never central to the foreign policies of European governments. The apparent exception of the two Germanies proves the rule in that, while human rights issues have on occasion been central to intra-German relations, this concern has been limited to Central Europe and has not become a central plank of the diplomacy of either German state. It is not possible to even describe all the views, as they have developed over time, of all the governments in Europe. Instead I shall try to concentrate on what they have in common, in all making in various ways the claim that they are protecting in law rights that should be inherent in all human beings independent of any juridical act.

Roots

Among the factors which might explain this development I shall emphasize three: European traditions of philosophy and law, the experience of Hitler's Europe, and American leadership of Western Europe. At a basic level of political culture all Europeans reject slavery, ostracism, exposure of infants and, more recently, the idea that non-Europeans are by nature inferior. More indicative of the novel prestige of human rights is that a writer in an academic review can assert 'Human rights is the dominant political philosophy in the world today.'[3] In 1689 perhaps Europeans felt similarly surprised by Locke's ahistorical thesis that toleration was the chief characteristic mark of the true church, religion being a sphere prior to and immune from the jurisdiction of magistrates. In Europe this separation of the two realms of church and state has provided an important precedent for accepting the humanist notion that there is a sphere independent of the wills of the particular states. More profoundly, the long tradition of Christian belief has prepared the ground for the general acceptance by secular states that individuals are, if not in the image of God, at least ends in themselves. The European reception of this Enlightenment outlook still contains within itself two strands of philosophy which have been separable since the eighteenth century.

The dominant school is that of natural rights, owing much to the Common Law tradition of rights prior to statute. Such rights are necessarily various in their origins and their nature. They may be rights which historically have been universally enjoyed by individuals considered abstractly, or which some positive authority considers ought to be so enjoyed. The characteristic form of expression is a list. Thus the list in the UN Covenant on Economic, Social and Cultural Rights is still sometimes contrasted with the

UN Covenant on Civil and Political Rights as representing different emphases on human rights in Eastern and Western Europe.

The 'list' approach raises difficulties which bring the subject of human rights into disrepute. Competing lists raise the question of overlapping categories. Should the right to form a trade union be regarded as social and economic, or civil and political? A more fundamental difficulty is that the concept of human rights as innate in the human condition can quickly become devalued by arguments which pertain more to civil rights, willed by positive authority, than human rights, which obtain irrespective of the wills of positive authorities. For example to claim that the right of Radio Free Europe not to be jammed is a human right is to claim too much; it is conceivable that men could be free and equal during the period of jamming. However as a civil right this could be given status by the positive agreement of the states concerned in particular circumstances like détente. Lawyers in the Anglo-Saxon tradition try to avoid this problem by subsuming human rights under political rhetoric: in their view claims only become rights when particularized and incorporated into enforceable domestic law. However, the undesirable effect is to assign all power over rights to the politician. To deny that there can be rights inherent in human beings by virtue of their humanity is to allow societies to withdraw all rights from some people if they should so will.

The alternative tradition is that there is only one innate right, freedom, 'independence from the constraint of another's will insofar as it is compatible with the freedom of everyone else in accordance with a universal law'. This Kantian approach simplifies the problem of relevant criteria for those who can accept his unproveable wager that the purpose of human life is to realize a capacity for freedom which logically exists prior to the state. All rights decreed by the civil authority in their domestic or international capacities are to be justified or not by reference to the question whether in their time and place they secure the conditions for realizing this innate freedom better than any practical alternative. Plenty of scope is left for controversy. Not all, for instance, would go as far as Rousseau in his notorious secularization of the Christian maxim that the way to save one's life is to lose it, 'Les clauses du pacte social, bien entendu, se réduisent à une seule, l'aliénation totale de chaque associé avec tous ses droits à toute la communauté.'

These two traditions of European thought are uneasily combined in the Final Act of Helsinki, 'They will promote and encourage the effective exercise of civil, political, economic, social, cultural and other rights and freedoms, all of which derive from the inherent dignity of the human person and are essential for his full and free development.'

A completely different root of the European concern for human rights issues derives from the memory of what Hitler's fascism meant in Europe.

His assertion of his own will as untrammelled by the rights and dignity of others, his disregard even in Germany of the rules of the German army, administration and judiciary, his contempt – reminiscent of classical Greece – for minorities and inferior peoples, have induced in Europeans a correspondingly deliberate emphasis on the need to institutionalize protection of the rights to freedom of individuals, communities and peoples. Another consequence is that Europeans tend to be more distrustful than Americans of fascist regimes in Latin America, Iberia, or Greece.

Secondly the defeat of Hitler in war entailed both a reversal of European patterns of migration as Germans, Jews, Poles and Russians moved from East to West and the imposition by arms of new social, economic and political regimes. The resulting disputes and human misery underlie much of the concern in Central Europe for human rights. The Berlin Wall and the mining of the frontier that divides Europe into East and West symbolize divided families as well as regimes.

A third cause of Western Europe's interest in human rights is that as a bloc it is led by the United States. In particular an unforeseen consequence of the Civil Rights movement in America has been that in the last decade human rights became for the American Presidency the rhetorical equivalent of Woodrow Wilson's 'Democracy' and Franklin Roosevelt's 'Four Freedoms.' European governments have had to take account of this American enthusiasm despite a sceptical awareness that the United States has itself failed to become a party to most multilateral treaties concerning human rights.[4]

Implementation

CONSTITUTIONS

Objective assessment of national performance in human rights, comparable to national economic indices, is not possible. However the prominence of human rights thinking in the immediate post-war years at the political level can be shown by the constitutions of the new liberal states of Western Europe and of the Peoples' Democracies of Eastern Europe. The famous preamble of the French Constitution of 1946 became the model. It revived the sweeping rhetoric of 1776 and 1789 except that it did not stress the right of revolution. Even the East German Constitution of 1949 began, 'Resolved to ensure the freedom and rights of Man ...' which was preferred to the model of the Soviet Constitution of 1936. In West Germany the first two clauses of the first article of the Basic Law neatly repeat the two lines of Western philosophy discussed above,

> The dignity of man is inviolable. To respect and protect it shall be the duty of all state authority.

The German people therefore acknowledges inviolable and inalienable human rights as the basis of every community of peace and justice in the world.

The following basic rights shall bind the legislature, the executive and the judiciary as directly enforceable law.

This emphasis has to be qualified. For example even in theory the stress in East European constitutions is on the unified and supreme power of the state. In this the Polish Constitution is representative: human rights are 'not to be abused for ends contrary to the interests of Poland'. On the Western side the government of West Germany is not alone in its zeal for positive vetting to ensure the ideological conformity of state employees. As the memory of the war recedes, human rights have become less important. The 1958 French Constitution is more authoritarian, especially in its provisions for suspending the rights of citizens in emergency; and the 1968 East German Constitution distances itself from the bourgeois Weimar Constitution as much as from the Reich.

Nevertheless, if one considers the objective possibilities for abuse, the domestic record of European states in safeguarding the rights of citizens and aliens within their jurisdictions has been good, albeit better in Northern than in Southern Europe, Western than Eastern. Moreover the protection of human rights has been developed as societies have changed. Apposite examples might be the developing protection of privacy threatened by computer technologies, or greater care in defining rights of peaceful assembly.[5] Underlying these developments has been a convergence in domestic legal systems. The distinctions between the Romano-Germanic family of law and the Common Law have been blurred by borrowings relevant to our present purpose like the Ombudsman and legal aid. The notion that there are general principles of law in Europe has been boldly promoted by the Community's Court at Luxembourg and by the Court of Human Rights at Strasbourg.

THE EUROPEAN CONVENTION ON HUMAN RIGHTS

The acceptance of general principles is bound up with a guarded and limited reception of a collective European responsibility for the protection of individuals against abuse by their own governments. The scope of the Convention is less extensive than the range now recognized in UN declarations on human rights taken as a whole. The Convention is not an international legal act in the sense of establishing reciprocal rights and duties. Rather it establishes a legal community. Article 1 of the European Convention on Human Rights requires the parties to 'secure to everyone within their jurisdiction the rights and freedoms defined in Section 1 of this Convention.'

How this is done varies from state to state. In Austria it has the status of constitutional law. In France it stands lower than the Constitution but higher than ordinary legislation. In Germany it is incorporated in domestic law. In Britain it has not been enacted and does not have the force of law. Despite this variety, states have agreed to amend their legislation, or acts of their administrative authorities or judgements of their courts at the instance of appointed international authorities – the European Commission on Human Rights, the Strasbourg Court, or the Committee of Ministers. In applying for investigations of the activities of the Greek government in 1969 or of the Turkish government in 1982, the three Scandinavian governments supported by the Netherlands did not have to fulfil the usual requirement of international law by showing any direct involvement of their own nationals. Collective responsibility was a sufficient aegis.

However the Greek case also shows the limits of this collective guarantee. It was up to the Greek authorities whether they cooperated with the investigating sub-commission. When the Greeks withdrew cooperation the sub-commission left, taking its ten proposals for reform with it. The only direct power available to the Committee of Ministers was expulsion from the Council of Europe which the Greeks pre-empted by withdrawal. There was no question of the kind of military intervention to which the Russians had been prepared to resort in defence of their security interests in preserving socialism.

Similarly a major innovation of the Convention has been the provision in Article 25 whereby states may allow that an individual, non-governmental organization, or group of individuals has the right to ask the Commission whether their case is admissible under the terms of the Convention. However the states have retained control of this development should it become embarrassing to them. Acceptance is for short periods of time, renewable only if the state concerned so wills. The gradual acceptance of Article 25 by most states, including France in 1981, was largely due to what Francis Jacobs has called the 'cautious policy of the Commission in its early years'.[6] It consulted the governments in determining whether the stringent criteria of admissibility, such as exhaustion of all domestic remedies, had been fulfilled. Should the case reach the court the individuals concerned do not appear before the Court but assist the Commission in its impartial review in court of the legal issues, including issues which may not have been raised by the applicant. Moreover a political body, the Committee of Ministers, instituted as an alternative route where states would not recognize compulsory judicial settlement, retains its role as an organ of decision as well as execution in that it may judge breaches of the Convention in some cases.

As a result of the Commission's Fabian tactics, the European Convention now has a prestige which makes it potentially 'the nucleus of a European constitution, laying down the fundamental principles of a European public law in the field of human rights'.[7] In its case law the Commission has asserted that interpretation of the Convention may legitimately be based not just on the wording of the Convention and its protocols, or other declarations like the European Social Charter and Code of Social Security, but on a common tradition of constitutional and other law. Some states, for example Sweden in relation to complaints about its labour practices, have even welcomed the involvement of the European Commission and withdrawn obstacles to the Court reaching a decision.

THE EUROPEAN COMMUNITY

The European Community remains a community of merchants and only potentially a community of the rights of man. There is no mention of human rights in the Treaty of Rome. Formally it does not have the ambition of a classic confederation of the kind proposed at de Gaulle's instance by M. Fouchet in November 1961, which aimed to 'contribute thus in the Member-states to the defence of human rights, the fundamental freedoms and democracy'. The Community is not yet a signatory of the European Convention. While the European Commission has recently followed the advice of its legal service and declared itself, like the parliament, willing for the community to accede, there remain considerable legal and procedural difficulties. The ex-President of the court in Luxembourg himself has stressed the incongruity of treating the Community as if it were a sovereign state. Moreover differences between the Member-states in defining economic and social rights make the Council of Ministers reluctant to grasp the nettle.

To the Commission's public regret the growing powers of the Community in legislation and administration are not contained by an adequate framework of clearly defined rights.[8] In general terms 'respect for human rights' was included in the declaration on 'European identity' at the Copenhagen summit in 1973. On 5 April 1977 the political institutions of the Community issued a joint declaration 'that respect for and maintenance of representative democracy and human rights in each member state are essential elements of membership of the European Communities'. This was reinforced in the Council's Declaration on Democracy in April 1978. It remains to be seen whether abuse of human rights could constitute grounds for expulsion in the absence of any provision in the treaties. And in external relations the Commission has conformed with the Council's general resistance to pressures that the Community should require observance of human rights by states to which it makes special concessions.

These pressures have been frequently expressed in resolutions of the European parliament condemning abuses of human rights. The European parliament treats separately human rights within the Community, the province of the Legal Affairs Committee, and human rights in other countries, which are considered first by the Political Affairs Committee and its active Working Group on Human Rights, set up in 1980.

The most successful approach to including human rights questions among Community concerns has been made by the Luxembourg court. In two judgements of 1969 and 1970 it was able to include respect for fundamental rights in the general principles of law, which it has a duty to see are observed in applying the Treaty of Rome. As Community institutions do not enjoy sovereign immunity for their acts and regulations, they could therefore be liable to damages should its work be construed as abuse of human rights.

Politically a collective commitment to securing democracy in Europe seems to have been uppermost in the Community's mixed motives in suspending the Greek application for membership for the duration of junta rule, and for welcoming Spanish and Portuguese applications after the return of democracy. On a more specifically human rights issue, the Community delayed fulfilling its financial protocols in respect of Turkey, apparently out of concern focussed by the treatment of Mr Ecevit the former leader.

From a human rights standpoint, one oddity of the European Community is that it separates the right to work in member-states from the right to vote in member-states. This separation may be part of the explanation for the weakness of the European record in treating migrant workers. A more long-term consequence may be that the settlement of many of the migrants, whose numbers peaked at ten million in the early seventies will, as in the United States, raise questions about the adequacy of the individualist tradition. For permanent minorities the securing of political representation or rights to education, housing or jobs may require legislation framed for named groups rather than abstract individuals.

PRESSURE GROUPS

Another indicator of the European reception of human rights as an issue is the creation of international pressure-groups devoted to this cause. Unlike the long-established International Red Cross, which is specifically Swiss in its composition, the newer non-governmental organizations are not exclusive to any nation. Four examples may serve to show the range of concern. The Human Rights International Documentation System was formally instituted in Strasbourg in 1982. The Rome Institute has done recognized work in enunciating rules of war that help to secure the rights of combatants and non-combatants. Amnesty International works privately in its concern for individuals in jeopardy all over the world. One wing of the European Nuclear Disarmament Movement holds that the development of human rights in Eastern Europe is the condition required if a popular movement in the East is to be imagined as capable of removing its dependence on the USSR simultaneously with independence from the United States in the West. This brings us to human rights as an issue in East–West relations in Europe.

East–West diplomacy

Like the seventeenth-century principle of toleration, human rights in Central Europe is simultaneously part of a continuing propaganda war and a healing philosophy. Basket Three of the Final Act, signed in 1975 by thirty-five states, contains much material for future disputes, some of which have been well aired at the follow-up conferences in Belgrade and Madrid. On the other hand there is the attempt to find in human rights a basis of agreement common to both sides of the European divide. United States emphasis on this issue is paralleled in the Soviet Constitution of 1977 in which rights and duties are promoted to chapters six and seven. Whether or not détente is equivalent to toleration, the Final Act resembles the Treaty of Osnabruck in not fully implementing the new idea that there should be protection in treaty form of a sphere immune from the magistrate's jurisdiction. Its human rights provisions have two separable thrusts, which relate respectively to the German and American provenance of interest in human rights.

From a German standpoint there is immediate humanitarian concern with the treatment of some two million Germans in the USSR, one million in Eastern Europe, and the problems created for families divided by the ugly frontier between the two Germanies. With the possible exception of the Germans in Hungary, all have suffered because they are Germans. There is also the long-term political question of the future of the two Germanies.

Put too simply, the logic of the easing of restrictions on movement is that Germans on both sides of the frontier will think of themselves in the all-German framework of a *Vaterland*. This logic is reinforced in the parallel treatment of intra-German trade as internal, subject to Value Added Tax, and not external, subject to tariffs. This conclusion is not altogether pleasing to the regime in East Germany, whose authority is threatened in proportion as the restrictions it imposed are to be eased. Nor is it pleasing to Germany's neighbours, who have ineradicable memories of German aggression and oppression.

For their part the Americans and their allies were making a major concession in finally accepting the Russian demand for formal recognition of the territorial changes made after World War II. The Americans wanted substantive amelioration of conditions in Central Europe in the hope of weakening Russian influence. The Western emphasis on Helsinki as oriented to the future rather than the past may bc seen as a continuation of Cold War objections to the nature and degree of Russian control. In this sense Helsinki is the continuation of a propaganda war over the East–West division of Europe, simply shifting the battleground from the United Nations to a succession of European cities. Historically both American sponsorship of the UN Declaration of 1948 and Russian objections that its terms did not preclude the reappearance of fascism were framed largely with European conditions in mind. The twinning of the Covenant on Economic, Social and Cultural Rights with the more individualist Covenant on Civil and Political Rights reflected the East–West division. And the UN Committee set up in 1967 to receive reports on human rights violations has a membership whose composition shows the undue weight ascribed to Europeans and their division between East and West. Five West Europeans were appointed, four from Eastern Europe, and only nine from the rest of the world.[9]

One novelty of Helsinki is that broader strata of opinion now involve themselves in this propaganda war. President Carter's personal interest seems to have inspired books by Brezhnev (1980) and British Foreign Secretary Owen (1978). The European states built on the political cooperation machinery of the Community to take the lead, with American acquiescence, in Basket Three negotiations. A variety of groups have with American encouragement been strident in demanding fulfilment of the ambiguous agreements associated with Basket Three. On the other side I have already mentioned the participation of the populists of the Campaign for European Nuclear Disarmament.

The sensitivity of the German problem, and the real possibility of humanitarian gains in Central Europe have made this the one area where the human rights issue has been central to the foreign policies of European governments. The scale of German migration and movement since Helsinki has been attributed to that agreement and the new atmosphere which made it possible. Lest they damage this flexibility on the part of the East European governments the West German government and non-governmental organizations of the stature of the International Commission of Jurists and Amnesty have distanced themselves from the propaganda barrage.[10]

North–South diplomacy

In contrast human rights has not been central to European foreign policy in North–South relations, despite some appearances to the contrary.

Thus on the one hand the constitutions of ex-colonies bear witness to European traditions. In Africa particularly the two lines of European philosophy are easy to trace. Ex-French colonies celebrated their independence with commitments of general principle, often repeating the formulae of 1789. Ex-British colonies tended to enshrine more detailed rights in their constitutions. However no European power has made future relations or future aid specifically conditional on the new states' good behaviour in fulfilling their human rights obligations. In contrast to American conditionality for military aid to Latin America, Europeans regard such measures as insulting and ineffective. The toppling of the Emperor Bokassa or the severing of relations with Amin's Uganda may be dramatic instances of the limits of European toleration of abuses of human rights, but they are exceptional.

In UN terms, the Europeans were disposed to follow American universalist rhetoric in the Charter, the UN Declaration of 1948 and in the long process of agreeing the UN Covenants of 1966. They may have been better disposed to agreeing on implementation procedures than the United States government itself which has been somewhat behindhand in this final stage of its own three-stage programme for an International Bill of Rights.[11] But the Europeans have been much more uncomfortable with the General Assembly's initiatives in the last decade. Resolution 32/130 of 1977 did not reflect European interests in its stress on economic rights against the depredations of Western companies and in the essential priority it accorded to the realization of the New International Economic Order. The right to development suggested by the UN Commission on Human Rights may have evoked sympathy in Scandinavia but more significant of European indifference was the negative response it evoked in Britain and West Germany.

This is not to say that there has been no movement in the European view. In the disputes over trading and sporting links with South Africa, the unanimity in condemning apartheid shows that the sovereignty of the target country is not an insuperable barrier to collective concern. But the interests of the three larger West European countries have pragmatically succeeded in keeping the content of declarations lukewarm. Only Sweden has banned investment in South Africa. Barriers have been more effective in sport than in industry. The Code of Conduct for EEC firms operating in South Africa may provide a precedent for US foreign policy (including human rights) controls over American firms operating in Europe, but in itself it is a weak mechanism of control. The reporting procedure is governmental, fraught with technical and legal obstacles. It appears that only Germany and Britain have dutifully collected information.

The activities of the European Community illustrate both the rhetoric and pragmatism of European concern. On the one hand the powerless parliament has been ready to pass more than seventy resolutions condemning abuses of human rights all over the world. On the other hand, the reports of the Commission are silent on the subject. The Foreign Ministers of the Community, under the procedures for European political cooperation, rejected the parliament's suggestion of an annual report to the European Parliament on the lines of the US State Department's annual report to the US Congress. The Lomé Convention contains no machinery for sanctions against participating states for abuses of human rights.

Conclusion

While it has not been easy to discuss the response of Europe as a whole to human rights, the fact that it has been possible at all is significant. The formulation and reception of the European Convention has provided the nucleus of a European Constitution. But equally the absence of a European Constitution makes the protection of human rights against state governments largely a matter of goodwill among all the states. As the Greek case showed, when protection becomes necessary, it is not effective. The full external protection of the rights of all inhabitants against the national states would require the creation of a European Confederation, a stage not reached in either Western or Eastern Europe. To rely on international law is to rely on the mobilization of sufficient power by interested neighbours. Since 1945 European states have had experience of having their regimes and frontiers externally guaranteed. But as the Russian guarantee of the regimes in Eastern Europe and American support of fascist Spain have shown, it does not follow that the rights of Czechs or Basques will be better protected. While a full-scale change of regime may seriously involve the security interests of powerful neighbours, human rights as such is too dilute an interest to arouse the mobilization requisite for enforcing international law.

The centrality of the human rights issue for Germany is fraught with ambiguity. In view of its non-binding nature, the quantity of legal ink expended on the Helsinki Final Act is extraordinary. It reflects both wide publicity for Principle VII, aimed at distracting opinion from what might otherwise be considered a peace treaty about frontiers and communications, and doubt on states' ability to implement or even agree on its generalities. With regard to the rest of the world, the human rights issue is peripheral and so dominated by considerations of pragmatism that it cannot be claimed that Europeans or their governments display a strong sense of obligation to the victims of abuse.

Notes

1 T. van Boven, 'Allocution à la cérémonie de remise du Prix de la Fondation Louise Weiss 1982'.
2 S. Bastid, 'The Special Significance of the Helsinki Final Act', in T. Buergenthal, ed., *Human Rights, International Law and the Helsinki Accord*, NY, 1977, p. 16.
3 M. Donelan, 'Reason in War' *Review of International Studies*, vol. 8, no. 1, January 1982, p. 57.
4 I. Brownlie, *Basic Documents on Human Rights*, 2nd edn, Oxford, 1981, p. 320.
5 British Institute of Human Rights, *The Right of Peaceful Assembly*, London, 1982.
6 F. Jacobs, *The European Convention on Human Rights*, Oxford, 1975, p. 275.
7 Ibid., p. 277.
8 COM(79)210.
9 A. Robertson, 'The Implementation System.' in L. Henkin, ed., *The International Bill of Rights*, NY, 1981, p. 338.
10 K. Birnbaum, *The Politics of East–West Communication in Europe*, Hants, 1979, p. 26.
11 J. Starke, 'Human Rights and International Law' in E. Kamenka and A. Tay, eds., *Human Rights*, London, 1978, p. 122.

11 The Third World

J. A. FERGUSON*

For an entity so much discussed, the Third World is surprisingly difficult to define. It is certainly a far less homogeneous body than the so-called First and Second Worlds. Perhaps the easiest way to describe it is to say that it encompasses everything outside those two more easily identifiable groups of states. It includes a number of remarkably wealthy countries, others with levels of per capita income approaching those of developed countries and fairly high levels of industrialization, as well as a substantial number of desperately poor, unindustrialized states. It includes a diversity of political and economic systems.

The term probably has most meaning to the states which make up the Third World. Despite their differences, they do share certain characteristics and, more important, certain attitudes. In comparison with developed Western countries, most experience a relative lack of local capital formation and low levels of domestic consumption, high levels of population growth, substantial inequalities in income distribution, low standards of social welfare and education services. Many Third World countries are important resource producers, but most suffer from low levels of industrialization or resource-processing. Few maintain effective, pluralistic political systems based on broad community participation.

The great majority of Third World countries have been colonies. Even amongst those which have been independent for years many have experienced, or believe they have experienced, degrees of quasi-colonialism, usually through forms of economic dependence. Whatever its form, the Third World is united in opposition to colonialism. A second common attitude is the demand for a better deal for Third World countries themselves in the international economic system, normally expressed by the phrase a 'new international economic order'. A third common feature is strong

* The views expressed in this chapter are those of the author, and do not necessarily represent those of the Australian Department of Foreign Affairs.

opposition to racism. The people of the Third World are overwhelmingly non-Caucasian, in contrast to their colonial rulers who, at least in modern times, were invariably Caucasian. Sensitivity about racism is closely connected to sensitivity about colonialism and it has been the Third World countries which have been principally responsible for making racism a major issue in international affairs.[1]

In the Western consciousness, the Third World is where some of the most obvious and well publicised abuses of human rights have taken place in recent years. For their part, it seems to many Third World states that the Western attitude towards their failings in protecting the political rights of individuals is unbalanced and neglects issues of importance to them such as racism, colonialism and the effect of the economic environment on human rights. It is this dichotomy between the attitudes of the West and those of the Third World that I wish to examine. Much of it has been expressed in stimulating intellectual debate which has nevertheless done little to further the welfare of the oppressed. It has been a debate complicated by East–West tensions, often distorted for political purposes. In the process of examining it, I will attempt to suggest appropriate responses to some of the major issues in this debate which might assist towards establishing a more understanding and cooperative attitude between the two sides. I write essentially from a government perspective, which is no doubt circumscribed by political realities to a greater extent than that of non-governmental organizations, but the basic principles are the same. Although the view has been contested, I assume that human rights is a proper subject for consideration in the field of international relations. Given the amount of time spent on it in the international arena, I can hardly conceive that any other view could prevail.

The Third World perspective on human rights issues

The issues of concern to Third World countries can be identified most readily through an examination of recent debates in various international organizations, principally the Third Committee of the General Assembly and the UN Commission on Human Rights. The most important are racism and the associated concern with colonialism, though this is hardly a direct human rights issue; the relationship between human rights and development, which involves also the relationship between civil and political rights and economic, social and cultural rights; concern that established approaches to human rights are based on Western ideals which do not take sufficient account of cultural diversity; the question of selectivity, of particular concern to some Latin American countries, which believe they have been unfairly singled out for criticism; and the broader consideration of how human rights problems should be dealt with.

RACISM, COLONIALISM AND SELF-DETERMINATION

Racism and colonialism have been of prime concern to African countries. Most endured a form of colonialism which at best was benevolently paternal but in which, nevertheless, the black colonial peoples believed they were regarded as inferior. Racism is kept alive as an international issue of importance by the continued practice of apartheid by South Africa and that country's continued occupation of Namibia in defiance of UN resolutions and world opinion. To black Africans, apartheid can only be an abomination, which must command a large part of their attention. Their frustration that no real progress has been achieved towards the removal of a system which institutionalizes the denial of the most basic rights on the basis of race is understandable.

There is, nevertheless, little change in the resolutions adopted year after year on racism and colonialism in international forums and little prospect of change, peaceful or otherwise, in South Africa itself. It has been difficult to identify any further specific action that might effectively be taken. Resolutions condemning apartheid are adopted by substantial majorities. Western abstentions or negative votes are not because of any support for apartheid or colonialism but because of problems caused by the relevant resolutions containing the advocacy of armed struggle, the specific condemnation of Western countries and Israel for maintaining commercial and other links with South Africa, or resolutions equating Zionism and racism.[2] Many Western countries do not have clear positions on the question of armed struggle and the issue of a 'just war' is complicated and not addressed by governments if they can avoid it. Western states are naturally wary of phenomena such as social unrest, subversion and terrorism and are concerned that support for armed struggle in one area would lead them into the impossible position of having to decide on a host of cases in other areas of the world. In the South African context there is also a recognition that armed struggle could well end in a conflagration with unpredictable consequences. In the United Nations these issues are avoided and objection is made to references such as armed struggle, not because of clear opposition to the concept itself, but to the fact that it is called for in a resolution of the United Nations, a body supposedly devoted to the peaceful resolution of conflict.[3] In fact many Western governments recognize that the situation in South Africa will lead to violence. That may not be condoned on principle but it is understood.

Western and Third World governments also have different public points of view on commercial links with South Africa. While the black African attitude in its strictest form is that commercial relations strengthen the forces of repression, many Third World states maintain commercial and other ties with South Africa. So, indeed, do many socialist states. Western states see it as hypocritical, therefore, to condemn their commercial contacts, especially as they do not accept the contention that trade invariably favours the white population at the expense of the black. It is also a reasonable proposition that, should one state suspend its commercial relations with South Africa, its place would quickly be taken by another and it would have achieved nothing but damage to itself. This is interpreted by black Africans as the West putting its own commercial interest before the eradication of apartheid. Most other Third World states pay lip service to that view, but there is little evidence that they are unduly worried by it.[4]

The question of the identification of Zionism and racism has been more difficult. The argument is subjective and, despite the occasional disclaimers, is an attempt to equate Israel with South Africa. It has led Western countries to emphasize that the intrusion of a gratuitous political posture is diverting attention from the real issues. The linking of Zionism to racism is of political importance to Arab nations, but not of great interest to others in the Third World, most having no basis on which to judge the facts and many maintaining diplomatic relations with Israel. Provided the references in resolutions in international forums are not too extreme, however, or are included amongst broader issues, Third World countries will prefer not to break ranks but to support them despite their individual reservations. Western countries, because of their closer relations with Israel, the general Western support for Israel in the context of East–West relations and because they believe the allegations are politically motivated and not sufficiently clear to warrant specific condemnation, have objected more strongly to what they claim has led to the politicization of the racism issue to the detriment of its intention.

The related issue of colonialism, or self-determination as it has been expressed in recent years, is of broader importance to most of the Third World. With the emergence of Zimbabwe and the independence of all but a few remaining colonies, it has largely ceased to be a question of colonialism in its original form, at least as expressed in UN Resolution 1514 (XV) – the 'Declaration on the Granting of Independence to Colonial Countries and Peoples.' While nine Western countries abstained on that resolution, the concept as endorsed in it is now universally accepted and Western countries are no less keen than their former colonies to invoke it when it suits them.

There is, nevertheless, a school of thought in the West that self-determination hardly qualifies as a human right. To Third World countries it is, however, an important collective right. The concept is difficult and the various international instruments that embody it do so in such a direct and authoritative way that it is not at first evident that many of the crucial terms are not adequately defined. In fact, it is still in the process of definition. Its original conception had a political motivation, namely to further the cause of independence movements, and it became accepted in the sense of a right of peoples already within a clearly defined homeland. It was not intended to cover ethnic groups across state borders, often arbitrarily defined, or minorities within existing borders. There are from time to time suggestions that it should, but any use of the concept in this form would be highly disruptive, particularly for Third World states themselves, and is likely to be resisted by them.[5]

Self-determination has, however, taken on new meaning in the sense that the concept has been accepted internationally as applying to cases where the independence of a people, in the sense of a pre-existing state, has been removed or placed in jeopardy by foreign interference. This new idea has been given expression in Resolutions 35/35B of UN GA 35 in 1980 and 36/10 of UN GA 36 in 1981. These were originally intended to cover the situations in Afghanistan and Kampuchea and were thus identified in a number of statements and explanations of vote. There has also been some talk in the West about the concept applying to government by consent, meaning that a population should have the right, through the exercise of some appropriate act, to decide what government it wants.[6] This is in some senses an extension of the concept, embodied in General Assembly Resolution 2625 (XXV),[7] that the political unity of a sovereign state that could not be disrupted by a call for self-determination from internal groups depended on the existence of a government which represented 'the whole people belonging to the territory'. This is obviously a concept with which Western democracies can feel comfortable. On the other hand, while many Third World countries are perhaps attracted by the idea in theory, many would obviously find it difficult in practice. They can be expected to approach it cautiously and it is doubtful if this rather extreme extension of the concept will find much acceptance at the political level.

SELECTIVITY

Although it is of special concern for Latin American countries, the problem of selectivity involves wider implications for the handling of human rights issues, which impinge directly on the relationship between the Third World and the West. In recent sessions of the General Assembly and the Commission on Human Rights, much attention has been given to the failings of authoritarian right-wing military governments of Latin America. Chile, Argentina, Bolivia,

El Salvador, Guatemala, Paraguay and Uruguay have all come in for critical attention. Non-governmental organizations, such as Amnesty International, seem to take a special interest in Latin America. At recent sessions of the General Assembly many governments, mostly from Latin America but also some from outside the region, have complained bitterly that this selectivity ignores flagrant and obvious abuses of human rights in other parts of the world and, in concentrating on the failings of right-wing governments, the excesses of the left, which are at least as bad, have been overlooked. As the US Permanent Representative, Mrs Kirkpatrick, put it in her address to the Third Committee at the 37th session, those countries introducing draft resolutions on situations in Latin America were thus perpetrating 'a double-double standard'. She unleashed her considerable invective against an unnamed Nordic state which had been prominent in promoting resolutions on Guatemala and El Salvador but which, she claimed, was not prepared to take action in respect of Cuba, Nicaragua, the Soviet Union, Kampuchea, Iran, or any one of half a dozen situations in Africa.[8]

This apparent bias, based on political motivation rather than humanitarian concern for individual rights, has led many countries, particularly in the Third World but also in the West, to question the way in which alleged abuses should be handled. There is undoubtedly some truth in the assertion that countries which do not have the protection of powerful blocs or important trading relationships are more vulnerable to condemnation. In the United Nations condemnatory resolutions against South American regimes of the right will normally receive support from the activist Europeans, genuinely concerned about violations, as well as from all the socialist states and their radical Third World allies who will vote on principle against any regime of the right. In the case of Latin America, local political rivalries also come into play. In many cases the facts, where they do not support the political inclinations of the protagonists, are simply ignored. This was the case in respect of the General Assembly Resolution on El Salvador in 1982, which took no account of the positive comments made by the Special Representative appointed by the Commission to investigate human rights in that country, nor of his explanations of the circumstances in which violations of human rights were taking place. There may well be a certain attraction for some Western governments in attacking abuses of human rights in Latin America because the issues are well publicized but the political and commercial consequences usually limited. There are more votes in making a fuss about abuses of rights in Guatemala than in a rarely noticed central African republic, or a country which provides an important market.

It is a reasonable proposition that the unbalanced treatment of human rights should not be used as a pretext for exempting known violations from critical scrutiny. And it is probably true that attention to selected cases in Latin America in the General Assembly has opened the way for the Commission on Human Rights to deal with a considerably wider range of situations. What is worrying, however, is that the politicized approach evident in this selectivity is damaging the traditional Western concern for individual civil and political rights. Many Third World countries, not least those which fear they might find themselves suddenly in the spot-light, are finding more attraction in the collective expression of rights, in which abuses against individuals tend to be lost sight of, and in support for the thesis that economic development is a precondition for the observance of human rights. And it is often pro-Western countries, many struggling to cope with serious social upheaval, which are criticized. At the same time, the denial of the necessary economic conditions to allow the full flowering of human rights is presented as being the result of the Western economic system.

It is also this concern about an appropriate approach to dealing with specific cases which is behind the assertion frequently advanced in the Third World that attitudes to human rights are dependent on social and cultural differences. The problem of selectivity thus goes to the basis of the way in which human rights should be approached internationally and to the differences in approach between Third World countries and the West.

CULTURAL DIVERSITY

The view has been expressed that universal human rights standards cannot be defined but that attitudes depend on cultural and social differences and that, further, if this is not recognized, any human rights policy will be doomed to failure. It has been proposed that, to have any practical import, human rights must reflect the reality of national cultures and not be imposed through artificial instruments negotiated by diplomats often remote from the actualities of their own countries or the voices of Western liberals who want to reform the world in their own image. These sorts of views were put most starkly by the Iranian delegate in the Third Committee at UN GA 37 who argued forcefully that international human rights standards, as exemplified by the Covenants, were derived from Western, Judeo-Christian values and should not be imposed on different cultures.[9] The delegate of Pakistan,[10] while acknowledging that it was necessary to establish common standards, also mentioned the importance of taking cultural and social differences into account.[11] On a more practical note, at that session a large group of Third World states expressed opposition to a West German proposal for the abolition of the death penalty, on the basis of arguments derived from religious and cultural differences.

Eight states (including the East Europeans) abstained on the Universal Declaration on Human Rights because it reflected Western liberal principles; and that at a time when there were far fewer Third World members of the United Nations than now. That the United States would not go along with the Covenants in turn reflected a shift of power away from Western attitudes. As at March 1983, a total of seventy-seven states had become parties to the Covenant on Economic, Social and Cultural Rights and seventy-five to the Covenant on Civil and Political Rights. Thus only half the UN membership accepts them and a number of important Third World states are conspicuous by their absence.[12]

It is, of course, undeniable that certain communities have their own indigenous practices relating to their social order, religion, and relations between individuals. Some societies stress a communal social order in which responsibility to the group is important, in contra-distinction to Western individualism. Cultural mores can be of great importance to certain groups, often constituting the very essence of their group identity. However, while it can be accepted that cultural differences may provide strong reasons for a sympathetic approach to certain aspects of the rights laid down in the Covenants, they do not in themselves provide convincing reasons for invalidating universally accepted norms regarding a range of human rights. Indeed, a good argument can be made for identifying a distinction between universal rights and what might rather be described as cultural modes of behaviour.

Third World countries, including some which might reasonably be expected to regard themselves as culturally distinct, played a leading role in the formulation of the international instruments and, despite the relatively small number of Third World states which are parties to the Covenants, they have been ratified by a representative sample from all regions of the world. Further, the constitutions of many recently independent states contain references to guaranteeing fundamental rights and freedoms in similar terms to those employed in Western constitutions, while their laws are often closely tied to European models. Most regional organizations have elaborated or are in the process of elaborating declarations on human rights which, while sometimes containing some rather self-conscious references to such concepts as collective or communal rights, nevertheless in everyday practice reflect closely the main ideas and principles of the Covenants.

It seems fairly clear, therefore, that although there are obvious differences on issues like marriage customs, religions, social organization, the treatment of women and so on, which constitute a large part of the Covenants, in reality all people subscribe to certain basic universally held ideals. These become obvious when they come into conflict with other groups within the same tradition. Ugandans being persecuted by Idi Amin, for example, did not excuse him on the grounds that he was acting in accordance with some indigenous cultural tradition. The test of cultural relativism is whether a customary law is still held valid by those in the same cultural group who suffer from it. The evidence is heavily in favour of the contention that certain basic rights, such as the right to life, and to freedom from arbitrary physical abuse etc., are held valid across cultural differences.

The real world

This discussion of cultural relativism does, however, raise a central question about how the international instruments should be regarded; about what can be expected of them and how realistic it is to accept them as universal standards for human behaviour. Although they do constitute a body of international law supposedly binding on states which have ratified them, it is one which is clearly far from universally accepted. The instruments are basically exhortatory. They represent an ideal and few countries can meet their exacting standards. While, therefore, they are important guides to behaviour, they must be viewed realistically. It would be unwarranted and simply impractical to base a governmental human rights policy on a call for close observance of all the provisions of the Covenants. Indeed, for many of its provisions to have meaning the Covenant on Civil and Political Rights must be regarded as being based on certain assumptions implying the existence of an ordered society, relatively secure in public order and in which the rule of law is generally respected. How then should it be regarded when such conditions do not apply? Equally, the economic and social Covenant assumes a certain level of development and social and economic infrastructure which does not exist in some Third World states.

Some Western governments regard it as little short of heresy to suggest any tampering with the international instruments. But such an attitude assumes an order and rationality that does not always exist. That does not mean, however, that all human rights are meaningless. What it does mean in a practical sense is that attention should be devoted to those rights which are universally accepted as basic or primary rights, which apply regardless of cultural differences or social order, such as the right to life, and the right to freedom from torture, slavery or summary execution. In the economic and social field, rights essential to human dignity might include a minimum standard of living, to freedom from hunger, to basic education and health care, for instance, though there may be some doubt as to whether these are really human rights, rather than simply laudatory recommendations. It is, in fact, the abuse of these basic rights in particular cases which in practice exercises the international community.

While the validity of the standards embodied in the Covenants can be accepted without difficulty, to attempt to judge Third World countries by them too closely is a somewhat pointless exercise. To talk of the 'sanctity' of the Covenants, as some Western representatives do, must look to most Third World countries as either ignorance of reality or hypocrisy. It is, after all, only fifty years since the most appalling abuses of human rights took place in Europe on a scale that so far no Third World country has been able to match.

It is not, however, the somewhat heated rhetorical atmosphere of the United Nations or the philosophical contemplation of human rights theory that is important. What is at issue are the lives of individual people living in the real world. Much Western criticism of Third World countries in relation to human rights does not take account of realities and misunderstands the nature of human rights abuse. Violations of human rights take place for all sorts of different reasons: where one group revolts against subjugation by another, where there is political or racial turmoil, in some cases as a result of the actions of a bloodthirsty or deranged tyrant, in cases of invasion or occupation, or in the course of civil wars. In many cases, including a number which have received international attention recently, violations have taken place in a climate of general violence in circumstances where levels of education and social responsibility are low and poverty distorts respect for individuals, where law enforcement officers are poorly educated and lowly paid, where corruption is endemic and social and legal systems are weak. Once the spiral of violence starts it is difficult to stop. In some cases in recent years violations have occurred in response to terrorism in societies which have not had institutions strong enough to withstand the assaults made upon them.

It is hardly necessary here to describe the conditions which exist in much of the Third World.[13] One quote from the Brandt Report will suffice: 'In the North, the average person can expect to live more than seventy years; he or she will rarely be hungry, and will be educated at least up to secondary level. In the countries of the South the great majority of people have a life expectancy of closer to fifty years; in the poorest countries one out of every four children dies before the age of five; one-fifth or more of all the people of the South suffer from hunger and malnutrition; fifty percent have no chance to become literate'.

In an interesting statement before the Third Committee in 1982 the delegate of Colombia[14] spoke about the difficulties encountered by developing countries in the struggle for peace and the observance of human rights. For them, the functioning of European models of democracy required enormous effort which those born into an historical and cultural tradition of democratic principles, for whom law was an automatic functioning of institutional machinery, sometimes lost sight of. It was a system requiring a sophisticated approach, education and freedom from hunger. Many Third World countries were struggling to operate such systems as well as deal with major economic and social problems, often under assault by forces intent on fomenting violence.

The extent to which a government can be held responsible for acts which occur within its jurisdiction is an important issue in determining a reasonable approach to human rights. It has been a general Western view that, since the Covenants define the relationship between individuals and their governments, it follows that only governments can be responsible for abuses of human rights. This is an assumption frequently found in Western writings. An example of it was a statement by the Delegate of Ireland before the Third Committee at the 37th Session where he defined human rights as resting principally on the proposition that 'the individual had rights in relation to governmental authority'; and 'human rights violations were committed or permitted by authorities and not by groups or individuals'. Offences not committed by state power were to be regarded as crimes, not violations of human rights.[15]

This seems a reasonable point of view, but it is too restricted and it assumes an ordered government in full control. Its narrow interpretation would mean that many activities currently regarded as breaches of human rights could not be so considered. It suggests that states initiate abuses of human rights, when in fact they frequently occur by default. Clearly, there are some activities committed on the direct authority of the state; such as psychiatric treatment for dissidents, institutionalized torture or arbitrary execution, which are undoubtedly abuses of human rights and for which governments must remain responsible. There are certainly cases where violations of human rights are direct consequences of deliberate government policy, such as in Nazi Germany, or Uganda under Amin, or Kampuchea under Pol Pot. The situation is not so clear, however, when what are normally regarded as crimes are carried out by individuals engaged in the state apparatus. It is unrealistic to say that a robbery committed by an individual policeman is a crime but that the torture of a suspect by an individual policeman acting on his own initiative is a breach of human rights. Both are crimes, in relation to which, governments have a responsibility to take action against the perpetrators. If they do not do so, however, there is no inherent reason why the case of torture should be regarded as a breach of rights and the robbery as something different. The individual rights of the victim have been violated in both cases. More dramatically, the same is true of the activities of death squads. Often these are composed of policemen and soldiers who have decided to take the law into their own hands, sometimes acting without authority from the state, sometimes with its passive complicity. They are able to operate with impunity when the normal forces of law and order cannot cope.[16]

The state has an obligation to protect individuals, not only by refraining from harmful actions itself but by preventing actions intended to undermine the rights of its citizens. Just as the state has an obligation to protect individuals against death squads, so does it have an obligation to protect them against robbery or terrorist attack. In fact there is little difference between the activities of death squads and those of terrorists. Rights apply regardless of whether it is the state or some other entity which denies them. The individual has a responsibility to other individuals in accordance with the law and the state has a responsibility to uphold the law.

Many serious abuses of human rights, however, occur where the system of law and order has broken down, when disciplinary control is lost, when judges and magistrates are unable to function properly, or when individual citizens or the police take the law into their own hands in frustration because they know the legal system will not protect them. To create such a situation is the specific purpose of terrorist activity, as has been clearly set out in the 'Minimanual of the Urban Guerrilla.'[17] If human rights belong to individuals, however, then abuses of individual rights, by whomsoever they are committed, should be condemned. To put all the onus on governments, often struggling against enormous odds including terrorist assault, corruption or poverty is unrealistic and unfair. Many Third World governments which in recent years have been the subject of international condemnation feel aggrieved that failure to apportion the blame fairly has been to weight the dice and provide a propaganda victory for the forces of terror. The readiness of many Western governments to condemn, on the principle that state responsibility should not be diluted, without taking account of the complexities of the problems facing countries where human rights abuses are occurring has been a major reason for Third World disillusionment with human rights procedures.

It cannot be expected, of course, that Western governments should simply give the game away and refuse to take an interest in human rights. What they can be expected to do, however, is to remember their own violent histories and take account of the difficulties for Third World countries in trying to deal with the major social and economic problems confronting them. For a state to interfere in the internal affairs of another state is a serious business. States which have responsibly accepted international instruments on human rights have done so on the assumption that they themselves will be treated responsibly. Governments should therefore be expected to attempt to ascertain the full facts of what are almost invariably complex problems before rushing to judgement. They can employ private representations rather than public condemnation. In the drafting of statements or resolutions on specific cases in international forums there is no reason why helpful formulae more likely to assist in rectifying situations which have given rise to abuses cannot be used instead of condemnation, which is often employed selectively on the basis of short-term political advantage. It should be realized, in the eagerness to support movements to liberate oppressed people, that the liberators are frequently seeking power rather than genuine reform and are often as brutal as those whom Western idealists seek to have them replace. While diplomatic and trade relationships need not be barriers to expressing concern about human rights, they are less likely to be damaged if concern is expressed carefully, responsibly and sensitively and is clearly based on a humanitarian concern for individuals.

Neither should Western attitudes be based on approval or disapproval of the types of governments often found in Third World countries. That different countries have different forms of government is a fact of life that must be accepted. A foreign policy cannot be formulated on the basis of a like or dislike towards different forms of government. Apart from the fact that, in the broad sense, authoritarian regimes curtail certain freedoms treasured by Western democracies, such as the right to vote, there are often perfectly legitimate reasons for military or single party governments in the Third World. Not all are hostile to their citizens and some can even be said to reflect the broad will of the nation. It is what governments do rather than what they are which is of primary importance in the human rights context.

This approach does not, of course, apply only to the West. It applies also to Third World countries themselves, many of which are not averse to throwing stones from their own glass houses.

Human rights and development

The relationship between human rights and development has been a particularly contentious issue between the West and the Third World, the more so because it is closely related to the further divisive issue of the notion of collective as opposed to individual rights.

The Covenant on Economic, Social and Cultural Rights calls on states to do what they can to provide such rights as 'the right of everyone to the opportunity to gain his living by work which he freely chooses or accepts' (Article 6); to 'a decent living for themselves and their families ... safe and healthy working conditions ... rest, leisure and reasonable limitations of working hours and periodic holidays with pay' (Article 7); 'the right of everyone to an adequate standard of living for himself and his family' (Article 11); and 'to free and compulsory primary education' (Article 13).

These are not obligatory rights which states undertake to observe. There must be, indeed, some doubt as to whether there is a right to a decent wage, or to paid holidays and if there is, how the level of a decent wage might be determined. It has nevertheless been accepted in the United Nations that all human rights are indivisible. This has caused a good deal of concern to some Western countries which suspect that the Third World will use its lack of development as an excuse for not observing civil and political rights and, in turn, use human rights as an argument for international economic reform. For their part, many Third World countries believe that, with its emphasis on civil and political rights, the West pays only lip service to the theory of the indivisibility of human rights but is not prepared to acknowledge the effects of under-development or do anything serious to improve the ability of developing countries to observe their economic and social obligations, for example, through a restructuring of the world economy, which would in turn allow the creation of conditions in which civil and political rights had the chance to flourish.

It can hardly be denied, however, that there is less protection for the individual in countries where there is widespread poverty, where the general level of education is low and political institutions, often in rapidly changing societies, are weak. Prison conditions are usually poor; institutionalized corruption denies many the access to genuine legal equality; administrative inefficiency prevents the effective operation of courts and normal avenues of redress for the individual; uneducated police are more likely to commit crimes or employ objectionable practices such as torture.

The issue is further complicated by the realization that, in order to meet its economic and social obligations a government may, wittingly or unwittingly, have to compromise on political rights. One of the first priorities of any government in a poor country is to feed its population, raise its nutritional levels, in some cases even to prevent starvation. Some governments have found it difficult to fulfil their responsibilities to make their economies run efficiently for the ultimate welfare of their people without taking measures which the West considers authoritarian. The crunch often comes when the International Monetary Fund is called in. In order to meet the IMF dictates and stay in power, itself a necessity for carrying out the IMF programmes, governments may have no alternative but to curtail certain civil rights. How should a government, which has raised food prices by removing subsidies at the instigation of the IMF, deal with the resulting riots? It is no answer to say that they should not have got into such a situation in the first place. Frequently, the government spooning out the medicine has inherited its problems.[18]

Developing countries often see these conflicts as being forced upon them by the developed world and the perpetuation of an economic system in which they are vulnerable to rapid fluctuations in commodity prices outside their control, protectionism, and the effects of economic policy decided in Washington, Brussels, London and Tokyo. They are then criticized for not measuring up by those Western countries which, they believe, have contributed to their depressed state. It is not surprising that this feeling has given rise to a tendency on the part of some Third World countries to claim that development must be a prerequisite for the exercise of basic rights and fundamental freedoms. It is a thesis encouraged by the Soviet Union and the Eastern bloc as useful propaganda against the West, with the claim that underdevelopment in the first place is the result of Western capitalist imperialism. It is the predominant motivation behind the notion that the so-called new international economic order is essential for the full observance of human rights and it has been central in promoting the concept of the 'right to development'.

Both these concepts were central to United Nations Resolution 32/130, which has been interpreted by both its supporters and its detractors as an attempt to lay down new principles for the consideration of human rights. It declares the indivisibility and interdependence of human rights and calls for equal attention to be given to economic and social rights and civil and political rights; claims that the realization of the new international economic order is an essential element for the effective promotion of human rights; and speaks of the rights 'of the human person and of peoples'. This resolution was adopted in Committee by 126 in favour, none against and 11 abstentions, all of which were Western states.

It is said by some Western commentators that the resolution represents a dramatic change in emphasis to a stress on economic, social and cultural rights with the result that 'rather than parts of a comprehensive approach ... they have become the sum and substance of the UN's human rights program [so that] ... today in the UN little attention is given to any rights other than economic, social and cultural rights'.[19] Such claims, including that noted here, are exaggerated and usually backed up by selective quotes from the more radical side of the debate. Even some opponents of Resolution 32/130 accept that, today, in many instances civil and political rights are of little meaning in the absence of basic economic, social and cultural rights and the satisfaction of fundamental human needs.[20] In opening the debate on 32/130, Cuba pointed out that it was an attempt to redress the balance because the United Nations had drawn too little on the experiences, personnel and institutions of the developing countries in the field of human rights.[21] It was not advanced as a complete reappraisal and it must be remembered that the resolution was put up specifically as a counter to a Western draft on a High Commissioner for Human Rights which embodied a traditional Western approach to international action on civil and political rights. More recent attempts have been made to consolidate the intention of Resolution 32/130.

Resolution 37/199 of 1982 is a case in point. This resolution was adopted by 113 in favour, 1 against (United States) and 26 abstentions, all Western states. Objections to the resolution were various, but almost all singled out the formulations relating to the new international economic order, to the concept of the 'right to development' included in the resolution and to the suggestion, implicit in the text though explicit in the statements of the co-sponsors (and clear from the original draft) that the rights referred to were to be seen as collective rights, applying to 'peoples' rather than 'individuals'. The intention of a number of the more radical co-sponsors of this resolution was to consolidate the move away from what the Third World sees as the Western stress on civil and political rights towards economic, social and cultural rights and away from an emphasis on the individual nature of human rights towards their collective expression. Both tendencies, of course, are more attractive to countries likely to come under the spot-light for abuses of individual civil rights.

The proposals for a new international economic order cover a variety of issues such as commodity trade, aid, investment, exchange rates, debt relief, food and agriculture, industrialization, transfer of technology and so on. The aim of the proposals is to meet the development needs of the Third World through an increased transfer of resources from the developed countries and preferential treatment for it in international economic decision making. Its rationale is the claim that the external environment, rather than domestic conditions, is the cause of underdevelopment. The basic text for the doctrine is the Declaration on the Establishment of a New International Economic Order, which was adopted by the General Assembly at its sixth special session. It is associated with the Programme of Action on the Establishment of a New International Economic Order and the Charter of Economic Rights and Duties of States.[22]

Without going into the proposal in detail, there are three general criticisms that can be made of the NIEO, namely: that it fails to recognize the degree of interdependence between developed and developing countries; that by concentrating on external factors it obscures the fact that a country's growth is heavily dependent on its own policies and efforts; and that it wrongly assumes that economic advantage obtained by one partner in a transaction is necessarily at the expense of the other. This is not to deny, however, as is pointed out in the Harries Report, that some of the NIEO proposals are politically and economically sound.[23]

Although when first developed the proposals were enunciated in a radical way and couched generally in anti-Western rhetoric, since the mid-70s the objectives of the NIEO have been pursued with greater moderation, emphasizing incremental adjustments and changes in existing arrangements rather than through radical reform. The detailed proposals are rather vague and have been interpreted differently, with different countries selectively drawing on individual elements when they are judged helpful and rejecting or ignoring those which are not. In the ten years since the concept was introduced, the world and general attitudes to the NIEO on the part of both developed and developing countries have changed. As a result of the Brandt Commission report and other studies, the issue of the new international order has been largely subsumed into the discussion of global negotiations and the North/South dialogue.[24]

This, however, does not mean that the original initiative was misplaced. The proposals in fact had the useful result of stimulating a major debate on international economic cooperation, which encouraged a greater determination to work for reform and did much to create the climate for further efforts. Many developing countries, not all radicals, were strongly attached to the NIEO. It is unrealistic to expect them to put the term aside. Claims that it represents a system at odds with the West are exaggerated. As pointed out in the Harries Report,[25] the more moderate proposals would not involve radical change or fundamentally alter the essential character of the present economic system. Further, a strong case has been made through such studies as the Brandt Report that, in the interests of our own prosperity, the West should be more accommodating to the demands of the Third World for a more equitable distribution of economic opportunity.

In the human rights context the term is vague and it is used, as in Resolution 37/199, in the sense that it is a precondition for the 'full' realization of human rights. It is not, except in its most extreme expression, advanced as an excuse for not observing civil obligations at all. To accept it as expressed in the broad terms of the Third Committee, if necessary with some public reservation, would not commit Western states to any special attitude to each and every one of its details. References to the NIEO in the human rights context are not solely motivated by the desire for economic reform but probably just as much by an intention to keep the pressure on developed countries to take into account the economic and social dimension of human rights.

Similar considerations apply to the concept of the 'right to development'. This is also an attempt to express briefly an attitude to the relationship between human rights and development. It has now been enshrined in UN terminology and a Working Group of the Commission on Human Rights is currently engaged on elaborating a clear definition of the concept and of what obligations might flow from it. It has been claimed by some Western countries that, as the concept has not been defined, it should not be accepted. That is an arguable view, but unless the general concept is first accepted in principle it is hard to see how it could ever be amplified. Further, other concepts now considered legitimate rights, such as the right to self-determination, have been developed in similar manner and are in fact still being interpreted and reinterpreted.

A more telling objection has been that it is not possible to speak of such a 'right'. Again, this is an arguable point. But it prejudges, in a pessimistic way, what the concept might entail. If it means that all people should have a right to equal access to the means to allow them to maximize their development, that is a democratic concept to which no capitalist should object. If it is taken to mean that they have a right to be developed, whatever that might mean, with no effort on their part, that would appear to be an absurdity.

The more important element in considering the right to development is whether it should be regarded as an individual or collective right. If it is accepted only as a collective right, as many radical Third World states and the East Europeans would obviously like, it would become an adjunct to the radical interpretation of the NIEO. If the right to development is an exclusive right of 'peoples' or even of states, then the clear implication is that all the obligation falls on the developed world to provide the means whereby the developing countries will become 'developed'. There would be no obligation on developing country governments themselves to meet their individual responsibilities to comply with the provisions of the economic Covenant. In both senses the proposition is absurd.

There need be, however, no objection to a collective right in itself and no reason why the right to development cannot also apply collectively, provided it is not confused with a state right. Human rights, as the expression makes clear, apply to humans. States, clearly, cannot have 'human rights'. The concept of the rights of states is different. Only if collectives or 'peoples' are regarded as groups of individuals with common characteristics does it make sense to talk of human rights collectively. It is only in this way, for instance, that the right to self-determination makes sense. This view was clearly expressed by the Indian delegate in the Third Committee of UN GA 37 when, arguing that an individual could not be denied the right to development, she said that 'society was a conglomeration of individuals'.[26] The Irish delegate at the same session elaborated this by pointing out that collective rights were the rights an individual exercised with the collective. Such a right was that to a national, political or cultural identity.[27] In this context there need be no objection to a right to development as a right pertaining to 'peoples'.

The important point is that it must also be seen as an individual right. If 'peoples' have a right, then so do the individuals that make up the collectivity. This is the way the Covenant on Economic, Social and Cultural Rights is expressed and it is the view accepted by the majority of moderate Third World states.

It is basically because of the importance of this problem of definition that Western countries should not stand aside and adopt a rejectionist attitude to the right to development. That they have largely done so seems to have led to the debacle on this issue at the Commission on Human Rights in early 1985. The concept has come to symbolize the difference in approach to human rights between the developed and the developing countries. In the interests of human rights it is vital that the gap be bridged to prevent a permanent division between the Third World and the West. At UN GA 37 Australia, together with Ireland and Italy, played a prominent role in seeking to bring the two points of view together. Resolution 37/200 on the further promotion and protection of human rights and fundamental freedoms, covered some of the issues also dealt with in Resolution 37/199 but in a manner more acceptable to Western delegations. Its adoption by 81–38–20 was a clear indication that, while recognizing the importance of development to human rights, its central theses, namely that a lack of development cannot exempt a state from its obligations to ensure respect for basic human rights and that human rights are individual possessions, are accepted by the vast middle ground of moderate Third World opinion.[28]

This moderate attitude has been made perfectly clear by many in the Third World. Although countries such as Cuba stress the importance of the community over that of the individual, many Third World spokesmen have accepted the individuality of rights.[29] Likewise, they have accepted that a lack of development does not excuse the protection of individual rights. One of the conclusions of the Seminar on Human Rights, Peace and Development, held in New York in 1981, and accepted by the large number of Third World representatives present, affirmed that 'the absence of peace, or the achievement of development by a people, can not exempt a state from its obligation to ensure respect for the human rights of its nationals'. What Third World countries want is better understanding for their problems and a more balanced approach. A great many support the view advanced during the debate on Resolution 32/130 by the Barbados delegate who spoke of the stress on civil and political rights as ignoring experience and being of limited use for the multitudinous problems of the world; while the contrary stress on economic, social and cultural rights reduced all men to 'economic man' who could only be explained in terms of economics and ignored many other essential facets of life.[30]

There is no reason why Western states cannot accept that there is a far better chance for basic civil and political rights if development (roughly equated with economic and social rights) can be maximized, poverty reduced, education improved and economic and political stability maintained. Without increased development the rapidly growing masses of the Third World will remain condemned to live without the opportunity to exercise many of their recognized rights. There is equally no reason why Third World states cannot accept that a collective expression of rights does not preclude their application to individuals, or excuse the use of psychiatric abuse against dissidents; or that a lack of development justifies the killing of political opponents, institutionalized torture by the state or the deliberate denial of due process.

The West should stop preaching to the Third World about human rights while at the same time doing little to assist them bring about the conditions in which human rights would have a better chance to flourish. On the other hand, however, Third World governments cannot be excused their obligations to provide as best they can for their citizens. It is no excuse to claim that nothing can be done without a new international economic order. A glance at many developing countries around the world is enough to demonstrate that that claim is not true. There is, however, a need for Third World elites to do a lot more to improve conditions in their own societies, to redistribute income and to give the poor a better chance to maximize their own development potential. If the world economic order is unjust so is the local economic order in many Third World countries. If the mass of individuals are denied the opportunity to play a more constructive role in the political, economic and social life of their countries, instability will persist. And with it will persist the conditions in which human rights are abused.

Conclusion

It is evident that the West and the Third World have different perceptions of human rights. There is misunderstanding on both sides. That is not surprising, because they see the world from different perspectives. In fact, the gap is not so wide. A widening of it however, would be to the benefit of neither side nor of the individuals whose rights we are interested in protecting.

There are undoubtedly cases where human rights are blatantly abused by conscious government action, situations which demand attention and condemnation. Indeed, such cases are all too frequently overlooked. Many abuses of human rights in the Third World, however, occur by default. Countries experiencing such situations are not helped by self-righteous criticism from the West, often misinformed or made for domestic political consumption. Whilst it is recognized that an approach to any situation where human rights abuses are taking place will involve a number of conflicting considerations, including domestic pressures and the attitudes of other countries, it is important for Western governments to realise the complexity of human rights situations. If there is a real desire to be helpful these issues must be approached cautiously, sympathetically and from a constructive rather than condemnatory point of view.

The conflict that developing countries often experience between their obligations to make their economies work efficiently and at the same time meet their civil obligations must be squarely faced. Attention should be focused on serious abuses such as institutionalized torture or indiscriminate murder, which cannot be excused on such grounds. There is a good case for greater recourse to individual observers or representatives of the UN Secretary-General, if possible before situations have developed beyond repair. Aid programmes could take into account the desirability of promoting human rights with special training for police or other 'front line' groups. More can be done to elaborate codes of conduct for law enforcement officers or to improve prison conditions. There are good grounds for encouraging human rights institutions at a regional level which can assist in the dissemination of information and can provide a quieter environment for the consideration of problems amongst countries with cultural similarities.

Most importantly, however, the West must be prepared to recognise the link between human rights and development. This is an important issue to all developing countries and is a major cause of polarization. Nevertheless, the differences in approach are not great, at least between the West and the more moderate countries of the Third World, which constitute by far the majority of that group. Almost all support similar notions of democracy and individual liberty. If the West continues to stress the civil and political nature of human rights in a manner which does not give due and reasonable regard to their economic, social and cultural background, the gap between the two groups will widen. While economic and social reforms are necessary in many countries and should be encouraged, strong elements of conservatism must be recognized, including among the peasants whom reform is intended to help. Reform cannot take place overnight and radical reform frequently leads to social dislocation.

Countries of the Third World, too, must attempt to take a non-political view of human rights abuses. Some should look to their own failings before criticizing those of their neighbours. They need also to take a more forthcoming attitude to the West as well and must realise that most Western states, even those with an unfortunate tendency to self-righteousness, are seriously and sincerely motivated in their desire to see a better, more peaceful world. They also need to look more to the economic distress of many of their own people.

There will probably never be a complete consensus on human rights. There are too many vested political interests involved. But a large degree of consensus is possible and a serious and urgent effort must be made to overcome the current differences between the West and the Third World which are harming the cause of individual rights, through sincere, sympathetic and understanding approaches on both sides.

Notes

1 For a useful discussion of the basic features of the Third World, see 'Australia and the Third World – Report of the Committee on Australia's Relations with the Third World'; Chairman, Prof. Owen Harries, Australian Government Publishing Service, Canberra, 1979.

2 UN Resolution 3375 (XXX) in 1975 first equated Zionism with racism. This was a major reason for the failure of the First World Conference to Combat Racism and Racial Discrimination of 1978. At the Second World Conference, which took place at Geneva in August 1983, references to racism and the legitimacy of armed struggle were not included in the Programme of Action for a Second Decade, though Western states abstained on the accompanying Declaration which did contain such references.

3 See, for example, the Australian explanation of vote on Resolution 36/9 of UN GA 36 A/C 3/36/SR.

4 It must, however, be recognized that in recent years pressure in Western countries for forms of commercial sanctions on South Africa have increased, including in the United States. Much of this pressure seems to have resulted from concern that to attack apartheid through limiting sporting contacts has led to an inequitable and apparently hypocritical situation where the burden of such policies has been borne by relatively small groups in the population.

5 Indeed, claims of self-determination have in recent years been frequently advanced in favour of various minority groups within state boundaries, particularly for indigenous peoples. It is not at all clear what is proposed by such claims unless it is to provide minority groups with their own internal 'homelands'. These calls have not been widely accepted.

6 See the Australian statement on item 86 at UN GA 38 (A/C.3/38/SR.5) which suggested that the right to self determination can be exercised by the people in freely choosing the form and manner of their government and in pursuing their economic and social development.

7 The Declaration on the Principles of International Law concerning Friendly Relations between States. The concept is alluded to in Art. 21 of the Universal Declaration of Human Rights, which provides that 'the will of the people shall be the basis of the authority of government'.

8 A/C.3/37/SR.66.

9 A/C.3/37/SR.56.

10 A/C.3/37/SR.40.

11 See also the statement by Saudi Arabia A/C.3/32/SR.43.

12 Of course cultural diversity is not the only reason for the relatively small number of states parties to these instruments. Some states have simply not regarded them as of particular priority, others no doubt do not wish to have their provisions quoted back at them.

13 *North–South: A Programme for Survival*, Pan Books, 1980 and *Inside the Third World*, Paul Harrison, Pelican, 1979, provide accurate descriptions.

14 A/C.3/37/SR.63.

15 A/C.3/37/SR.69.

16 I recognize, of course, that in some cases death squads may actually be directed from the highest authority; Uganda under Amin is a case in point. Recent evidence suggests a high level of complicity at least in the activities of some of the death squads in Argentina during the most recent years of military rule, though it must also be acknowledged that other death squads, from both right and left, were operating before the coup of 1976. But this certainly does not seem always to be the case, as is sometimes suggested by Western human rights activists.

17 This document, an instructional manual for terrorists, by Carlos Marighella, can be found reproduced as an annex to Adelphi Paper No. 79 'Urban Guerrilla Warfare.' Institute of Strategic Studies, London, 1971.

18 This relationship between the IMF and governments seeking access to its funds in times of difficulty has attracted particular attention in recent years as a result of the so-called 'debt crisis' and the resulting debate on IMF 'conditionality'. No-one would deny that countries which run into serious problems have to undertake difficult processes of adjustment. The implications, however, are complex. If IMF conditionality is too severe, not only might it impede future growth but it could also directly affect the viability of the government concerned. The problem needs to be treated with great sensitivity as, by and large, it has been. It is strange, however, that the issue has been largely regarded as an 'economic' issue rather than one with potential implications for human rights.

19 Jack Donnelly, 'Recent Trends in United Nations Human Rights Activity: Description and Polemic' in *International Organisations*. vol. 35, no. 4, Autumn, 1981.

20 Recognized by Donnelly, Ibid.

21 A/C.3/32/SR.43.

22 Respectively, Resolution 3201 (S-VI) of 1 May 1974; Resolution 3202 (S-VI) of 1 May 1974; Resolution 3281 (XXIX) of 12 December 1974.

23 The Declaration and the Programme of Action on the Establishment of a New International Economic Order were adopted by a consensus decision of the General Assembly. The Charter of the Economic Rights and Duties of States (Resolution 3281 (XXIX)) was adopted by the Assembly by a vote of 120–6 with 10 abstentions. In each case there were a large number of reservations expressed. Most of these related to specific provisions of the proposals; in the case of the Charter, concentrating on issues such as foreign investment or the question of state sovereignty over natural resources. In the case of the Declaration and Programme, reservations referred to issues such as sovereignty over natural resources, compensation in cases of nationalization, the establishment of producer associations, etc., in short many of the then controversial North/South issues that have now largely disappeared from the international debate. Even though many Western states voted against or abstained on the Charter, they nevertheless expressed support for the initiative and the basic objectives of the document, described by Canada as the formulation of principles and guidelines to enable the international community to establish and maintain an equitable distribution of the world's wealth. Japan, stating that it was in full agreement with the objectives of the Charter, expressed the hope that efforts would be successful for a universally acceptable solution of the economic and social problems facing all states in an era of growing interdependence. This seems to suggest a clear Western acceptance that there are faults in the international financial system. This has also been recognized by recent Economic Summit meetings. The differences in the current debate have been about how to rectify them. (See *Yearbook of the United Nations*, 1974, vol. 28, Office of Public Information, UN New York, 1977.)

24 Global negotiations have stagnated and the character of the North/South dialogue itself has changed. There has been a concentration on different issues as a result of the international recession, the debt problem and growing levels of protectionism. These have replaced many of the previous elements of the debate, such as discussion on the Common Fund and efforts to even out commodity price fluctuations. Further, the obvious economic successes of some developing countries, which have for the most part followed open, export-oriented policies, have demonstrated conclusively that it is not just the international order which is at fault but also the domestic policies followed by many of the protagonists for an NIEO. The concentration on the NIEO has been replaced by a more constructive emphasis on how the international monetary and trade systems can better operate for the well-being of all nations. From this perspective the NIEO is an interesting historical development. The human rights debate has simply not caught up but this does not mean that the background to the NIEO is less relevant.

25 Harries Report p. 68, see note 1 above.

26 A/C.3/37/SR.40.

27 A/C.3/37/SR.40.

28 At the 38th session of the General Assembly it was possible to bring the two sides closer together and secure the adoption of one resolution (38/124) though even so the United States voted against and thirteen Western delegations abstained, mostly because of the references to the right to development and to the New International Economic Order being described as 'an essential element' for the full enjoyment of human rights.

The attempt by some Western states to seek to deny acceptance of the right to development by delaying study of the concept in the working group established under the CHR seems to have resulted in the Commission, at its 1985 session, agreeing to refer the issue back to the General Assembly.

29 For example Sri Lanka A/C/3/37/SR.40; Colombia A/C.3/37/SR.63; Pakistan A/C.3/32/SR.53 and A/C.3/37/SR.40; Philippines A/C.3/32/SR.49; Mali A/C.3/32/SR.49.

30 A/C.3/32/SR.53.

12 The United Nations

ROBIN CHATTERJIE*

The United Nations is the only worldwide international organization dealing with human rights. There are regional bodies or agreements, for example, the Conference on Security and Cooperation in Europe machinery which resulted from the Helsinki Agreements and which although confined to East–West relations, specifically covers human rights and has a review process; there is the European Convention on Human Rights (which came into force in 1953 under the auspices of the Council of Europe) and which is not only exclusively concerned with human rights, but also provides for individuals to seek redress through its machinery including its court (at present this right of individual petition is accepted by seventeen of the twenty-one member states of the Council of Europe). Other regional human rights machinery includes the Organization of American States (OAS) Convention and Charter, and the newly adopted African Charter on Human Rights drawn up under the auspices of the Organization of African Unity (OAU). These will not be looked at here.

The United Nations Charter

Largely as a result of the appalling violations of fundamental human rights in certain countries immediately before and during World War II, the need to try to protect human rights at least in some measure was recognised when the United Nations came to be set up.[1] Unlike the Covenant of the League of Nations which did not mention human rights, Articles 1.3 and 1.4 of the UN Charter state that it is an objective of the United Nations:

1.3 To achieve international cooperation in solving international problems of an economic, social, cultural or humanitarian character, and in promoting and

* The views expressed in this chapter are those of the author and do not necessarily represent those of the Foreign and Commonwealth Office.

encouraging respect for human rights and for fundamental freedoms for all without distinction as to race, sex, language or religion; and

1.4 To be a centre for harmonizing the actions of all nations to the attainment of these common ends.

Altogether the Charter contains seven specific references to human rights,[2] and two of the main bodies established by the Charter, namely the General Assembly and the Economic and Social Council are specifically charged *inter alia* with promoting respect for human rights. Some states have however tried to qualify the UN's competence in this area by referring to Article 2(7) of the Charter which states 'Nothing contained in the present Charter shall authorise the UN to intervene in matters which are essentially within the domestic jurisdiction of any state ...'

Nearly all the human rights[3] with which the United Nations deals were set out in general terms in the Universal Declaration of Human Rights adopted by the General Assembly in 1948. This Declaration was drafted by the Human Rights Commission, a body which had been set up in 1946 by the Economic and Social Council in accordance with Article 68 of the Charter which requested that commissions be set up 'for the promotion of human rights'.

Although the Declaration was not legally binding (unlike a Covenant or Convention) and was adopted with eight abstentions,[4] it has had great moral force and even legal significance since it provided the framework for future international legislation and was intended as the first step in the formulation of an International Bill of Human Rights. It also inspired much national legislation.[5] Several countries which abstained when the Declaration was adopted called attention either directly or indirectly to the fact that it represented only Western values and patterns of culture. This was true and almost inevitable since even at the end of 1949 there were only fifty-nine member states of the United Nations, among which those with a western tradition and culture clearly predominated. This slight note of discord however was not repeated when the two UN Covenants, one on Civil and Political and the other on Economic, Social and Cultural Rights were adopted unanimously by the General Assembly in 1966. The Declaration, the two Covenants and the Optional Protocol[6] to the Covenant on Civil and Political Rights together constituted the Bill of Human Rights foreshadowed by the Declaration.

The Covenants actually entered into force in 1976 when a sufficient number of states had ratified them. They are legally binding on those states that do ratify them and to date about half the UN membership has done so including the East European countries, the United Kingdom and most other western countries.[7] Both Covenants start with Articles proclaiming the right of peoples to self-determination and then go on to detail a list of mainly individual rights which include, for example: the right to join the trade union of your choice, the right to education, to social security, the right to life, to a fair trial, to liberty of movement, to freedom of thought and religion and the right to peaceful assembly. The extent of these rights and the limits states may impose on their exercise are set out clearly. So, states do, in ratifying the Covenants, accept specific undertakings or obligations, not merely the statements of principle that were contained in the Universal Declaration. It is inevitably not easy to ensure that these obligations are lived up to, but each Covenant has its own separate machinery to monitor implementation by the states concerned. The rights set out in both Covenants also have to be exercised without discrimination as to race, colour, sex, language, religion, political or other opinion, national or social origin, property, birth or other status. It is also specified separately that men and women have an equal right to the enjoyment of these rights.

The Civil and Political Rights Covenant specifies that certain rights it proclaims are so fundamental that no derogation from them may be made even in times of public emergency. These include the right to life, the right not to be tortured; the prohibition on slavery and on imprisonment for failure to fulfil a contract; the right of everyone to equal recognition before the law; and freedom of thought, conscience and religion. It is these rights which are often invoked when human rights issues are raised at the United Nations.

States that have ratified the Civil and Political Rights Covenant elect a body called the Human Rights Committee composed of eighteen experts (traditionally lawyers) who, although nominated by states party to the Covenant, sit in their personal capacity and report to the Economic and Social Council. The Human Rights Committee considers reports which have to be submitted regularly by all states party to the Covenant and may address general comments (or advice) to these states as well as to the Economic and Social Council. The committee which operates by consensus has so far confined itself to establishing a dialogue with the reporting states, asking them for supplementary reports when this is thought necessary. The representatives of the states presenting the initial reports are expected to answer detailed and searching questions about their obligations under the Covenant. The committee has also drawn up some general guidelines on how the reports should be prepared. In this way it has established a high reputation for the professional and objective way in which it performs its task.

The Covenant on Economic, Social and Cultural Rights requires states to take certain measures 'progressively' to ensure that their citizens can enjoy, for example, just and favourable conditions of work, the highest attainable standard of health and education, an adequate standard of living, social security and freedom to join the trade union of their choice. It is worth noting that the 'right' to own property (Article 17 of the Universal Declaration) is not set out in either Covenant.

States that have ratified the Covenant on Economic, Social and Cultural Rights undertake to submit periodic reports to the Economic and Social Council on measures adopted and progress made towards realising these rights. The council has the power to make general recommendations and may promote appropriate international action to assist states party in these fields. The record of the Economic and Social Council has however been unimpressive compared with that of the Human Rights Committee. The council effectively delegates its task to a fifteen man working group of the council, whose consideration of reports has been superficial. The group, composed of governmental representatives rather than independent experts, often with little expertise in the subject, has met for only one session per year compared with the Human Rights Committee's three.

In an effort to improve matters, the 1982 spring session of the Economic and Social Council passed a resolution which, while keeping the group a governmental body, emphasised the need for people of relevant expertise and provided that they should be elected by the Economic and Social Council for a term of three years. This should help the group in its work, although many countries consider the best solution could be a body analogous to the Human Rights Committee.

There has been a tendency among some Western theorists to see the two covenants as containing two different types of rights with civil and political rights being 'essential' rights which are easy for the state to guarantee negatively. This is done by not torturing, by not interfering with thought or religion and by not discriminating before the law. The rights in the Economic and Social Covenant are seen however as vaguer or lesser rights demanding positive action by the state to ensure, for example, an adequate standard of living or education.

Such a distinction is too stark and misleading. Some commentators[8] have argued that satisfying the most basic right, the right to life requires more than merely ensuring people are not being arbitrarily killed. It also implies ensuring access to adequate food to sustain life. This in turn may entail positive moves by government, for example, to prevent one person being deprived of his source of food by another. So the right to life becomes, in effect, an economic and social as well as a civil political right.

The relationship between the rights set out in the covenant is complex and cannot justifiably be described by making one set contingent upon the other. The Marxist view which emphasises the duty of the individual citizen to his country and state presupposes that civil and political rights only have meaning when economic and social rights are realized. Many Third World countries while not necessarily simply accepting a Marxist analysis have tended to emphasise the need to realise economic and social rights which they see as their more pressing problem. Moreover it is then often argued that to fully realise economic and social rights changes are required in the world economic order including the financial institutions. Thus the link is then made with development and with the responsibilities of developed countries to agree to the 'necessary' changes in the world order.

Most Western countries have argued that both sets of rights, civil and political, economic, social and cultural, should be implemented together, that they are 'indivisible' in the sense that you cannot pick and choose which to allow or which to pursue. This approach does permit a necessary flexibility in implementation since by their nature some rights are dynamic (e.g. the right to education) and may need to be implemented 'progressively' over a period of time while others (e.g., freedom of religion) can normally be realised speedily and more easily. It would be misleading however to think that there are clearly drawn lines of interpretation on human rights among different groups of countries. The position is rather that while the expression of human rights in the Covenants is that of the Western individualistic tradition, shared by Europe and the whole American continent, it is not necessarily the language or expression of many African, Asian or Islamic societies. While their values and priorities may not run counter to those expressed in the Covenants, at the same time they may not appear to be adequately covered by them. However, although these countries arrived on the world stage too late effectively to influence the drafting of the UN human rights instruments, they are now actively involved in their interpretation and implementation with the consequent differences of emphasis and priority.

The Optional Protocol

The Optional Protocol to the Covenant on Civil and Political Rights is, as the name suggests, not a compulsory part of that Covenant. Only twenty-eight states have become a party to this Protocol. It enables the Human Rights Committee to consider communications from private individuals who allege that they are the victims of a violation by a state party to the Protocol of any of the rights set forth in the Covenant. Individuals must however have 'exhausted all available domestic remedies'. In many respects, the provisions of the Optional Protocol are similar to those provided in Article 25 of the European Convention which antedates it. Both allow the individual to appeal against the actions or decisions of a state to a judicial or semi-judicial body which is outside the jurisdiction of that state, and show an unprecedented recognition of the rights of the individual in international law.

Human rights and development

In the 1960s while the drafting of the two Covenants was being finalised, a debate was taking place in another field of foreign affairs about the nature of 'development', at least for purposes of the international aid effort. There appears never to have been an agreed international definition of development, but by the 1960s most development specialists agreed that economic growth by itself was not a sufficient definition.

In 1976, the Tripartite World Conference on Employment under the auspices of the International Labour Organization (ILO) adopted what was called a 'basic needs strategy' (BNS) in the form of a Declaration of Principle and a Programme of Action. The concept of a BNS (and the ILO is only one but perhaps the most representative definition) concentrated on the essential needs of the individual, especially of those most in need. It also acknowledged that the satisfaction of 'non-material' needs was vital. It was generally agreed that minimum basic needs consist of food, health, housing, sanitation and education, but participation and self-determination were also considered to be a necessary part of a basic needs strategy. BNS is now regarded with some reservation by many developing countries who prefer to emphasise the need for reform of the world economic order and existing institutions. Nevertheless it still plays a role in development thinking, e.g., in the United Nations and its agencies, in the OECD, and bodies like the World Bank. It is of interest because although the BNS was, and is, an approach to development, not a formulation of human rights standards, the strategy assumed that development necessarily involved an awareness of, and respect for, human rights. One commentator has stated that 'A comparative survey of the provisions of the BNS with those of the International Bill of Human Rights reveals that the objectives of the BNS have much in common with human rights objectives in terms of certain economic and social rights such as those relating to food, health care, housing, clothing and education, and, to a larger extent, to culture. Civil and political rights, on the other hand are only dealt with in so far as they are included in the strategy's concern for participation in decision-making.'[9] It is significant that even if only to this limited extent, human rights are being built into central areas of international action such as development policy.

United Nations human rights machinery

In addition to the two bodies established to monitor the UN Covenants, there are other organs dealing with human rights. The main ones are:

The Third Committee of the General Assembly. The Assembly which meets annually, normally only between September and Christmas, divides into at least six committees all with universal membership, in order to deal more easily with the diverse and complex subjects which come before it. The Third Committee deals with human rights and humanitarian and social affairs.

The Economic and Social Council (Ecosoc) restricted to fifty-four members was established by Article 62 of the UN Charter which also set out its functions and powers: 'The Economic and Social Council may make or initiate studies and reports with respect to international economic, social, cultural, educational, health, and related matters and may make recommendations with respect to any such matters to the General Assembly, to the Members of the United Nations and to the Specialised Agencies concerned. It may make recommendations for the purpose of promoting respect for and observance of, human rights and fundamental freedoms for all. It may prepare draft conventions for submission to the General Assembly, with respect to matters falling within its competence. It may call, in accordance with the rules prescribed by the United Nations, international conferences on matters falling within its competence.' Ecosoc meets twice a year and reports to the General Assembly. The spring session which is held in New York deals mainly with human rights and social affairs; the summer session in Geneva deals largely with economic matters.

The UN *Commission on Human Rights* established by the Economic and Social Council in February 1946 (restricted to forty-three members). The Commission which meets every year for six weeks in February/March in Geneva was set up to prepare recommendations and reports regarding an International Bill of Rights, International Declarations or Conventions on Civil Liberties, the Status of Women, Freedom of Information and similar matters, the Protection of Minorities, the Prevention of Discrimination on the basis of Race, Sex, Language or Religion and any other matter concerning human rights.

The *Sub-Commission on Prevention of Discrimination and Protection of Minorities* (set up by the Human Rights Commission) is not a governmental body since although its members are nominated by governments, they serve as experts in their personal capacities. The Sub-Commission meets for four weeks every summer in Geneva.

Thus there is a regular cycle of UN human rights meetings throughout the year with the General Assembly meeting in the autumn as the body with overall supervisory power, the Human Rights Commission meeting in

February/March and carrying out the more detailed work on human rights and frequently following up instructions given by the Assembly or the Economic and Social Council. The Human Rights Commission is also the body to which the Sub-Commission reports. The Economic and Social Council (spring meeting) receives the report of the Human Rights Commission but it normally has a predominantly procedural role – it receives for example the reports from the two bodies which monitor the UN Covenants. Most initiatives and drafting of texts on human rights matters are therefore usually undertaken at the Human Rights Commission or the General Assembly. Resolutions on human rights questions can come from the Human Rights Commission, the Economic and Social Council or the General Assembly. However, resolutions such as these are not mandatory for the international community (unlike some resolutions of the Security Council) and they only have moral or persuasive authority. If a resolution is adopted by consensus it is more likely to command much authority than one adopted with a large number of abstentions or votes against. There is thus an increasing tendency to strive for consensus since it is believed that the chances of a successful follow-up on questions such as these are thereby increased.

The machinery in practice

There is increasing competition to be elected to bodies like the Human Rights Commission. Moreover, at the 1982 meeting some sixty observer states took their seats, bringing the total attendance to two-thirds of the UN membership. The work of the commission is therefore attracting increased interest. It is also increasing the range of its interests and not dwelling only on South Africa, the Middle East or Latin America. In recent years it has adopted resolutions on Afghanistan and Cambodia and in 1982 and 1983 it adopted human rights resolutions on both Poland and Iran.

Another sign that states are not indifferent to the machinery of human rights is their increasing concern not to be subject to the so-called confidential or '1503 procedure'. This interesting mechanism takes its name from resolution 1503 (XLVIII) adopted by the Economic and Social Council in 1970 which was set up within the UN machinery to examine 'communications' on human rights (letters or case-studies alleging violations) from individuals and non-governmental organizations (NGOs). Unlike the Optional Protocol to the Covenant on Civil and Political Rights, or Article 25 of the European Convention, it is not designed or able to deal with alleged violations of human rights by a state against an individual. Its remit is to consider cases, or even a case, which suggests a 'consistent pattern of gross and reliably attested violations of human rights and fundamental freedoms'.

In 1982, over 27,000 communications relating to 76 countries were received by the UN and 318 replies were received from 41 governments. Those considered *prima facie* to be within the remit of the 1503 procedure are sent to the Sub-Commission where they are considered by a five-man working group and then in plenary. The Sub-Commission decides, by a vote if necessary, whether or not to forward a complaint against a given country to the Human Rights Commission. If it does so, the allegations against that country are examined by a further working group of the Commission which makes a recommendation, for example that the situation should be kept under review, or, if the state concerned agrees, that an *ad hoc* committee of enquiry be appointed or even that discussion should now be concluded. The final decision is taken by the Commission as a whole in conclave, after representatives of the country in question have had an opportunity to present their case and answer questions

It cannot be said that this process is completely objective since the Commission is a body of governmental experts whose voting will reflect, in differing degrees, the interests of their governments. Even some members of the Sub-Commission are not immune to such considerations. The confidential nature of the proceedings is designed to prevent the proceedings and discussions from being disclosed to the public or press. Nevertheless, in recent years the Commission has adopted the practice of listing the names of those countries discussed at the end of its session. Moreover in 1979 the refusal of the then government of Equatorial Guinea to cooperate with the Commission led to the transfer of discussions from the confidential to the public forum. This precedent has given the Commission useful potential leverage with recalcitrant countries. In fact, states are increasingly concerned not to be subject to the 1503 procedure and tend to lobby strenuously if they are due to be considered. While by no means comprehensive, this procedure has in the last few years become increasingly more even-handed and has considered countries from Eastern and Western Europe, Asia, and Africa as well as from Latin America.

The existence of this procedure is significant. Firstly it means that even if other governments do not initiate action no country accused of 'consistent patterns of gross violations' can be sure that it can evade scrutiny as a result of petitions from individuals and NGOs. Secondly the existence of this private procedure has also made it easier to promote public debate, in both the Commission and the Sub-Commission on world wide human rights violations. An umbrella agenda item covering human rights violations throughout the world has been inscribed in both bodies since 1963. Thirdly the practice established under Ecosoc Resolution 1503 marks a decisive advance in the evolution of the Commission's earlier view of its role as illustrated by Ecosoc

Resolution 75(V) of 1947 when it stated 'that it had no power to take any action in regard to any complaints regarding human rights'. The Commission now has some of the characteristics of a quasi-judicial, though not (since it is governmental) independent, body. It may receive complaints, it has procedures for classifying them, and initial preparatory discussions take place in sub-groups before the full discussion takes place confidentially in the Commission in the presence of a representative of the accused country who is invited to answer questions.[10]

The United Nations and South Africa

Together with the Middle East, this is one of the two major questions dominating the United Nations. In the case of South Africa the pursuit of human rights by the international community has gone far beyond the normal parameters of such questions. The legality of the South African government has been questioned, and it has been suggested that the apartheid policy of South Africa represents a threat to international peace and security. Calls for economic and trade sanctions have been made persistently. Calls for action against South Africa and apartheid permeate almost every UN organ. However, although there is consensus at the United Nations that human rights are violated in South Africa, there is disagreement over what policies to adopt to improve matters. Thus, not only can some countries not accept some of the specific calls for action, but also certain of the statements made regarding South Africa, e.g. that it is a colonial situation are in their view inaccurate and unacceptable.

Consequently, although resolutions on South Africa automatically pass, since there is a built-in majority in favour of them, Western countries, because of the language (descriptive or prescriptive), in certain parts of the resolutions, often abstain or vote against. However, Western caution is related to the terms of most of the resolutions rather than implying support for South Africa's policies and practices; western countries do vote for resolutions condemning human rights violations in South Africa if the wording is not in their view extreme. At the 1983 Human Rights Commission a resolution condemning human rights violations in South Africa was supported by all Western countries on the Commission, although some felt it necessary to say, in separate statements, that they could not endorse every point in the resolution.[11]

The reasons why the United Nations as a whole has homed in on South Africa are not difficult to find. The growth in the number of African and Caribbean countries which became independent in the 1960s and subsequently members of the United Nations pushed the issue of apartheid to the forefront of the organization. Then the link was made with the Palestinian question and the Afro-Arab nexus was formed on both these questions. However the main philosophical reason is that the nature of the human rights violations caused by apartheid in South Africa are unique in that they are the product of institutionalized racism. Condemnation of this cuts across all ideological boundaries at the United Nations, and apartheid finds no public apologists there. The divide in the international community is over means rather than ends.

Notwithstanding this divide a mandatory arms embargo was imposed on South Africa in 1977. This was the outcome of a decision of the Security Council and it therefore needed and obtained the support of the five permanent members. However there have been continued calls for trade, economic and financial embargos. Such calls have been resisted, mainly by Western countries who have argued that sanctions were unlikely to be effective and that maintaining contact and dialogue with, and at the same time pressure on, South Africa was more likely to achieve results. Western countries are accused of hypocrisy by those who call for further sanctions and they cite the willingness of the West to use sanctions (though not through the United Nations) in other cases. The calls for stronger UN measures against South Africa stem from a need to be seen to be trying and from the perception many countries have that only by maximizing their demands can they make even limited headway.

The USSR and Eastern Europe

The first public resolution to be passed by a UN Human Rights body on an Eastern European country was the resolution on Poland passed by the Human Rights Commission in 1982, which expressed concern at events there and asked the Secretary-General to prepare a report to the next Commission. There are several reasons why only recently an East European country has been examined in this way. Resolutions on specific countries (apart from South Africa and the Middle East) are a relatively new phenomenon. Many of the most significant attempts to change regimes in Eastern Europe (e.g., the 1953 uprising in East Germany; Soviet invasions of Hungary in 1956 and Czechoslovakia in 1968) and the subsequent oppression, occurred before the United Nations began to look at individual countries. Non-western members of the United Nations have not been keen to get involved in what they consider East–West disputes, and Soviet and East European stress on the 'freedom from interference in domestic affairs' interpretation of article 2(7) of the Charter is not without appeal to many Third World countries.

Moreover the USSR and Eastern Europe have always tried to deflect potential criticism of their observance of civil and political rights by pointing to the economic and social progress that has been made in Eastern Europe and to the liberties proclaimed in the constitutions of East European countries. They have sought to create a mutuality of interest with Third World countries over human rights, by stressing economic and social rights and showing 'solidarity' over the New International Economic Order (NIEO) as well as giving unstinting rhetorical support on South Africa and the Middle East. Eastern Europe is of course a relatively closed system (unlike Latin America), and it has often been difficult to establish the truth or the exact facts of any case. Moreover many countries perceive changes in Eastern Europe as being essentially within the same political system and therefore not so easy to slot into the accepted patterns of human rights violations. The United Nations has been slow to respond unless the status quo is visibly overthrown (as is often the case in Latin America), and is often reluctant to ask questions unless there is a clear international dimension.

The USSR's lack of success in preventing a resolution on Poland in 1982 probably reflected a number of factors. The invasion of Afghanistan had done considerable damage to its image, particularly with Islamic countries. The strength of popular feeling in Poland was evident. And the West confined itself to strong lobbying for a mildly-worded resolution expressing concern rather than condemnation, which was therefore more difficult to oppose.

Latin America: Chile

After the *coup* which overthrew President Allende, Chile was indicted for human rights abuses at the Human Rights Commission, the Economic and Social Council and the General Assembly. In 1975 the Human Rights Commission instituted a special item on Chile, most unusually since apart from the separate items on South Africa and Palestine, all individual countries are raised at the Commission under one general agenda item. Chile's treatment remains separate.

Chile complains of 'victimisation' and indeed, has been singled out for special treatment. Why was this? The glare of world publicity under which a previously well-known South American democracy became a military dictatorship confronted member states at the United Nations with a highly visible new situation. Many had their own reasons for reacting. The East European countries had an obvious reason for denouncing human rights abuses perpetrated by a right-wing dictatorship, particularly one with which they did not have significant trade. Western countries to a lesser degree had similar political reasons, as well as humanitarian ones. At the time the Latin American Group was not well organized or powerful at the United Nations and was in any case divided. It therefore failed to protect Chile, in the way that the Africans and Arabs have tended to protect each other. Chile, like most of Latin America, remained a relatively open society (unlike much of South East Asia, Middle East or Africa). Credible reports therefore trickled out through many sources, for instance the Catholic Church. Well organized and powerful pressure groups sprang up in many Western countries and these had an important influence on the positions taken up by western governments at the United Nations. Significantly the United Nations paid scant attention to countries where such powerful lobbies did not exist (e.g., Cambodia or Equatorial Guinea) even though their human rights situation was worse. Availability of information and the extent of publicity are therefore important elements in determining the level of UN interest.

Black Africa: Uganda

No public resolution was ever adopted condemning the human rights abuses of the Amin regime. The United Kingdom sponsored a resolution on Uganda at the Human Rights Commission in 1977. Canada independently sponsored another. However, after it had been pointed out that a draft resolution was also to be considered by the Commission under the related (confidential) 1503 procedure, it was decided to continue consideration in closed session. A draft resolution on the Protection of Human Rights in Uganda was then placed before the Third Committee of the General Assembly in 1977 but the sponsors did not press it to a vote, on the understanding that the concern expressed therein would be taken into account when the Human Rights Commission resumed consideration of the question again in closed session. Why did the United Nations react in this way? Specific condemnations (except for Israel and South Africa) were still very rare. Chile was the glaring exception. There was also a general sense of Afro-Arab solidarity, especially for recently independent ex-colonial countries. The East European countries remained aloof and domestic pressure groups in Western countries were not as vocal as for Chile. Nor was the flow of information as reliable.

Asia: Cambodia

A similar situation arose in relation to the atrocities committed by the Pol Pot regime in Cambodia. The United Kingdom raised these at the Human Rights Commission in 1979 but the draft resolution was defeated by the combined votes of the Third World and East Europeans.

Bolivia

Lest it be thought that there are no happy endings it is worth looking at the case of Bolivia. The General Assembly in December 1980,[12] asked the Human Rights Commission to review at its next session the human rights situation in Bolivia. Although Bolivia had voted against this resolution at the Assembly, it subsequently cooperated with the Commission. At its meeting in 1981, the Commission adopted a resolution[13] by which it appointed a Special Envoy to make a thorough study of the human rights situation in Bolivia and requested him to report to the Commission in 1982. The Bolivian government was invited to submit material to the Special Envoy and to comment on the contents of his report.

In 1982 the Commission adopted without a vote, a resolution which noted the report of the Special Envoy,[14] in particular his conclusion that since 4 September 1981 there had been an improvement in the situation of human rights in Bolivia. It also welcomed the cooperation extended by the Bolivian government to the Special Envoy, urged the government to take 'further practical measures to implement its stated resolve to ensure full respect for human rights' and decided to extend the mandate of the Special Envoy for a further year.

In 1983, the Commission adopted without a vote a resolution[15] which concluded its consideration of human rights in Bolivia. In the resolution the Commission took note of the Special Envoy's conclusion that 'particularly since 10 October 1982 the constitutional government of Bolivia demonstrated a complete respect for human rights'. It welcomed inter alia the setting up of a national commission to investigate cases of disappearances, and also Bolivia's accession in 1982 to the two International Covenants on Human Rights and the Optional Protocol. This was the first time that the Commission has ended its public consideration of a country in the light of improvements in its human rights situation.

Northern Ireland

Although references have been made in the United Nations to the human rights situation in Northern Ireland no resolution on Northern Ireland has ever been adopted. The last attempt to introduce such a resolution was made by the USSR at the Human Rights Commission in 1980. The draft resolution was tabled, but withdrawn by the USSR before it could be put to the vote when it was realised that it did not enjoy enough support to pass.

New developments

Apart from the individual country resolutions, a more thematic and humanitarian approach is being developed in the United Nations and particularly in the Human Rights Commission. A great deal of work is done on the question of refugees. Prince Sadruddin Aga Khan has produced a study on 'Massive Exoduses'. Other resolutions have commissioned guidelines for states to try and prevent the abuse of psychiatry. A Special Rapporteur has been commissioned to examine what can be done about summary executions; and a working group of experts was established in 1980 on the problem of 'the disappeared'. Such resolutions are generally adopted with very few or no dissenting votes. This was the case with the Working Group on 'Missing and Disappeared Persons' which was set up with the purely humanitarian aims of persuading governments to investigate cases under their jurisdiction, of putting a stop to the practice, and of giving information to relations and families. This group has had its mandate renewed annually by consensus and has had more success than was initially expected. It has persuaded an increasing number of governments to cooperate, and, by its prompt reaction has in some cases undoubtedly saved lives. Furthermore, work continues on exploring the viability of an idea which originated in the 1960s, that of having a High Commissioner for Human Rights, which would enhance the importance of the subject within the United Nations and the possibilities for effective action.

Effectiveness

The effectiveness of international concern about human rights is difficult to measure. It is tempting to say merely that the situation would undoubtedly be worse without it. However the examples given here have provided some concrete illustrations of how concern for human rights is making a difference. There has been increased acceptance over the last thirty years that human rights is a legitimate subject for international concern and discussion. This is reflected in the increased calls for action, which may often be the limit of what the United Nations can do. Much of what happens at the United Nations in this field is rhetoric; but rhetoric should not be scorned. It is rhetoric which produces the awareness and establishes – if only by dint of repetition – the frames of reference within which problems are considered and judgements made. Rhetoric may be a feeble substitute for action but it is often a necessary precursor. It could be argued that the Universal Declaration and the two UN Covenants on Human Rights are in effect examples of rhetoric codified into international law.

The bite that these and other measures have depends, as with national laws, not only on the degree to which they can be enforced but on the degree to which they become norms by which societies live. Probably no form of international concern (except force) could prevent another Amin or Pol Pot. Some countries that can exist on the fringes of the international community may remain impervious to what is said about them at the United Nations and elsewhere. However the increasingly interdependent nature of the world makes it more difficult for countries to be totally impervious to world opinion for any great length of time. Most governments feel under some pressure, often internal, to avoid the shadow that is cast on their respectability or even 'legitimacy' by being in the dock on human rights at the United Nations. This is not to exaggerate the power or influence of the United Nations which as far as human rights are concerned, does not command any divisions. Nevertheless it would be a mistake to dismiss the debates and machinery which the member states of the United Nations have evolved as being of no avail. The United Nations may only be one factor, and rarely a decisive one in the complex of factors which influence governments. But some people do owe their lives or liberty to the effect of UN action. Maybe in time more will.

Notes

1 For a very valuable general treatment of the place of human rights in the contemporary international community, see Karel Vasak (gen. ed., rev. edn. Philip Alston) *The International Dimensions of Human Rights* (2 vols. Westport, Conn., Greenwood Press, for UNESCO, 1982).
2 In the Preamble, and in Articles 1, 13, 55, 62, 68 and 76.
3 The big exception was the right of peoples to self-determination, which was later enshrined in the two UN Covenants.
4 The USSR, the Byelorussian SSR, Czechoslovakia, Poland, the Ukrainian SSR, the Union of South Africa, Saudi Arabia and Yugoslavia.
5 See Egon Schwelb and Philip Alston, 'The Principal Institutions and Other Bodies Founded upon the Charter' in Vasak, *The International Dimensions*, vol. 1, p. 245.
6 Adopted in 1966 by the General Assembly: 66 in favour, 2 against, 38 abstentions.
7 The United States has signed but not ratified the Covenants.
8 Henry Shue, in *Basic Rights: Subsistence, Affluence and US Foreign Policy*, Princeton, 1980..
9 Philip Alston in 'Human Rights and Basic Needs: A Critical Assessment'; *Human Rights Journal*, vol. 12 1979.
10 For a detailed discussion, see Schwelb and Alston, 'The Principal Institutions' pp. 270–77.
11 Human Rights Commission Resolution 1983/9.
12 GA Resolution 35/185.
13 By a roll-call vote, 17:8:6.
14 Human Rights Commission Resolution 1982/33.
15 Human Rights Commission Resolution 1983/33.

13 Non-governmental organizations

J.D. ARMSTRONG

Four general questions are addressed in this chapter:

1. What kinds of non-governmental organizations (NGOs) are concerned with human rights issues and on what specific rights do they concentrate?
2. What is the validity of the claim frequently advanced by NGOs that they play an important, indeed crucial, part in the international protection and promotion of human rights?
3. What has been the role and function of two specific human rights NGOs, Amnesty International and the International Committee of the Red Cross (ICRC), in relation to the issue of political prisoners?
4. How might we assess the work of NGOs? How can we judge their effectiveness in relation to their goals? What are the relative merits of the ICRC approach to promoting human rights through quiet and discreet diplomacy as against the Amnesty approach, with its greater emphasis on exposing the wrongdoings of states?

Organizations and rights

In one sense, all private organizations have some relevance for human rights since they all depend for their existence on certain basic rights, such as freedom of association.[1] Even if we narrow the field to include only those NGOs which are directly involved in the promotion of human rights, the number is still very large, especially if we take a broad definition of human rights to include such claims as the right to an unpolluted environment, as well as various social and economic rights, not to speak of the 'traditional' political and civil rights. All trade unions, all political parties and all ideological or religious organizations, as well as numerous single-purpose bodies like the Campaign for Nuclear Disarmament or the Friends of the Earth, would in some sense qualify for inclusion in a list based on the criterion of direct involvement in the furtherance of human rights.

Hence, drawing up a typology of NGOs in accordance with their relevance to human rights would oversimplify a complex reality. However a number of basic distinctions might prove of some use in fitting NGOs into a framework for analytical purposes, with the proviso that the true picture is considerably more blurred than this scheme of classification might suggest. The first distinction is between those NGOs which are essentially national in their field of operation, such as national trade union federations, and those which in some fundamental sense (e.g., their aims or their membership) are 'international', such as Amnesty or the ICRC. Secondly, one may make a distinction between NGOs which are exclusively concerned with human rights, like the International Commission of Jurists or the International League for Human Rights and those which pursue a wider range of activities, of which the furtherance of human rights is only one, such as the Roman Catholic Church. Thirdly, NGOs may be distinguished according to whether they seek to advance the rights of a single section of society, like the Minority Rights Group or the women's liberation movement, or whether they have a more general concern with human rights as such. Finally, NGOs may be concerned with different kinds of rights. Indeed this last distinction has been the source of an intense debate amongst NGOs themselves, with some activists strongly urging that NGOs should reflect the shift in the United Nations' approach to human rights away from the 'traditional' rights and towards such new demands as the 'right to development' or the 'right to peace'.[2] Others have been equally adamant that political and civil rights, such as freedom from torture and arbitrary arrest and the right to a fair trial, retain their former primacy.[3]

These distinctions enable us to narrow our focus to a point where we may concentrate upon a manageable number of NGOs rather than attempting the impossible task of comparing the thousands of NGOs with some relevance to this issue. I propose here to concentrate on NGOs which meet four conditions. First, they should be concerned with the *international* protection of human rights. This has been an important growth area since 1945 and one which raises several fundamental questions for the present sovereignty-based international society. Secondly, they should be exclusively involved with the protection of human rights. Thirdly, they should be concerned with rights as such rather than the rights of particular sections of society. In the latter case NGOs function essentially as interest groups and hence belong to a distinct analytical category.

It should be noted that these three criteria are not intended to act as a measure of a NGOs importance in the human rights movement. Indeed some NGOs which would be excluded by them might well be of far more significance in terms of real influence and impact on events than others which would be included. For instance, the Roman Catholic Church, omitted because it has other goals and functions, has had a very considerable role to play in pursuit of human rights in Latin America, Eastern Europe, Northern Ireland and elsewhere. The criteria are simply designed to spotlight those NGOs which can unambiguously be termed international non-government organizations for the protection of human rights.

The fourth condition set here for the inclusion of an NGO is more controversial. It is that the principal focus of the NGOs considered should be the civil and political rights emphasized in the West rather than the social, economic, cultural and collective rights that are currently stressed by the Third World majority in the UN General Assembly and also by the Soviet bloc. The reasons for advancing this criterion, which clearly involves taking sides in one of the major controversies in relation to human rights, cannot be treated adequately here but a few basic points may perhaps be made.

The prevailing Third World approach to human rights is encapsulated in the title of a seminar organized by the UN Division of Human Rights in 1980. The title reads 'Effects of the existing unjust international economic order on the economies of the developing countries and the obstacle that this represents for the implementation of human rights and fundamental freedoms.'[4] This is in line with the generally successful attempt since the mid-1970s to shift the emphasis in the work of the United Nations in connection with human rights away from the political and civil rights of the individual to social, economic and cultural rights and the rights of collectivities (especially the Palestinian Arabs and the black majority in South Africa).[5] This movement has been accompanied by two constantly reiterated arguments: first, that in the Third World context, economic development is not only a precondition for any significant progress towards ensuring the rights of the individual but suppression of basic civil and political rights may be justified in its name; secondly, that the creation of a new international economic order has priority over instituting a system for the international protection of human rights. Those human rights NGOs which enjoy consultative status at the United Nations have come under particular pressure since 1975 to tone down their advocacy of civil and political rights.[6]

There is little point in disputing the obvious fact that the basic human needs for food, clothing, shelter and medical care are more fundamental to human existence than are the basic political and civil rights. But the dichotomy between needs and rights that is often implied, if not directly stated, by the General Assembly majority seems to be a false one. As one NGO puts it: 'No persuasive evidence has been advanced that basic civil and political rights need to be derogated or sacrificed to meet essential human needs.'[7] Indeed the reverse argument might equally easily be put: the denial of basic rights might simply be one aspect of an incompetent government's attempt to conceal its failures on the economic front from its own populace and an atmosphere that encourages the free expression of opinions might be more conducive in the long run to economic growth than one in which people were reluctant to say anything that might contradict the current government line.

A second problem with the Third World approach to human rights concerns the extreme difficulty of obtaining any international consensus as to how economic, social and cultural rights should be implemented. Basic civil and political rights can be granted by the act of any sovereign legislature, and indeed such *de jure* rights exist in most countries. They depend for their practical attainment most of all upon an effective, impartial and independent legal system but even this is not a hopelessly unrealistic dream for any country, however poor. In contrast, the achievement of economic rights such as development is far less straightforward. At the most basic level, there is a sharp ideological divergence between those who argue that economic growth depends on free market conditions and those who advocate central planning. There is even less agreement on the specific causes of economic inequalities in the world today. Some talk of an exploitative international economic system, others stress inefficient and corrupt practices in the developing countries themselves. Given such fundamental differences of opinion, it would clearly be impossible to decide which NGOs should be the focus of this study if it were to encompass economic as well as civil and political rights. According to one's ideological perspective, a case could be made for examining relief agencies like OXFAM, national liberation movements in the Third World or political groups working towards the overthrow of the existing political and economic system in the West.

However the main reason for concentrating on political and civil rights is not that they are easier to attain than other rights but that they may be considered 'primary or elementary' rights in the same sense that Hedley Bull talks of 'primary or elementary' goals of society.[8] There are two main reasons for conceiving of civil and political rights in this way. The first relates to one of the philosophical origins of the doctrine of human rights: the assertion that men have natural rights and that any society must be founded in some sense upon a contract between state and individual which defines the limits to the state's arbitrary power. In this sense, political and civil rights are fundamental to any society. Secondly, political and civil rights may subsume or be logically prior to other rights. Rights accorded to collectivities, such as trade unions, are first dependent upon the existence of such individual rights as freedom of speech and freedom to associate. Cultural rights, such as a national minority's right to national self-expression likewise depend upon the prior existence of a right to free speech, legal protection from official harassment, the right to a fair trial etc.

Employing these four criteria for choosing NGOs enables us to arrive at a manageable number of organizations which are directly and exclusively concerned with the protection and/or promotion of basic political and civil rights. Two of these, Amnesty and the ICRC, are considered elsewhere. This section concludes with a brief review of some of the other principal NGOs in this category: the Anti-Slavery Society, the International League for Human Rights (ILHR) and the International Commission of Jurists (ICJ).

Slavery involves the most unambiguous denial of all basic rights and some of the earliest human rights NGOs were concerned with this issue.[9] The Anti-Slavery Society was founded in 1839 and merged in 1909 with the Aborigines Protection Society. Its current aims are defined as: 'to eliminate all forms of slavery and forced labour, to promote the well being of indigenous peoples and to protect human rights in accordance with the Universal Declaration of Human Rights, 1948, especially those of people who have no voice of their own'.[10] It has come increasingly to concentrate upon the rights of aboriginal peoples but retains its earlier concern with slavery, which it sees as persisting today in the thinly disguised forms of debt bondage and serfdom as well as in such practices as child labour, the exploitation of prostitution and the traffic in migrant labour. It was one of three human rights NGOs (together with Amnesty and the ILHR) to be singled out for criticism by the Soviet delegate to the Social Committee of Ecosoc in May 1977:[11] part of a major onslaught during 1977–8 on the consultative status of human rights NGOs at the UN.

The ILHR (originally the International League for the Rights of Man) was founded in 1942 and soon developed a major emphasis on working within the UN system.[12] It had some influence on the drafting of the references to human rights in the UN Charter and also in the adoption by the United Nations of agreed international standards of human rights and the codification of these standards in the various UN Declarations and Covenants of human rights. Like the ICJ, its chief focus has been civil liberties and the rule of law but in the 1950s and 1960s it paid particular attention to the decolonization issue, since it saw the colonial system as involving one of the largest scale violations of basic rights. During the 1970s the ILHR became somewhat disillusioned with the inability of the United Nations to make much impact on human rights, with the increasing tendency of the UN Human Rights Commission to attempt to curtail the consultative role of NGOs and with the general politicization of the human rights issue at the United Nations, with only alleged violations by Israel, South Africa and Chile standing much chance of being discussed.[13] Dissatisfaction with the United

Nations had led the ILHR to attempt to expand its limited role in investigating and following up specific areas of human rights violations that are reported to it.

The ICJ, which was founded in 1952, is an organization of forty lawyers drawn from several countries, with a secretariat in Geneva.[14] Its primary concern is to promote the widest possible acceptance of the rule of law as *the* fundamental principle of any society, and it defines the rule of law in terms of the classic civil rights that developed in Western countries as a counter to arbitrary government. It has consultant status with several international organizations and access to the legal elites of several countries. It holds regular conferences, publishes periodicals and special reports, sends out investigative missions and observes trials. Like the Red Cross, its primary emphasis is on quiet diplomacy rather than publicity, although it does occasionally publicize particular cases of violations of human rights. Of all the human rights NGOs it has probably aroused the most suspicion from communist countries that it is a disguised Western propaganda agency, and, certainly in its earlier years, it did tend to concentrate its attention on violations of human rights in Eastern Europe, although since then it has broadened its focus in a conscious attempt to appear more even-handed. As with all the NGOs being considered here, it has been criticized for having too Western an outlook and during the 1970s it tried to enlarge its concept of the rule of law to encompass social, economic and cultural rights. It also went some way towards an implicit acknowledgement that the principle of the rule of law can operate in a one party state as well as pluralist democracies.

The significance of NGOs

Before looking in detail at the work of the two NGOs selected for fuller scrutiny here, it may be appropriate to ask first the question why NGOs are worth considering at all. Four general arguments might be advanced as to why such organizations are important to the international protection of human rights. First, and most basically, there is the nature of politics as such. Any political process works in practice through the activities of organized groups of one kind or another. Ideas about human rights do not simply emerge from abstract speculation. They arise out of the experience of actual wrongs and the demands relating to the redress of those wrongs that are advanced by organized groups. For example, agitation against slavery in the eighteenth century came first from organized groups like the Quakers, who were prominent in setting up NGOs that were specifically directed against the practice of slavery.

The second reason for regarding the human rights NGOs as significant derives from the fact that the United States is both a particularly open society and an extremely important actor in world politics. Its political system is highly responsive to the activities of various pressure groups which can influence American foreign policy and so have an impact on international relations as a whole. When the Carter administration took up the human rights cause, many NGOs were placed in a unique position to influence the course of American foreign policy – for example in the allocation of aid. Reports by Amnesty and other NGOs were frequently cited as evidence in US Congress debates and the impact of NGOs on international relations reached a peak. Of course, as an open society, the United States also nurtures pressure groups which would prefer *not* to see the human rights records of foreign governments influence American foreign policy where other interests are involved which in their view are overriding. Under President Reagan such groups have been more prominent. But the essential point is that the American political system is responsive to pressure from NGOs and while the United States remains the most important single force in world politics, some of whatever influence NGOs have on the promotion of human rights will be channelled through Washington. It may also be noted that some other governments, such as the Canadian and Swedish, have also actively pursued the human rights cause and they too have worked with the human rights NGOs.

The third argument, and a very popular one with NGOs, is that it is unrealistic to suppose that the rights of an individual *vis-à-vis* the state can be effectively protected either by the state itself or by international governmental organizations (IGOs).[15] Friendly governments will tend to be reluctant to accuse each other of human rights violations where to do so might damage a relationship that was seen as important to strategic or economic interests. Conversely, where an adversary relationship exists between two states, accusations of human rights violations can easily be dismissed on the grounds that they stem from thinly disguised political motives. IGOs, as the creations of states, will inevitably reflect both problems. NGOs also claim that as their members are volunteers, they will work with more commitment than paid officials and as they have similar views and interests, there will be less conflict amongst them than, for example, in a government bureaucracy.[16]

Finally, NGOs claim to have acquired much greater legitimacy in the post-war world than they had previously. This enhanced legitimacy can be demonstrated in several ways, most notably by the extent to which international law now formally acknowledges NGOs. The Covenant of the League of Nations formally recognized the special role of only one NGO, the Red Cross, but Article 71 of the UN Charter provided for NGOs as such to have consultant status with the Economic and Social Council of the United

Nations.[17] The fact that a number of states have tried so vigorously to emasculate this role so far as human rights NGOs are concerned is perhaps some evidence that consultant status at the United Nations is seen by those states as indeed conferring international legitimacy on NGOs. Several regional organizations have similarly granted consultant status to a number of NGOs, including Amnesty. Another indication of legitimacy came in 1977, when a committee of the International Court of Justice suggested that NGOs (as well as states and IGOs) should be enabled to ask the court for advisory opinions relating to human rights and also to submit memoranda to the court.[18] The NGO with by far the highest status in this respect is the ICRC, which is explicitly given various functions to perform by the Geneva Conventions and which can even be said to have a quasi-legislative role inasmuch as it has always played a crucial part in the actual drafting of the Conventions.

Each of these four propositions about the significance of NGOs may have some validity. But a distinction should be drawn between the first two, in which the importance of NGOs is directly related to the nature of the modern state and the extent to which some states promote human rights internationally, and the last two, which downplay the significance of the state in international relations and envisage by implication a 'transnational' world in which the state is merely one out of many actors. This latter perspective reflects a somewhat idealistic view of the realities of world politics adopted by many human rights activists, a view encapsulated by the words of one of their number: 'For me, states are temporary historical accidents, not very useful units for planning the welfare of peoples.'[19] In fact the state is all too durable and what it has given – such as legitimacy – it can also take away. NGOs may well be correct when they assert that the state and inter-state institutions are unlikely to produce an effective international human rights system of their own initiative. But to ignore the reality of state power is equally implausible. The most successful NGOs – like Amnesty and the Red Cross – have learnt to tread a delicate path between accommodating the real world of states and being subservient to it.

Amnesty and the Red Cross

One of the most unequivocal violations of basic rights occurs when an individual is imprisoned for the non-violent expression of his beliefs. This is the issue that Amnesty International has made its own but it is less well known that the ICRC, in addition to its more famous work in connection with the laws of war, has also concerned itself with the problem of political prisoners for many years.[20] But the two organizations have adopted very different approaches to this issue and a comparison of their work raises some fundamental questions about the role of NGOs in the international protection of human rights.

Amnesty was founded in 1961 with the aim of working for the release of 'prisoners of conscience'.[21] These were defined as persons who 'are imprisoned, detained or otherwise physically restricted by reason of their political, religious or other conscientiously held beliefs or by reason of their ethnic origin, sex, colour or language, provided that they have not used or advocated violence!'[22] This last point about violence was to be the origin of several controversies within Amnesty. From very small beginnings the organization grew rapidly, especially during the 1970s. As Martin Ennals, its Secretary General from 1968–80, points out, in 1970 the international budget of Amnesty was £28,741, its International Secretariat employed 19 people and there were 27 national sections with 850 groups between them. In 1980 its budget was close to £2 million, the International Secretariat employed 150 people and there were 39 national sections, subdivided into 2,200 groups. Ennals claimed that this meant that 'In the seventies Amnesty International became the first organization in the field of human rights to collect, systematically and impartially, information about the violation of a very limited number of human rights.'[23]

Amnesty's basic methods are by now well known: it is organized into many small groups who 'adopt', to use Amnesty terminology, a political prisoner and bombard him with letters of support and the authorities with letters demanding his release. As well as working for the release of prisoners, Amnesty also tries to provide some material relief for them and their families and it presses for all political detainees to receive a fair trial. More recently, Amnesty has campaigned against capital punishment and the use of torture or cruel or inhuman punishment in all cases, not just political prisoners. In all of its activities, Amnesty tries to adhere to a few basic guidelines, especially that it should always appear to be non-ideological and impartial. In pursuit of this aim, there are rules that the adoption groups cannot adopt a political prisoner in their own country and that groups should balance the geographical-political nature of their detainees – one is to be from the West, one from the East and one from the Third World.

The question of Amnesty's effectiveness is considered in the next section, which also compares Amnesty's approach with that of the ICRC. But a number of basic issues may appropriately be discussed here. First, Amnesty's stipulation that it should take up only the cases of nonviolent prisoners has caused some strain within the organization as well as encountering criticism from outside it. The paradox that Amnesty is obliged to confront is that the more repressive a regime is (and hence the more likely to need Amnesty's attentions) the greater the probability that violence may be the only means left for those committed to resisting the regime. This issue was sharply posed for Amnesty members in 1964, when there was an internal debate in the organization over whether to continue support for the black South African leader, Nelson Mandela, after he shifted from his earlier position of nonviolence.[24] The dissatisfaction of Amnesty members with Amnesty's decision not to continue treating Mandela as a prisoner of conscience was in large part responsible for Amnesty's expanding its area of activities to include pressure for fair trials and the non-use of torture. The violence issue arose again in a different form in the 1970s when Amnesty took up the case of the Baader-Meinhof terrorists who some Amnesty members claimed were being ill-treated in prison.[25]

A frequent criticism of Amnesty, especially from some of its targets, is that it lacks political balance. It has been suggested that by treating the world as divided into three equal parts so far as human rights violations are concerned, Amnesty, in the effort to appear impartial, is indulging in the hypocrisy of pretending that the assault on basic rights is in reality of identical proportions in its three regions.[26] Some have gone further than this to charge Amnesty with a deliberate left wing bias. For example, an analysis of Amnesty's 1977 Report noted that the space devoted to West Germany was equal to that given over to Cuba, Kampuchea and North Korea combined.[27] This was at a time when the Kampuchean government was being widely accused of committing murder on a genocidal scale. Amnesty itself has pointed to a rather different problem of balance arising out of the practical difficulties of operating in a Third World context:

> Amnesty International could not be identified and harnessed in Third World countries in the same fashion and with the same methods as in the highly developed economies of the West. It was a point of principle to have sections in Asia, Latin America and Africa but the differences of culture, finance, attitude towards non-governmental organizations and means of expression were not always appreciated in either practical or conceptual terms. At the same time it became accepted that there were countries where Amnesty International could develop and countries where it would be impractical.[28]

The charge of deliberate bias is unwarranted, although it is true that some individuals will have been drawn into Amnesty because its specific purpose was seen as according with their left wing ideology. But whether or not an imbalance is built into Amnesty's way of demonstrating impartiality, the only logical alternative would be, as an act of policy, to concentrate on one or two areas, which would be hardly likely to increase Amnesty's credibility in those areas. A more serious problem for Amnesty, which may sometimes produce an appearance of bias, is that it can only act on the basis of reliable information and this may not always be forthcoming in a form acceptable to Amnesty. The 'disporportionality' in its treatment of West Germany and Kampuchea largely stemmed from the difficulty of obtaining information that satisfied its own rigorous standards, rather than from any pro-Kampuchean sentiments in the organization.

A final problem is that Amnesty may have been most effective in its earliest days when governments were perhaps less aware that the flood of letters they received on behalf of certain prisoners originated from an Amnesty campaign. Familiarity may since have bred a degree of contempt. Most of the violators of human rights have now learnt to pay some attention to public relations but often their concern has not extended beyond this. A former political prisoner addressing an Amnesty meeting at Birmingham University in 1982 tells a story that indicates how well some governments may have learnt to play the new game of demonstrating their reformed characters to Washington and the NGOs. She claims that one week before the arrival of an Amnesty mission in 1975, the inmates of her prison (in the Philippines) were approached by important officials who promised their release if they did not give evidence to the mission. Most refused and were harshly treated after the mission left. Before it arrived, there was a considerable improvement in prison conditions but these deteriorated sharply when the mission departed.[29]

Where Amnesty operates in part by publicising and making enough noise about political prisoners to embarrass governments into releasing them, the ICRC has adopted a completely different approach. It was founded in 1863 by a group of private Swiss citizens and it remains an exclusively Swiss organization – a source of some criticism in recent years.[30] The ICRC is one of three wings of the Red Cross movement and it should be noted that these wings are independent of, and sometimes work at cross purposes with, each other.[31] The other two wings are the national Red Cross societies, which often cooperate closely with their own governments, and the League of Red Cross Societies, which is the federation of the national societies.

The traditional function of the ICRC is, of course, in relation to the laws of war, which it has played a significant part in drawing up. It has the roles of monitoring the treatment of prisoners of war to ensure that it is in conformity with international humanitarian standards and of providing material assistance in time of war. As part of this responsibility it has the unique right under international law of access to prisoners of war and it is a development of this right that has led to the ICRC's involvement with political prisoners.

The ICRC's first visit to political detainees came about accidentally after the Russian revolution, when an ICRC delegate visited a Russian hospital ward containing not only prisoners of war but also some Russian political detainees.[32] Its first initiative that was purely on behalf of political detainees came in 1919, in the aftermath of the Hungarian revolution.[33] It received a quasi-legal basis for intervening in internal conflicts from resolutions adopted by the International Red Cross Conference (which included states as well as the ICRC and the national societies) which urged the ICRC to aid the victims of 'social and revolutionary disturbances'.[34] Provision for ICRC involvement in internal strife was written into its 1928 Statutes.[35] But between the wars the ICRC only engaged in occasional initiatives in this area: the real growth took place after World War II since which time the ICRC has visited more than 300,000 detainees in over 70 countries in situations not covered by the Geneva Conventions.[36]

The expansion has not just been in numbers but in terms of the range of situations in which the ICRC has sought the right of access to political prisoners. The *raison d'être* of the ICRC has always been to work for the maintenance of minimum humanitarian standards in wartime. After 1945 there was a great increase in internal conflicts, especially arising out of the process of decolonization. If hostilities in such conflicts reached a high degree of intensity, the ICRC had the right to offer its services under Article 3 of the Geneva Conventions of 1949 but very many situations were occurring in which the ICRC could not claim this right although a clear danger of inhumane treatment of detainees existed. Often such cases did not even involve armed conflict as such between a government and a disaffected group, so the ICRC's right of access was legally dubious as well as carrying potentially disturbing implications for governments. It might, for instance, be seen raising the status of a group of opponents of a government by according it some degree of legal status. Yet as early as 1955, a Commission of ICRC experts appointed to consider such questions decided that: 'It does indeed appear consistent with the interests of humanity as well as with the standards of civilization that the humanitarian safeguards should be applied to persons at strife with their own government on political or social grounds.'[37]

The situations outside the Conventions in which the ICRC felt justified in offering its protection were termed 'internal disturbances and tensions'. In 1970 the ICRC attempted to define these terms more precisely but ended up with a very broad definition, especially of 'internal tension', which was said to exist 'when, without internal disturbance, force is used as a preventive measure to maintain law and order'.[38] The ICRC's Annual Report of 1978 spelt out the sorts of individuals encompassed by this definition: 'A general characteristic of internal disturbances and tensions is the imprisonment of certain categories of people by the authorities. These people all have this in common: their acts, their words or their writings are considered, by the authorities, to be such an opposition to the existing political system that they must be punished and deprived of their liberty.'[39]

The ICRC's rationale for its ever increasing involvement in ensuring humane treatment for political prisoners is interesting. Its starting point is that traditional distinctions between internal and international conflict have become blurred and are no longer appropriate:

> The fact is that, in a world in a state of almost permanent revolution, it is now becoming increasingly difficult to distinguish where the struggle for change in the social order has gradually shifted from the national to the international level, from internal to international conflict. The political prisoner is often a professional revolutionary engaged in a transnational civil war. Even where he is but the innocent victim of his government's arbitrary action, he willy-nilly plays a passive part in a larger battle.[40]

So the ICRC could legitimately interest itself in a wider range of situations than those involving conventional interstate warfare. But it was not to comment upon the reasons for a prisoner's detention or press for his release. It stood for the 'international interest': the few matters on which there could be genuine agreement among all states; but in its view 'unanimity is achieved only on the lowest common denominator ...'[41] And this certainly did not encompass questions into which ideology entered, such as the reasons for the detention of political prisoners or even the definition of the term 'political prisoner'. What was important so far as the ICRC was concerned was that there was a tendency in some countries to deal particularly ruthlessly with opponents of the government held in prison. Hence the ICRC should be concerned solely with the conditions of detention and its efforts have consistently aimed at the observance by states of certain minimum rules to ensure the humane treatment of political prisoners.[42]

The ICRC's operational principles in this work are derived from its traditional approach to prisoners of war and from its determination to avoid political controversy. It sees its function as the pragmatic one of bringing material relief and some measure of protection against inhumane treatment, not as asking awkward questions about the fact of detention. It regards its special relationship with governments as due in large part to its own insistence on discretion and not publishing its findings, which are sent confidentially to the government concerned. In general it stresses cooperation with governments rather than opposition to them. Its underlying philosophy is summed up by what one writer terms the 'one more blanket' theory: it believes it will have achieved its purpose if it can succeed in bringing one more blanket (or some additional material relief) to one prisoner.[43] This approach has inevitably brought it some criticism on the grounds that it avoids confronting the larger moral questions concerning political prisoners. Some would go so far as to suggest that the ICRC's determination to 'see no evil' may actually serve to underpin the unjust governments and political systems that created the need for its services in the first place.[44]

The ICRC would maintain that it owes its unique position in both international law and international practice to four factors. First, and most obviously, it has existed longer than the other NGOs and has built up its position over a number of years. Secondly, its membership is all Swiss, and so it is able to benefit from the traditional neutrality of a country which has no quarrels with anyone. Thirdly, it is obsessively discreet and fourthly it stresses cooperation with governments rather than confrontation. Its critics regard these very qualities as its major drawbacks, at least so far as its work with political prisoners is concerned. Because it is exclusively Swiss it is thought by some to have a narrow and somewhat elitist outlook. Moreover, to some in the Third World the image of Switzerland is not that of the benevolent neutral but of a major centre of Western capitalism. The ICRC encountered great difficulties during the Biafran War in Nigeria and the African political scientist Ali Mazrui has suggested that this was because it was out of touch with attitudes in the Third World.[45] A more frequent criticism has concerned its emphasis on discretion and cooperation with governments. The fact that it opts for a moral position which accepts one evil – an unjust government – in order to ameliorate another evil, some of the specific consequences for individuals of that government, may help to legitimize the more fundamental evil.

One case in particular illustrates the complex issues involved in assessing the ICRC's work for political prisoners.[46] During the period when Greece was under a military dictatorship, Amnesty cooperated fully with the Council of Europe in its investigations into the Greek government's violations of human rights. The ICRC, in contrast, refused to divulge information to the Council of Europe and indeed the fact that Greek prisoners were being visited by the ICRC was used by Athens to block attempts by other NGOs and by the Council of Europe to gain access to the prisoners. However, when the Greek junta published a brochure in which it denied charges of human rights violations, it quoted selectively from the confidential ICRC report which, in accordance with normal practice had been sent privately to it. The ICRC protested about this and the Greek government's response was to sign a unique Accord with the ICRC in which the ICRC was given guaranteed access to any place where political prisoners were held, to all police stations and to the families of detainees. This was something entirely novel in international relations: the supervision by an international NGO, by legal agreement, of a country's army and police on a day to day basis. Its results were mixed. Allegations of torture almost ceased in the year following the agreement but the junta did not renew the Accord after the year during which it was operative. It is also relevant to mention the fact that the American State Department during Richard Nixon's presidency partly based its case for improving relations with Greece on the argument that the ICRC had not been able to confirm the use of torture by the junta.

So, on the one hand, the ICRC was granted a unique access to political prisoners by Greece, an access which no other NGO, and certainly not Amnesty, would have received. It is also undeniable that some good – perhaps quite a lot of good – was done as a result. On the other hand, the Accord was used by the junta to strengthen its internal and international legitimacy and it helped Washington to justify its policy towards Greece.

We shall return to this question in the conclusion but it may be noted finally that the ICRC's work with political prisoners inevitably touches upon sensitive political areas whether the ICRC is prepared to admit it or not. Governments have refused the ICRC access to political prisoners on the grounds that such matters fall entirely within their sovereign prerogative, or that ICRC access might give detainees international legitimacy or the status of prisoners of war or that there is no such thing as a political prisoner in the country concerned.[47] Governments have misrepresented ICRC reports as being more in their favour than they are and have incurred the ICRC's one sanction of publishing the report in full.[48] In one case – that of the Irish Republican Army – the prisoners concerned showed hostility towards the ICRC delegates because they were afraid that its report might show that, contrary to their propaganda, they were in fact being humanely treated.[49] Hence the ICRC's work does not simply have political implications but it impinges upon two fundamental political areas. First, although the ICRC itself is concerned only with ensuring the observance of basic humanitarian standards – with the human right to some dignity whatever the circumstances – some governments clearly perceive an indirect criticism of political imprisonment as such and hence believe the ICRC's work to have implications for the more delicate area of political and civil rights. Secondly, its work affects in two respects the most sensitive of all matters for governments: the doctrine of sovereignty. The ICRC stands for the *international* as against the purely national protection of human rights and it also claims for itself, a nongovernmental organization, a significant role in ensuring such protection.

Conclusion

Measuring the effectiveness of the human rights NGOs is not the easiest of tasks. Apparent improvements occur every year: prisoners are released, laws are changed and international organizations expand their activities. But to attempt to attribute any of this directly to the efforts of one or more NGOs raises insuperable problems, not least the fact that few, if any, governments will admit to having been influenced by NGOs. As two of the leading

American authorities on the subject point out, NGOs attempt to change the repressive behaviour of governments 'either through shame – that is, appeal to internalized norms – or by damaging their reputation in the eyes of relevant others – for example, the internal populace, politico-military allies, trading partners, the international business investment community or the World Bank'.[50] Success in such endeavours is hardly likely to be acknowledged by target governments.

But there are many grounds for believing that NGOs do make a significant contribution to the furtherance of human rights, however difficult this may be to quantify. Many thousands of political prisoners have been released and Amnesty can claim some of the credit for this. Even where it does not succeed in achieving its primary goal it has undoubtedly brought both psychological and material help to prisoners and their families. Similarly the ICRC points to many instances where its observers have witnessed a radical improvement in prison conditions, apparently in consequence of ICRC visits. Amnesty and the other 'pressure group' organizations have also had an impact on the foreign policies of several Western governments. Amnesty's revelations about human rights violations in the Central African Empire helped to bring about a change in French support for the country, while the influence of NGOs perhaps reached a peak during the Carter Administration when Congressional decisions about American aid allocations were in part based on evidence that was presented by Amnesty and other NGOs. In general terms, the activities of the NGOs may also be said to have helped to shape public debate about human rights. But there is also a negative side. For every released prisoner there are more new detentions. Indeed some repressive regimes have even been said to welcome Amnesty campaigns as identifying for them the particular individuals they should regard as most dangerous.

Would Amnesty benefit from emulating the ICRC and seeking to acquire greater international legitimacy and the trust of governments – in short, to become respectable? Or should the ICRC become more like Amnesty and reveal its findings in order to bring greater pressure to bear on governments? This can only really be answered with the platitude that the world is probably large enough to contain both approaches and perhaps more besides. If the ICRC followed Amnesty's path and publicly criticised governments, it would simply lose its access to many detainees and it is difficult to discern what good that would do. The ICRC's prestige and special status derives in large part from its image of total discretion and a shift away from a policy of discretion would mean a loss of its present standing. While there are many vociferous NGOs there seems little point in the ICRC changing. Even its Swissness is important: the Swiss government guarantees the inviolability of ICRC property – it promises not to raid the files – and only a neutral government could be trusted by other governments to keep this sort of promise. Conversely, there would be little point in the other NGOs trying to become like the ICRC. Its unique international legitimacy is the end product of a hundred years of history which commenced when there was a considerably greater degree of international consensus than exists today. Besides, the cost of legitimacy may be restricted freedom of action. NGOs today perform quite different functions but all contribute to what amounts to a working, albeit hardly perfect, system for the international protection and promotion of human rights.

Notes

1 On this point, see P. Archer, 'Action by Unofficial Organizations on Human Rights', in E. Luard (ed.), *The International Protection of Human Rights*, London 1967, p. 161.
2 E.g. A. Cassese, 'How Could Nongovernmental Organizations Use UN Bodies More Effectively?', in *Universal Human Rights*, vol. 1, no. 4, October–December 1979, pp. 73–80. See also L.S. Wiseberg and H.M. Scoble, 'Recent Trends in the Expanding Universe of Nongovernmental Organizations Dedicated to the Protection of Human Rights', in *Denver Journal of International Law and Policy*, vol. 8, 1979, p. 657.
3 E.g. the American Association for the International Commission of Jurists' statement on this issue, excerpts from which are reprinted in *Human Rights Internet Newsletter*, June–July 1980 pp. 18–19.
4 *Human Rights Internet Reporter*, September–October 1980, p. 8.
5 J.F. Green, 'NGOs' in A.A. Said (ed.), *Human Rights and World Order*, New Jersey, 1978, pp. 90–9; and A. Cassese op. cit. pp. 76–7.
6 J.J. Shestack, 'Sisyphus Endures: the international human rights NGO', *New York Law School Review*, no. 1 1978, pp. 90–1, 115–17.
7 American Association for the ICJ, op. cit. p. 18.
8 H. Bull, *The Anarchical Society*, London 1977, pp. 4–5.
9 P. Archer, op. cit. pp. 162–4.
10 Cited in the Annual Report of the Society, 1978, p. 15.
11 Ibid., p. 3.
12 For the history and work of the ILHR, see J.J. Shestack, op. cit. and also L.S. Wiseberg and H.M. Scoble, 'The International League for Human Rights: The Strategy of a Human Rights NGO', in *Georgia Journal of International and Comparative Law*, vol. 7, 1977; and R.S. Clark, 'The International League for Human Rights and South West Africa 1947–1957: The Human Rights NGO as Catalyst in the International Legal Process', in *Human Rights Quarterly*, vol. 3, no. 4, 1981.
13 Wiseberg and Scoble, ibid, pp. 301–6.
14 On the ICJ, see its *Quarterly Review* and Annual Reports.
15 For this argument, see D. Weissbrodt, 'The Role of Nongovernmental Organizations in the Implementation of Human Rights', in *Texas International Law Journal*, vol. 12, 1977, pp. 299–300; and H.M. Scoble and L.S. Wiseberg, 'Human Rights NGOs: Notes Towards Comparative Analysis', in *Human Rights Journal*, June–December 1976, pp. 617–8.
16 Clare Nullis, 'NGOs and Human Rights', unpublished dissertation, School of International Studies, Birmingham University.
17 For a discussion of this function, see J. Lador-Lederer, *International Non-governmental Organizations and Economic Entities*, A.W. Sythoff-Leyden, 1963, pp. 69–77.
18 D.P. Kommers and G. D. Loescher (eds.) *Human Rights and American Foreign Policy*, Indiana 1979, p. 154.
19 R. Wadlow, 'Review of a UN Report', in *Human Rights Internet Reporter*, September–October 1980, p. 7.
20 D.P. Forsythe, *Humanitarian Politics: The International Committee of the Red Cross*, Baltimore 1977, p. 59.
21 For the history of Amnesty, see E. Larsen, *A Flame in Barbed Wire. The Story of Amnesty International*, New York 1979, and J. Power, *Against Oblivion*, Fontana 1981. See also H.M.

Scoble and L.S. Wiseberg, 'Human Rights and Amnesty International', *The Annals*, May 1974, pp. 11–26.
22 Article 1 of the Statute of Amnesty International, Annual Report, 1982, p. 357.
23 Martin Ennals, 'Amnesty International in the 1980s', Annual Report, 1980, p. 6.
24 J. Power, op. cit. p. 23.
25 Ibid., pp. 126–35.
26 H.M. Scoble and L.S. Wiseberg, 'Problems of Comparative Research on Human Rights', in V.P. Nanda et al., *Global Human Rights: Public Policies, Comparative Measures and NGO Strategies*, Boulder, 1981, p. 149.
27 S. Miller, 'Politics and Amnesty International', *Commentary*, March 1978, cited in L. Hurwitz, *The State as Defendant*, London 1981, p. 184.
28 M. Ennals ,op. cit. pp. 8–9.
29 C. Nullis, op. cit.
30 Notably in a major review of the work of the ICRC by D. Tansley: *Reappraisal of the Work of the Red Cross*, See also the ICRC rebuttal of the Tansley Report's findings on this question in the *International Review of the Red Cross*, January–February 1979.
31 D.P. Forsythe, op. cit. pp. 5, 19–21.
32 J. Moreillon, 'The ICRC and the Protection of Political Detainees' in *International Review of the Red Cross*, November 1974, p. 588.
33 Ibid., p. 589.
34 J. Moreillon, 'International Solidarity and Protection of Political Detainees', in *International Review of the Red Cross*, May–June 1981, p. 127.
35 Ibid.
36 ICRC, 'Protection and Assistance in Situations not Covered by International Humanitarian Law', *International Review of the Red Cross*, July–August 1978, p. 213.
37 *Commission of Experts for the Study of the Question of the Application of Humanitarian Principles in the Event of Internal Disturbances*, ICRC, Geneva 1955.
38 ICRC Annual Report, 1978, p. 42.
39 Ibid., pp. 42–3.
40 J. Freymond, 'The ICRC Within the International System', *International Review of the Red Cross*, May 1972, p. 251.
41 J. Moreillon, 'International Solidarity . . .', op. cit. p. 126.
42 See the *International Review of the Red Cross*, August 1967, pp. 403–16 and the draft 'Minimum Rules for the Protection of Non-Delinquent Detainees', *International Review of the Red Cross*, February 1968.
43 D.P. Forsythe, op. cit. p. 65.
44 L.S. Wiseberg and H.M. Scoble, 'Monitoring Human Rights Violations: The Role of NGOs', in D.P. Kommers and G.D. Loescher, op. cit. p. 197.
45 D.P. Forsythe, op. cit. pp. 240–1.
46 The following discussion is based on the account in Forsythe, pp. 76–84.
47 J. Moreillon, 'The ICRC and the Protection of Political Detainees', op. cit. p. 173.
48 D. Weissbrodt and J. McCarthy, 'Fact-Finding by International Nongovernmental Human Rights Organizations', *Virginia Journal of International Law*, Fall 1981, pp. 86–7.
49 D.P. Forsythe, op. cit. p. 69.
50 H.M. Scoble and L.S. Wiseberg, *The Annals*, op. cit. p. 14.

14 Conclusion

R. J. VINCENT

We began with the idea that human rights might be to a twentieth-century international revolution what natural rights were to the eighteenth century. If so, the revolutionary institutions might be those of the United Nations: the Charter, the Declaration, the Covenants, the machinery for enforcement that Robin Chatterjie described in chapter 12. We have now to decide whether these institutions have established themselves, or whether they are only quasi-institutions, part of the paper world of the United Nations but no part of the life of a functioning world community.

Much of our discussion, especially in the issues section of this book, has shown how strongly the ramparts of international society are being defended against the invasion of the world community. The principle of non-intervention is invoked, in black Africa, to protect the integrity of local conceptions of human rights. In South Africa, as Dan Keohane pointed out in chapter 3, the idea that nations as culturally homogeneous entities possessing a collective identity should be allowed the institutional expression of their dissimilar aspirations, has spawned a homelands policy which might appeal to classical international theory, but which is undertaken in the teeth of the opposition of the world community. In chapter 6, Francisco Orrego wrote in the Latin American tradition of maintaining the non-interventionist line against the imperial colossus to the North.

If these are theoretical, or doctrinal defences of non-intervention, there has also been its practical vindication – the demonstration that change is an indigenous product and that outside interference does not work. It might even make matters worse for the target group, as Arfon Rees noted in his discussion of dissidents in the Soviet Union, allowing the regime to isolate what was already a minority group. Advocates of formal international intervention, Charles Townshend said in the chapter on Northern Ireland, have been denounced for their naivety on all sides of the Irish triangle. And from the other side James Mayall shows why a sanctions policy even against a pariah-state like South Africa is difficult for the United States and therefore for the international society acting collectively. The two difficulties reinforce each other: outside interference is hard to mobilize and unlikely to work.

Making sceptical remarks about the efficacy of humanitarian intervention, an activity that demands selflessness from institutions that exist to be partial, does not dispose of the question of the reception of human rights by international society. The persistence of non-interventionism has not ruled out the discussion of human rights. Nor, as is clear from James Ferguson's chapter on the Third World, have states been prepared to carry an argument about their different conceptions of human rights to the point of ending discussion. Third World objectives cannot be reached, Clare Wells adds about the debate on information rights in UNESCO, if Third World countries end up talking to themselves. So the plurality of cultures in international society has not made a conversation between them impossible. Moreover, James Ferguson applies a nice test for the argument of cultural relativism. Is it acceptable within the cultures claiming it? Ugandans being persecuted by Idi Amin, he says, did not excuse him on the grounds that he was acting in accordance with some indigenous cultural tradition. This supports Rhoda Howard's sense in the chapter on black Africa that the argument from cultural relativism should be treated sceptically as something which tends to find favour with elites interested in reducing criticism and entrenching their own positions.

The international community then discusses human rights. The discussion is not taken up simply with the declaration of irreconcilable positions. It is a directed discussion. It aims to produce conventions and declarations which shall have authority across international society. Since 1945 a number of conventions and declarations have been produced such that some argue there is no longer a need for lengthy discussions on the merits of individual or collective rights, or civil and political rights as against economic and social rights. The texts are there, Robin Chatterjie declared in the chapter on the United Nations, the task is to implement them.

The laying-down of these texts has expanded the scope of the idea of international legitimacy. Martin Wight defined this notion as 'the collective judgement of international society about rightful membership of the family of nations; how sovereignty may be transferred, and how state succession is to be regulated, when large states break up into smaller, or several states combine into one'.[1] In virtue of the establishment of international human rights instruments, the collective judgement of international society now involves questions about how states govern domestically. Rightful membership is now not merely about sovereignty but, in some degree, about the nature of internal rule. In contemporary international society, it may be argued, a rule against racial discrimination has become part of international legitimacy. There is evidence for this in the anti-racism of the Charter of the United Nations. And this doctrine has been spelled out in an International Convention on the Elimination of Racial Discrimination, and another on the Suppression and Punishment of the Crime of Apartheid. There is evidence too in the judgement of the International Court of Justice (in the *Barcelona Traction* case) which has interpreted the duty not to discriminate on racial grounds as an obligation of a state towards the international community as a whole.[2]

But the political weight behind the establishment of legitimacy is provided by the new states emerging from colonial status and remembering especially the racial insult involved in European imperialism.[3] It is for this reason that South Africa, as an 'internal colonialist', finds itself uniquely on the wrong side of the new legitimacy; the only country out of step. And, as Dan Keohane suggested above, it has not been allowed to forget it because of the natural alliance between its oppressed majority and the rest of the African continent which has already gained its freedom from the same oppression. The eastern bloc has been solid with the Third World on this question from the outset; and the West, under pressure, has gradually retreated from its non-interventionism in the 1950s. Elsewhere in the world the solidarity of international society on the question of racial discrimination is less noticeable.

Even in South Africa, as we saw above, the weight of international opinion has not been able to sink the regime of apartheid. Accordingly, our expectations about the effectiveness of international opinion on a question of racial discrimination which commanded less of a consensus (such as East African expulsion of Indians) would be less sanguine still. On the matter of human rights on which there was a clear division in the international community (such as Poland, or El Salvador), we might expect the issue to be lost in the political contest. And where, (as in Northern Ireland), there is a doubt even about what the basic rights issues are – economic, or political, or judicial – we might expect, with Charles Townshend, the lack of sophistication in the response of the international community to show itself.

Thus we cannot divorce the discussion of human rights from that of international politics. Their arrival on the agenda of the international community, as Christopher Brewin reminded us in the chapter on Europe, was a reaction to the consequences of allowing Hitler to rule by will without reference to rights. And they are kept on the agenda, as James Mayall pointed out in the chapter on the United States, as much by particular interest or ethnic groups using them to advance their own cause, as by human rights groups concerned with the equal rights of everyone. It is the politics of human rights that explains the absence of China from the conventional western list of human rights issues. It is not that there is no dissident movement in China, no oppression to create it.[4] It is more the position of the Chinese since the early 1960s as our principal enemy's enemy.

So talk of the establishment of an international human rights regime, or of the extension of the notion of international legitimacy to include the relationship between governments and governed, should not be exaggerated. The world society which exists in virtue of the arrival of human rights on the international agenda is uneven and sometimes scarcely visible.[5] In this regard it would seem more appropriate to speak of human rights as the vocabulary of our time rather than the idea of our time: it provides the terms in which the discussion of (individual and other) values in international politics is carried on. It is, again as Christopher Brewin reminded us, like the seventeenth-century principle of toleration, simultaneously part of a continuing propaganda war and a healing philosophy. It is a mistake to suppose that it is either the former (Enoch Powell, Daniel Moynihan), or the latter (Louis Henkin). It is both, and often both at the same time.

There is one sense, however, in which the arrival of the issue of human rights in international society may be regarded as wholly progressive. It is the sense in which the idea of human rights is borne by non-governmental organizations who act in defence of no sectional interest. International organizations have admitted the issue of human rights, and so made life between governments more uncomfortable. But those governments might still be suspected in their associations of arranging matters to suit their own convenience. NGOs, as David Armstrong points out, have intruded on the cosiness of the international club, and may be uniquely placed to further the interests there of oppressed individuals and groups. Left to itself, the club might take little more than formal notice.

We have in this book amended the liberal non-interventionist orthodoxy, but not overturned it. Human rights have arrived in international society. States take account of them in both domestic and foreign policy. There is some warrant for detecting the establishment of a world community of human rights in an early stage of its development in the progress made by human rights instruments since 1945.[6] But international society still predominates, and it is a gatekeeper in the way of the progress of world society. The domestic arena is still the crucial one. Like all good theories, this one has an exception. It is the case of the Palestinians. To the extent that the PLO has achieved a quasi-legitimate place in international society it has been the result of a movement in international and perhaps global society, not domestic society. They have not operated on a homeland so much as with a view to getting one back; like the Jews before them. As Sally Morphet documents it, theirs is a remarkable achievement, gaining legitimacy without territory. In order for human rights, the rights of all people, regardless of the accident of their territorial location, to become firmly established they must make a similar gain of legitimacy without territory.

Notes

1 Martin Wight, *Systems of States* H. Bull (ed.) (Leicester, Leicester University Press, 1977), p. 153.
2 See Louis B. Sohn and Thomas Buergenthal (eds.), *International Protection of Human Rights* (Indianapolis, Bobbs-Merrill, 1973), pp. 18–19.
3 See R.J. Vincent, 'Racial Equality' in Hedley Bull and Adam Watson (eds.), *The Expansion of International Society* (Oxford, Clarendon, 1984).
4 See Merle Goldman, 'Human Rights in the People's Republic of China', *Daedalus*, vol. 112, no. 4 (Fall 1983).
5 See R.J. Vincent, *Human Rights in International Relations* (forthcoming), chapter 6.
6 See C. Wilfred Jenks, *The Common Law of Mankind* (London, Stevens, 1958).

Index

Well-known terms which are used in abbreviated form in the text are indexed under their abbreviations, with no cross-reference made from the full form; *passim* is used to indicate scattered mentions of the subject, not necessarily on consecutive pages; *above* and *below* in cross-references indicate that the reference is to another sub-heading under the same heading, not to a separate heading.

Index